Democracy and Anarchy

At a time when democracy is under threat from new authoritarian forces and tendencies, this book looks back to the Greek dawn of the *pólis* to uncover an element of democracy that has been repressed for centuries: its indissoluble link to anarchy.

Whether *demokratía* is uttered with nervous enthusiasm or utter contempt, this word – whose semantic history is retraced here – points to two interconnected events: it evokes both the people's entry onto the stage of history and the destitution of every power that claims some original foundation. The spectre of anarchy unsettles the city. Democracy was feared by the tragedians, narrated by historians, and denounced by philosophers.

The *arché* of fathers, property owners, autochthons, and heirs was profoundly undermined and stripped of legitimacy, while the space of politics was inaugurated. Thus emerges the tragic condition of democracy, which is based on nothing certain, and risks even its own existence. Women are the protagonists of this story. It was a revolt of foreign women, fleeing domestic violence, that brought to the surface the compound term that names the people's capacity to assert itself. Democracy is born with hospitality. And the *dêmos* can never regress into *éthnos*, grounding itself in ties of blood and soil, nor can it suffocate conflict and division.

In this highly original analysis of democracy and its sources, Donatella Di Cesare brings to light a hidden and long-repressed feature of democracy and shows why it is relevant today, at a time when democracies face new and unprecedented dangers.

Democracy and Anarchy

Democracy and Anarchy

Power in the Polis

Donatella Di Cesare
Translated by David Broder

polity

Originally published in Italian as *Democrazia e anarchia. Il potere nella polis* © 2024 Giulio Einaudi editore s.p.a., Torino

This book has been translated thanks to a translation grant awarded by the Italian Ministry of Foreign Affairs and International Cooperation / Questo libro è stato tradotto grazie a un contributo alla traduzione assegnato dal Ministero degli Affari Esteri e della Cooperazione Internazionale italiano.

Polity Press
65 Bridge Street
Cambridge CB2 1UR, UK

Polity Press
111 River Street
Hoboken, NJ 07030, USA

ISBN-13: 978-1-5095-6724-9 – hardback
ISBN-13: 978-1-5095-6725-6 – paperback

A catalogue record for this book is available from the British Library.

Library of Congress Control Number: 2026933181

Typeset in 10.5 on 12 pt Times New Roman
by Fakenham Prepress Solutions, Fakenham, Norfolk NR21 8NL
Printed and bound in Great Britain by Ashford Colour Ltd

For further information on Polity, visit our website:
politybooks.com

Contents

Until now, Greek history has always been written from an optimistic perspective.
Friedrich Nietzsche

To be free meant neither to rule nor to be ruled.
Hannah Arendt

Preface

Greek democracy has been erected as a monument. It has been built up as an immovable archetype, and as a model fickle enough to be colonized by the so-called 'true' democracies of the modern age. The present study reflects the need to dig right to the bottom of this monumental history, seeking a way through its cracks and crevices in order to shed light on an element of democracy that has been repressed for centuries: *anarchy*.

Layer upon layer of diligently written histories and dusty traditions have stashed anarchy away in the oblivion of the archives. However, when we examine democracy's roots, its unbreakable link with anarchy becomes apparent. This makes it all the more remarkable that this connection has never been examined, let alone discussed in any depth. Even radical thought has overlooked this ancient Greek source. But all the adjectives that point to the conflict inherent in democracy – conceived as wild, untamed, insurgent, or emergent – are swept aside by just one other. This adjective does not fix the definition of democracy but instead points to its fundamental indeterminacy. For democracy is, at heart, *anarchic*.

When the word *demokratía* burst onto the scene at the dawn of the *pólis*, uttered with trepid enthusiasm or shocked contempt, its subversive breakthrough pointed to two connected events. One was the entry of the *dêmos* onto the stage of history; the other was the eclipse of the *arché*, the power that vaunted its own foundational status. The new compound *demokratía* used the verb *krateîn* to reject all absolute domination and to cast off all archic regimes, including for the future.

The spectre of anarchy, which disturbs and shakes the city, had already haunted the earliest documents, in texts authored by poets and historians, philosophers and tragedians. Even when the connection with anarchy is hidden, it appears between the lines. Not so unusually, it is democracy's detractors who reveal what might otherwise remain unseen. The ontological-political link between anarchy and democracy comes to the fore in the pages of Plato and Aristotle. Both were proud opponents of this bizarre government by the people – a non-government, an epochal disorder, the overturning of all principles. With democracy, natural relations are turned upside down. The *arché* of the fathers, of the propertied, of the natives, of the heirs, is profoundly undermined and stripped of its legitimate standing. The principle of birth that orders and fixes arrangements is abolished, along with all the archic forms of the community: the line of descent, patriarchal power, the transmission of property, the bonds of blood and soil, the code of autochthony, and the right of inheritance: in short, the archic form of community. This means chaos in the streets, and squares occupied by shameless women, insolent children, and stubborn donkeys. Plato cries scandal. Democracy is a real anarchy. Aristotle echoes him, denouncing this political form, a non-constitution, as the multitude turns *arché* to ruin. He indicts *eleuthería*, an an-archic freedom, which translates into a lack of command, or at most being commanded by turns. What makes power impossible to appropriate is not simply the rotation of offices, but also the drawing of lots, the sacrosanct reliance on fate. This is the hallmark of democracy: that those with no qualification to rule have the right to do so.

The decline of *arché* opens up a new scenario, in which the *pólis*'s forms of expression become open to debate. Now comes the space of politics. It is the antithesis of whatever is private, selfish, and self-interested: *political* is synonymous with *common*. A new community is formed, in which citizens, torn from their ancient family ties and drawn out of the reassuring shadow of the *oîkos*, the private space, are held together only by the new, political, bond. There is no other foundation. Thus emerges the tragic condition of democracy, which is based on nothing certain, and risks even its own existence. On closer inspection, this is the tragic condition of all political action. Hence the importance of tragedy, as that threshold that puts the city at a distance from itself and challenges its limits. Theatre, this transgressive gateway to the source of order, offers a glimpse of the backstage behind the city. The danger does not lie in the prestige of the illusion; the theatre is a stage on which fearsome ghosts perform, anarchic spectres ready to unmask the *arché*. Sophocles' *Antigone* is emblematic in this sense. But to understand the full significance of this epochal transition from *oîkos* to *pólis* we have chosen to read it through an engagement with an exceptional modern interpreter,

Hannah Arendt. Politics can only exist where human relations are no longer debased by subordination – where *isonomía*, equality, is doing its work. In the aftermath of the totalitarian experience, Arendt identified in *arché* the total command that puts an end to every beginning, that erases the human capacity to begin and begin again.

Women play a leading role in this book, through their challenge to their exclusion from the *pólis*. Women are traditionally figures of turmoil and agitation; neither inside nor outside, they confuse and undermine the androcentric order. It was the *stásis* generated by women that brought the democracy into existence. The women who broke onto the scene were foreigners, fleeing domestic violence and begging for political protection. Their entreaties were a test for the popular assembly, called to vote on whether to accept these women. A verse by Aeschylus provides the birth certificate for *demokratia* – a word that can only be glimpsed, perhaps because it cannot be established or defined, poised as it always is in the unstable balance between *dêmos* and *krátos*. The semantic investigation follows the ups and downs of this compound term and its two elements. It reappraises, in a political and philosophical reading, the account given by Herodotus, who raises the anarchic banner of democracy: *oúte árchein oúte árchesthai*, 'neither to rule nor to be ruled'. This is the theme at the heart of this study.

How long would this word, asserting the power of the people, go on being uttered as a matter of pride and satisfaction? Perhaps only for the heartbeat of a collective passion, for the span of a generation. Not only had democracy's detractors managed to blacken its name, but its supremacy brought to mind the division of the city, reawakening memories of the *stásis*.

Delving into the archives of democracy, going against the grain of the usual narrative, means scrutinizing the momentary points of insurgency. It means unpicking the sequences of rebellion within the tangle of the written stories, proceeding through the different scenarios and their sudden twists. The democratic history of the *pólis*, which began with the uprising of 508 BCE, led by the 'rest of the Athenians', passed through Ephialtes' 'absolute democracy' when the Areopagus, the last bastion of the *arché*, was abolished, and ended with the civil war of Corcyra in 427 BCE. It is a history of discord, conflicts, and bloody clashes. But to understand the *stásis* in its full, dramatic depth, we must move away from those approaches that see things through a modern lens. We have to look at the *pólis* as a non-state community: one capable of holding together in the absence of a coercive apparatus, united by the strength of political bonds alone. *Stásis* is a fundamental condition of the *pólis*'s existence, but also the abyss that lies beneath it, the inescapable threat of its dissolution.

So, what does *demokratía* – this self-evident label, this opaque passe-partout – really mean? To avoid leaving the *dêmos* without *krátos*, which is surely an increasingly acute risk in today's context, etymological analysis starts from the terms of power and examines the *pólis*'s elements of sharing and participation. From this it seems evident that the people does not establish itself in an *arché*, and that it keeps its distance from the archic logic of sovereignty. The people's power is always an-archic: it comes from a challenge to *arché* and itself remains under challenge; it is a precarious pre-dominance that is ever subject to recall. This is the light in which we should reconsider the *dêmos*, as it is not simply the majority, nor even a class. Cleisthenes' redivision of the *demes* was a revolutionary act which enabled the people to constitute itself against the beginning and against command, long before the modern beheading of the king. The *dêmos* are those who do not fit into the order of any *arché*, those who have no title to be counted. The *dêmos* is not *éthnos*: it is not based on ties of blood or soil. The people always comes into being in the unfounded place of politics. As such, the people has no pre-existing identity. Rather, it is constantly recomposing, dividing, and redefining itself.

The spectre of anarchy looms large in the contemporary landscape, with its proposals for norms of strengthened governability and airing of authoritarian solutions. Precisely because it is un-founded, democracy is held up by the political bond, maintaining itself in its structural an-archy. The opposite force, which is supposed to sustain it, instead walls it in, closes it off, and imposes its conclusion. It is possible, then, that the threat clouding democracy's skies may be the nightmare of *arché*.

1

DEMOCRACY IN RADICAL THOUGHT

1. Now that all other credible principles have lost their political legitimacy, power ultimately belongs to the people. This idea is commonly accepted, in the West but also beyond. Democracy has become an almost self-evident, unquestioned value. But alongside the apparent triumph of democracy, the overarching suspicion has crept in that the term is hollow, and that the people hold power in name only. Is democracy really reducible to electoral institutions alone? How have the rules of the market and authoritarian policies enacted in the name of 'security' undermined and trampled upon the ideal of democracy?

The word 'democracy' seems to refer not just to popular sovereignty but also to the possibility of fundamentally challenging that power whenever it makes decisions. This raises the question of whether democracy is a political regime akin to any other. Those who doubt such a claim look to its sources of conflict and rebellion – that is, to its origins. Yet, it does not seem that any absolute principle can be invoked in its justification. Democracy is at work when there is a continual discussion of what is legitimate debate on what is or is not legitimate. In this sense, democracy is incomplete. This explains both its fragility and the recurrent temptation to cast it aside.

2. Today, in the shadow of disenchantment, some are airing the idea of the death of democracy. It is both challenged from outside by authoritarian threats and undermined from within by technocratic governments, no less than by populist-type pressures. In an era like ours, it would seem almost obviously necessary to try to contain, regulate, and discipline democracy. That is what has happened in the

long tradition that stretches from the writings of Plato and Aristotle to the thought of John Rawls and Jürgen Habermas in the twentieth century, and then to a myriad of contemporary studies.

Although their approaches vary and their different hues cover a broad spectrum, in each case we can see a strongly normative inspiration. This tradition, which has dominated over the centuries and does so even today, judges democracy by the yardstick of its well-foundedness and stability. It evaluates democracy based on the criterion of command and the capacity to govern and administer; it conceives of democracy in view of a *télos* that transcends it, located in a consensual harmony in which all discord is dissolved. Unsurprisingly, these normative theories consider democracy as a political regime and as a set of institutions. They thus focus on principles; they question how this regime works, propose rules, outline its procedures, and develop a model political system. Hence the many attempts to define democracy, to fix its foundations, to give it firm underpinnings. Bound by the chains of the state and harnessed by institutional reins, democracy is forcibly reduced to a static idea, a solid and orderly design. The more chaotic and unstable it appears, the more attempts are made to fix and regulate it.

This book takes a stand at the opposite end of things, in the camp of what has been called 'radical democracy'.[1] In today's situation, we might be led to believe that moderation is more suitable and justified than radicalism. This perspective should be turned on its head: if democracy is dying, or self-destructing, this is not due to its impotence, ineffectiveness, or lack of rules, but because it is being stripped of its dynamism and inventiveness. It is the result of a lack, not an excess. Democracy is not democratic enough. Democracy needs to run both wider and deeper.

The many variants of radical democracy that have raised their heads mostly in recent decades do not constitute a single homogeneous and cohesive school of thought. 'Radical democracy' is more of a label applied to a movement made up of different tendencies, widely divergent orientations, and interpretations that sometimes conflict with each other. However, it is possible to identify at least three common themes: 1) With regard to normative foundations and the related obsession with definitions, these theories not only reject definitions and fixed assumptions, but recognize that democracy has no stable principle, no ultimate foundation. 2) The quest for a *deeper* democracy is accompanied by the search for a *wider-reaching* democracy, meaning that it cannot be reduced to a political regime, let alone to a set of institutions. 3) In the same vein, radical-democratic theories stand at the watershed of the now widespread distinction between *politics*, meaning its practice in institutions, and *the political*, referring to the extra-institutional and extra-state sphere, where subversive impulses would otherwise remain hidden.

3. What does 'radical' mean? The adjective comes from the Late Latin *radicalis*, which is derived from the noun *radix*, *-icis*, meaning 'root'. It means: that which gets to the root of things, that which penetrates the inner essence of something, that which renews from the ground up, that which acts in depth. The term often recurs in everyday language but it also has a specific meaning in linguistics, where it refers to the root of a word; it likewise has specific meanings in mathematics, chemistry, and medicine. From a literal meaning, related to the roots of a tree, it soon took on a more metaphorical one, with the effect that the figurative term 'radical' ended up becoming synonymous with 'fundamental'. This also happened in political terminology, where, particularly in eighteenth-century Britain, the term 'radical' gained currency within the growing movement for parliamentary reform. Associated with the idea of extreme change, or even an overhaul of the system's foundations, the term entered the lexicon of modernity, taking on different accents and nuances. It would play a leading role in the Russian Revolution (1905–17) and in the writings of Vladimir Lenin.

Still later in history, the term 'radical' remained connected to ideals of renewal. Those who do not abandon their principled positions are called radicals or champions of political radicalism. In the decades just before and after the fall of the Berlin Wall, as social democracy was diluted and dissolved into neoliberalism, 'radical' became a name for what remained of the left (and became synonymous with the extreme, the revolutionary, and the critical). But it was Karl Marx who first pinned down the political meaning of 'radical', as it is understood today, in terms of its disruptive force. He embraced the term in one of his youthful writings, the *Critique of Hegel's Philosophy of Right* of 1843–44. In his plea for the liberation of human potential from the chains that bind it – that is, in making his case for revolution – Marx called for a critical theory useful to political praxis. He termed this a 'radical' theory that made its case *ad hominem*, so that it would be able to grip the masses' attention and stir them to action. Marx wrote: 'To be radical is to grasp the root of the matter.'[2] As he put it in German: 'Radikal sein ist die Sache an der Wurzel zu fassen.'[3] Marx then pointed out: 'Die Wurzel für den Menschen ist aber der Mensch selbst.' 'But for man the root is man himself.'

This addition was decisive, because radicalism is not only a *vertical* movement, getting to the bottom of the matter. Marx was already proposing the overthrow of all the social relations in which human beings are degraded, enslaved, and trampled upon. Here, already, it became clear that such a radical move could have no criterion of judgement – and, above all, no base of support – other than human beings themselves. This was the new element introduced by the young Marx. It was a move that distanced him from Enlightenment critique, which still respected a dividing line between the reformable and the unreformable, between that which bears the stamp of human activity and that which is fixed by nature. Religion, the state, private property, and the institutionalized expressions of bourgeois society crumble one after the other: their legitimacy cannot be located in any natural order. Marx did not stop at scrutinizing these forms of domination, which are *verkehrt*, upside down – that is, as senseless as they are alienating. Nor could it suffice simply to appeal to a human essence, a notion which risked hardening into a rigid anthropological principle.[4] Marx went a step further in the pages of *The German Ideology*. Stripping the veil from the supposed naturalness of the dominant order, he demonstrated that it was a product of history, meaning the processes that had constituted the relations of production over time. Bourgeois society did not just appear inhuman and in contradiction with life and its flourishing; more than that, it was shown to be a form of society which had arisen in a specific period and which corresponded to the bourgeois class that gave it institutional form. In the *Communist Manifesto*, Marx and Engels forcefully denounced a world in which every sphere of activity is influenced, indeed permeated and turned upside down, by the relations of production proper to this bourgeois class. In short, the bourgeoisie 'creates a world after its own image'.[5] It then leads people to believe that this is the only possible order, the natural order, the best order, the one that represents order *tout court*.

In *Capital*, Marx undertakes a critical examination of political economy in which he deconstructs the self-image projected by bourgeois society. It becomes clear that this society's mode of production, far from representing the pinnacle of civilization, is in fact a system through which the bourgeoisie dominates the proletariat – a system built on violence and pivoting on exploitation and profit. From this perspective, it becomes clear that this system's workings are produced and reproduced by human beings themselves. They are not unchangeable. Society can assume a form other than the bourgeois one. Capitalism is not the ultimate horizon.

Understanding that this order is a product of history goes hand in hand with radicalism. No form of human organization can justifiably be considered eternal. The capitalist mode of production is not based on foundations that lie outside of history, that are ultrahistorical or somehow natural in character. Rather, this order's process of development, its constitution over time, and its historical character as such, make it possible to change it. Just as this bourgeois society arose in specific circumstances, so it can and must meet its end. Marx writes in his *Eighteenth Brumaire of Louis Bonaparte*: 'Men make their own history, but they do not make it just as they please; they do not make it under circumstances chosen by themselves, but under circumstances directly encountered, given and transmitted from the past.'[6] This clarifies what he meant by *ad hominem*: it refers not to an anthropological principle but to the human alone – that is, a theory having no foundation other than the human. But the human is temporal, historical, and finite.

The etymological connection of 'radical' to 'roots' fails to capture this element of contingency. Indeed, even beyond its naturalistic connotations and botanical hues, the metaphor risks being misleading for at least two other reasons. First of all, because it suggests a firm principle, a solid foundation that can be grasped. Secondly, because it conceals the work of radicalism, which is not just a vertical move to get to the bottom of things, but also an attempt to unmask what is considered natural and immutable, making clear its contingent nature. Faced with Marx's deconstruction of the supposed foundations, we may well wonder whether other words might have been more appropriate.

Recall the formula used by Dante Alighieri in *Convivio*: 'the root foundation underlying the Imperial Majesty'.[7] In democratic radicalism, this foundation, this *arché*, loses its force.

4. The need to radicalize democracy was already advanced by Ernesto Laclau and Chantal Mouffe in the subtitle of their 1985 book *Hegemony and Socialist Strategy: Towards a Radical Democratic Politics*.[8] Their explicit use of the adjective 'radical' suggests a project which – in contrast to the moderate and normative discourse espoused by Habermas – does not stop at examining the transcendental conditions and legal principles that are supposed to underpin democracy. Rather, it makes them questions of democratic debate. This was not just because of fears that these norms and presuppositions might end up domesticating the democratic conflict. Rather, the quest for principles and foundations itself proves superfluous, seeing as democracy is legitimized by its lack of foundations. In other words, to speak of 'radical' democracy is to suggest that it is rooted in no foundation other than its own realization. Hence the paradoxical meaning of this adjective, which becomes apparent even in this context.

For Laclau and Mouffe, in those transition years the radical-democratic project also and above all represented an alternative orientation for a 'new left'. They hoped that this latter would be capable both of overcoming neoliberal politics and of critically distancing itself from orthodox Marxism, which had found its own essentialist foundations in anthropology and the philosophy of history.[9] Yet these authors themselves remained caught in the impasse of looking for foundations.

5. The word 'radical' has been used in many different ways in connection to democracy. This is hardly surprising, given the limitations of a term of naturalistic hues, incapable of conveying the paradoxical meaning of a foundation that derives its legitimacy from its own lack of foundations. Hence the numerous attempts to find an adjective more suited to democracy – restless, unstable, never complete, always '*à venir*' (to come) according to Jacques Derrida's famous expression.[10]

The attempts destined to leave a trace came from what Ernst Bloch termed the 'warm currents' of Marxism. Through their libertarian reflection, they deconstructed the liberal glaciation of democracy and made it into something more fluid. As against an orderly and ordering conception of democracy, reduced to a code of principles, rules, and procedures, these approaches instead emphasized the political conflict and permanent disorder inherent to democracy. Considered in its subversive aspect, 'negative democracy' proves to be something like a challenge to or an interruption of power, even a development close to revolution.[11]

The most forceful and effective adjective was introduced by Claude Lefort when he spoke of a 'wild' democracy, thereby emphasizing its disturbing, unsettling nature and projecting it far beyond the bounds of the political regime and the right to govern.[12] Democracy is like a raging river that constantly overflows its banks. It cannot be tamed, brought back home, or made to fall in line. Miguel Abensour further stressed this indeterminacy: taking up Lefort's term *sauvage*, he interpreted it not as a synonym for the primitive or natural, but rather in the sense of a wildcat strike that breaks out spontaneously and builds in opposition to all authority. However, as early as 2004, in the preface to the second edition of his work *Democracy Against the State*, Abensour distanced himself from Lefort and from this overly ambiguous adjective, replacing 'wild democracy' with 'insurgent democracy'.[13] He chose the adjective 'insurgent' instead of the more customary 'insurrectionary' in order to emphasize the permanent nature of this democratic insurrection. This marked a break with Lefort that ran deeper than might be imagined, bound up as it is with the relationship between democracy and the state. Despite the emancipatory thrust of his political thought, Lefort did not free himself from the framework of the state, which he instead ended up reaffirming and reinforcing. This is, in short, the critique levelled against him by Abensour, who sees democracy as irreducibly in tension with the state. Insurgent, untamed, agonistic, and, ultimately, anti-state, in Abensour democracy winks at anarchy.

> Insurgent democracy is born out of the intuition that there is no true democracy without reactivating the anarchic impulse which first rises against the classic expression of arche – at once commencement and commandment – namely, the State. In this sense, insurgency is the live source of true democracy.[14]

Abensour was far from alone in embarking on this long path, where democracy finds its compass in non-domination. In those years, similar echoes could be heard from other voices, from Jacques Rancière to Jean-Luc Nancy.

The need for a politics that interrupts the logic based on the *arché* – the principle that defines who has the natural right to command – was outlined by Rancière in his 1995 book *Dis-agreement: Politics and Philosophy*.[15] Democracy is the name for the interruption of the *arché*. In the third of his 'Ten Theses on Politics', Rancière explains: 'Democracy is the specific situation in which there is an absence of qualifications that, in turn, becomes the qualification for the exercise of a democratic *arche*.'[16] It is thus no surprise that he also took the next step. In his 2005 essay *Hatred of Democracy*, he refers to the 'an-archic supplement signified by the word democracy'.[17] In short, with or without a hyphen, anarchy appears here and there in the texts of the authors whom we can associate with radical democracy. This is also true of Nancy, who just a few years later went so far as to assert the equivalence of the pair: 'democracy equals anarchy'.[18]

Yet, the relationship between the two terms is anything but clear. We still need to understand whether they are in inevitable tension or enjoy a fruitful convergence. Is anarchy the spectre that haunts democracy, undermining it from within and threatening its ruin? Or is it rather the absence of principle that preserves democracy's lack of foundation, the impossibility of command that holds every *arché* in check?

6. Taken back to its root, democracy reveals its connection with anarchy. All the adjectives used to evoke turmoil and conflict, to guarantee an inexhaustible reserve of disorder, are swept away. They are undercut by that single adjective which, instead of making democracy determinate, allows its fundamental indeterminacy to emerge. Wild, untamed, insurgent democracy – is it not, at heart, *anarchic*?

The most explicit answer came in a reflection by Abensour published back in 1993, entitled '"Savage Democracy" and "Principle of Anarchy"'.[19] The title points to the programmatic scope of an essay that mounts a detailed comparison of the positions of Claude Lefort and Reiner Schürmann. Abensour was dissatisfied with the adjective *sauvage* – which, even in a libertarian reading, does not convey the abyssal verticality of democracy – and this pointed him to the need to move away from Lefort's approach. This opened up a '*détour*', not a circumvention or a loophole, but rather a new path, albeit one at first glance hard to understand, given that it passed for a 'left-Heideggerian' interpretation.[20]

The key reference here was Schürmann's book *Heidegger on Being and Acting: From Principles to Anarchy*, first published in French in 1982.[21] Beyond the more or less successful attempt to democratize Heidegger's thought, Schürmann sought to show that the philosopher did not mythologize the origin, nor defend the principle, but instead conceived the anarchic dissolution of any *arché*. In seeking to highlight the disruptive force of this dissolution, Schürmann coined the expression 'principle of anarchy'.[22] The contradiction between the two terms is obvious – and it would be futile and inappropriate to chase after its reconciliation or overcoming. The principle of anarchy is an an-archic principle which, in deposing itself, prevents anarchy from rising up as a principle of its own.

It is to Abensour's credit that he followed this side avenue, which proved to be a real turning point. The insight lay in the 'perspectival alignment' of democracy and anarchy – the former understood as wild, free from reference points and constraints, and without foundation; the latter conceived as a paradoxical an-archic principle that dethrones and topples every principle. In other words, Abensour understood the need to go beyond a focus on democracy's forces of insurgency in order to examine its ontological dimension. Otherwise, there is a risk of remaining at the surface level of things. The *détour* was thus a passage from politics to ontology. But, on closer inspection, the reverse is also necessary. Only through the prism of the principle of anarchy can wild democracy be seen as a liberation from the *arché*, while only in democracy could the an-archic principle find the political path that it has not found. Here, Abensour levels an implicit criticism against both Lefort and Schürmann.

However, Abensour's programmatic essay was destined to remain just that. The ideas and insights contained in those promising pages were not taken up and developed further.[23] Abensour later turned towards a critique of the state, and 'insurgent democracy' assumed increasingly anti-state, or rather non-state, features. Many questions remain unanswered, starting with one Abensour himself posed: 'Can we consider savage democracy anarchic?'[24]

7. Democracy does not rest on a foundation, and nor is it part of a founding act. Any attempt to constrain or underpin it thus seems futile or even counterproductive. Considering democracy outside the normative cage that reduces it to an institutional system and a regime of government is necessary – but also insufficient. We need to radicalize our gaze, in order to examine democracy more deeply.

Ultimately, democracy proves to be without foundation – without a solid basis, a stable principle, or a constituted *arché*. A radical vision of democracy, which drives it forward without thereby distorting it, is radical in two senses. Firstly, because it is prepared to recognize that democracy is without foundations: it does not hedge around or try to hide this fact, but allows it to come fully into the light of day. Secondly, because it makes no claim that its own theory is based on unshakeable assumptions or universally valid axioms. Rather, it unhesitatingly puts its own foundationlessness on display.

8. As can readily be understood, it is impossible to discuss democracy without addressing the crucial philosophical question of the *foundation*. Otherwise, there would be a risk of misunderstandings.

Oliver Marchart helped to shed light on this issue in his study *Die politische Differenz*, in which he questioned the meaning of *Grund* and *Grundlosigkeit*. What does foundation mean, and how should its absence be interpreted? His pages do not offer a diagnosis of today's contingency, as one might imagine. Rather, they investigate the ontology at the heart of politics.

The key concept introduced by Marchart is *Postfundamentalismus*, which has been translated as *post-foundationalism*.[25] The German compound is derived from the English *foundationalism*, which, while likewise referring to a foundation, does not (as in German) imply misleading associations with fundamentalism.[26] This is not to rule out the possibility that fundamentalism, in its many contemporary forms, does indeed draw on foundationalist positions, which it then harshens. It is reassuring to believe that the world rests on firm bases, on sure principles. But the *chiaroscuro* of the present reveals quite how fragile this world is. Foundations split and crumble, revealing how they are ever-changing, decaying, and fading. Still, such a collapse cannot simply be blamed on the particular historical era in which we live. Indeed, that era differs from previous ones only insofar as it tears the veil from the repressed[27] abyss hidden beneath the foundation. Nor is it possible to go on skirting around the contingency that always already undermines principles considered unalterable.

None of this is to claim that the world is tipping into an abyss of nothingness. Foundations have not disappeared from view; rather, the important thing is that they should be read as constitutively *historical* in nature. What is in question is the *ultimate* foundation, not the existence of *any* foundation. Thus, Marchart's use of the term post-foundationalism is apt; here, the prefix *post-* refers not to posteriority – one thing following another in a temporal sequence – but rather to the acknowledgement of an event that the historical constellation invites us to recognize.

This move allows Marchart to distance himself from both foundationalism and anti-foundationalism. The first of these terms denotes positions that refer to fundamental principles, objective realities, and certainties immune to any revision. This is the attitude of those who, even when faced with splintering and shattering, insist on asserting the need for some ultimate, unyielding foundation, which reproduces itself in various spheres. Thus, in the case of political foundationalism, there is a search for a transcendental principle, an external fulcrum that will grant politics legitimacy. This is not uncommonly seen in the economic domain. Marchart finds an example of economic determinism in the Marxist tradition, which distinguishes between base and superstructure, identifying the former as the economy, guided by irrefutable laws of progress, and the latter in terms of a surplus of politics. Neoliberalism, which evokes the indispensable and imperative constraints of the market, passed off as facts of nature, is considered a special case. But there are also many examples elsewhere, from science to philosophy. Although Marchart considers the foundationalist paradigm exhausted, he does not see it as a relic of the past. Rather, it survives and remains, indeed plays a hegemonic role, taking on new guises which Marchart defines as neo-foundationalist. Here, the boundaries with fundamentalism are fluid. For an example of this, we need only think of the religious versions of the phenomenon – or even the political ones, of which the populist crusade to reassert national sovereignty is perhaps the most extreme. The search for the lost foundation still weighs on political life.

However, the critique of the idea of an ultimate foundation could give rise to the fatal misunderstanding that reduces 'post-' to 'anti-', i.e. that it opposes, denies, or inverts foundationalism. This is why Marchart stresses that post-foundationalism does not represent a 'counter-paradigm'.[28] This is a crucial point, even if the difference is surely a subtle one. It does not mean negating the foundation, as if contesting its necessity, but rather recognizing that the foundation is always *contingent*. This third way goes beyond the alternative between those who cling to an ultimate foundation and those who deny any foundation at all. Both end up sharing the same horizon. Locked into the same metaphysical schemas as the foundationalist, the anti-foundationalist becomes entangled in the same game. To maintain that it is possible to do without any foundation is to sign up to the ideology of 'anything goes' – that relativism in which any one thesis cancels out another in a carnivalesque farce. Dismissed as 'postmodern', anti-foundationalism is nothing more than a caricature, a parody aimed at disqualifying any criticism of metaphysics. Who could ever identify with such a position – which, not by chance, finds such scant representation on its own side? But, above all, it needs recognizing that the mere antithesis to foundationalism uses the same arguments and makes the same metaphysical moves; even in its defence of the anti-foundation, it reintroduces the idea of the foundation.

To get out of this impasse, we need to follow the strategy introduced by Heidegger, whom Marchart therefore sees as 'the most important pioneer of post-foundationalism'.[29]

Heidegger shared an important conviction with Husserl – that of the need to recover the world of life. Yet, he soon distanced himself from him. The reason was that, despite everything, to his eyes Husserl remained trapped in a Cartesian conception of philosophy which, being understood as a rigorous science, still required a *Letztbegründung*, an 'ultimate ground'. For Heidegger, however, it was time to bid farewell to this and other delusions of a metaphysics that believed it saw an unshakeable, stable and solid foundation, where on closer inspection the foundation proved to be shaky and precarious.

The event that shatters the ultimate foundation literally shakes philosophy to its core, leaving open cracks and fissures. The bottomless abyss of every foundation is thus opened wide. In pointing out this reality, Heidegger ventures hazardous rhetorical figures that revolve around the assonance between *Grund* and *Abgrund*, bottom and abyss. This is sometimes expressed in the typographical expedient of the hyphen: *Ab-Grund* is the name which, containing the fissure within itself, refers to what is now an abyssal foundation.[30] It is enough to realize that every *Grund* is at the same time *gründend*, grounding, and *grundlos*, ungrounded. No foundation is ever an ultimate foundation, because it is not grounded *in itself*, but is always already marked by the abyss. In this sense, there is no *Grund* that is not *ab-gründig*, no bottom that is not an abyss. The evocative ambivalence nestled within the term *Ab-Grund* does not somehow indicate an antithesis. Rather, it refers to an indissoluble intertwining. The foundation does not disappear, but is maintained within the hyphen.

So, this does not mean denying or refuting the existence of foundations. Instead, it must simply be admitted that there is no foundation that remains unshakeable. Heidegger limits himself to recognizing this much; he steers clear of any frontal attack on metaphysics, which cannot be overcome by sheer force of will without falling into an equally metaphysical gesture. This is the trap to be avoided. Therefore, he does not abandon the terrain of metaphysics, but remains there to trace its disintegration, scrutinize its foundations, and allow the abyss to emerge through the cracks. It is not an inversion but a deconstruction.

This makes it possible to grasp why Heidegger's deconstructive gesture becomes exemplary for post-foundationalism, which does not naively deny foundations, but reveals them to be ever-agitated and finite – that is, it insists upon their historical character. The rejection of an ultimate and final foundation – understood as something separate and above dispute – gives rise to a plurality of foundations which, insofar as they are always *penultimate*, cannot hide their own historical development, their specific contingency.

9. In 2001, Dominique Janicaud published his monumental research on the reception of Heidegger in France. In this study, he took up and reworked an expression that had for some time already been circulating back and forth across the Atlantic. It was, it seems, initially formulated to describe the position of Herbert Marcuse, who had outlined a radical critique of late capitalism on the basis of Heidegger's *Being and Time*. Marcuse's critique helped to ignite the 1968 protests and breathe life into the New Left.[31] Thus was coined the label *gauche heideggérienne* – not a title anyone claimed for themselves, but one which seem to fit quite a few voices in French philosophy. But what does *gauche heideggérienne*, 'Heideggerian left', really mean? Isn't it a contradiction in terms? Janicaud observed:

> The attempt to seek a convergence between Marx's goals of emancipation and the preparation of 'another thought' is not a reactionary or conservative attempt; rather, it is a more radical project than an enlightened liberalism or a social-democratic progressivism, not to mention its obvious refusal of fealty to Stalinist or 'revisionist' apparatuses.[32]

It is interesting to note that the first names mentioned by Janicaud are Derrida and Schürmann – who might be called left-Heideggerians *avant la lettre*. Over time, however, others joined them in an increasingly complex and variegated landscape. Marchart wonders what unites Ernesto Laclau, Claude Lefort, Jacques Rancière, Jean-Luc Nancy, and Giorgio Agamben, to name but a few. Linked by multiple family resemblances and situated in the same theoretical constellation, they share Heidegger's fundamental critique of metaphysics, that post-foundationalist thought that represents almost a point of no return.[33] In this sense, the left-Heideggerians seem to have even more heirs, whether explicitly or tacitly. But those enlisted – so to speak – in the Heideggerian left also took up this cause in the political sphere.

Heidegger was the trailblazer, the precursor, the pioneer of the deconstruction of cobblestones, *pavés*, and paving of all kinds. It can justifiably be argued that a kind of urbanization of the Black Forest, indeed one of a most radical kind, took place in 1968 on the barricades of Paris and in the street clashes in Rome. To bid farewell to centuries-old principles, to peer into the abyss of foundations that were once considered stable, is to open oneself up to a scenario no longer bound to metaphysics, one in which the gaze follows transitions and passages, and which requires decision, choice, and antagonism. It is no accident that left-Heideggerian thought has been so permeated by figures of contingency such as the 'event' – that which happens and takes shape outside of any foundational logic.

Derrida offers an exemplary description of the 'fracture' event that decentred the centre, deconstructed the structure, and opened up the abyss hidden beneath the foundation. It is an event that, as such, does not bear the signature of any single author. It occurred in a particular era, which it ultimately defined. However, it had always been at work and was thus always perceptible. In this way, Derrida avoids a spiral of historicism. The fracture was also present in previous eras, though they always sought to repress it. But in this era of crisis it can no longer be skirted around. Nietzsche with his unmasking of truth, Freud with his critique of consciousness, and Heidegger with his destruction of metaphysics all contributed to its emergence.[34] It was not an act of sheer will, nor was it a pious wish. Rather, the foundation had already been irrevocably shaken from its hinges. And this 'unhinged' metaphysics was sure to have effects everywhere.

If the reactionary reading of Heidegger emphasizes principles, Schürmann perhaps goes further than others in hermeneutically opening a window onto the absence of principle – onto the *an-arché*. Through the event at the heart of every phenomenon, foundations will sink, hegemonies will be shattered, and principles will fade away. Schürmann invites us to consider history as an alternation of epochs, each of which holds together and hardens around a principle. Living in the midst of an era, we experience the powerful archic grip of a foundation, which we thus tend to consider both first and last. As long as an *arché* – an epochal principle – holds, it is not even possible to imagine another order. But at the end of an era, the principle crumbles. Connections loosen and coherence becomes blurred; what had seemed above challenge is suddenly called into question. Seen from a distance, the principle turns out to be doubtful and provisional. Only when the *arché*'s domination is broken, when the principle no longer reigns supreme, does there open up a passage beyond, an interregnum. Ultimately, the theme of Schürmann's reflection is the an-archic transition.

10. The unstable complexity of democracy, the underlying contingency and indeterminacy at its heart, are sure to have repercussions on theory. If democracy is not rooted in any foundation other than its own realization, and if the absence of a principle maintains its foundationlessness, then it would seem difficult to trace it back to principles and foundations. It is no accident that no definition of it has ever been fixed.

This poses a problem for those political theories, whether normative or empirical, which do aim to establish foundations, to determine and to define. These theories take different forms and approaches – some arguing from assumptions and rules, others inductively from the observation of data. Still, they each purport to construct and elaborate upon models of democracy, whose advantages and disadvantages may then be weighed up. This is a debate between theoretical positions that might support and promote an ideal model. But this is exactly the problem: can democracy be reduced to an ideal model? Doesn't this end up missing the point, exactly when we think that we have grasped the truth? Is it not a way of exorcizing the unease of democracy, of softening all tensions, reducing all uncertainties? Rationalizing and formalizing democracy, focusing on its procedural aspects, is a means of skirting around its underlying aporia. These theories speak not of how democracy *is* but of how it *should be*, regimenting it into a rigid classification.

Yet, the indeterminacy that so pervades democracy ought to warn against any attempt to determine it. In its structural openness, in its temporality, in its incompleteness, democracy cannot be captured as if it were objectifiable. Still less can it be fixed and secured to fulcrums and hinges. More than that: it has no essence that can be grasped in a Platonic *eîdos*, an intelligible idea, a constitutive or constitutional paradigm. Nor does there even exist a democratic ideal.

This is why a theory that contemplates the dissolution of democracy's fixed points cannot make fundamental and systematic claims. It must follow the trail of democracy's unpredictable, incalculable adventure hermeneutically. It must critically monitor the bedrock of democracy so that it does not harden in place and close itself off in a totalitarian temptation. Such a theory, which is at the same time an interrogative praxis, submits to the foundationlessness of democracy. It brings out the tension that agitates democracy, the fracture that divides it, conscious that its openness is both a threat and an opportunity. The more democracy takes the risk of doing without principles and foundations, the more it frees up all possible aspirations – projecting itself towards new and unprecedented forms.

11. At this point, it seems useful to take up a distinction that has increasingly prevailed in recent decades, even becoming canonical, though it also has many important variations. This is the distinction between *la politique* and *le politique*, politics and the political. It took shape in the debates from 1980 to 1984 at the 'Centre for Philosophical Research on the Political'. Created at the École Normale Supérieure on the initiative of Jacques Derrida, and headed by Philippe Lacoue-Labarthe and Jean-Luc Nancy, the Centre was a gathering place for philosophers from Claude Lefort to Jacques Rancière, and from Jean-François Lyotard to Alain Badiou. They contributed, albeit with different approaches and varied outcomes, to the development of a new way of thinking.[35] The distinction had real explosive force, becoming something like a theoretical-ideal link between philosophers who otherwise differed in many respects, from Ernesto Laclau to Chantal Mouffe and from Giorgio Agamben to Roberto Esposito. It is no coincidence that the leading figures in the debates at the Centre are largely the same figures behind the various currents of radical democracy.

The motto coined by Philippe Lacoue-Labarthe and Jean-Luc Nancy read: *retrait du politique*.[36] Also understood as a response to the then widespread idea that everything is political, it lent itself – and still lends itself – to more than one misunderstanding, given the ambiguities and assonances wrapped up in the French phrase. It might be translated literally as 'the retreat of the political'. But this complex expression is used in at least two senses. The first owes to the fact that politics – not only in totalitarian regimes but also in Western democracies – seems to be consumed and dissolved in the spotlight of public space and its blinding self-evidence. Thus the political withdraws, recedes, steps back, drawing out of view. It is, therefore, a retreat both *of* and *from* the political. Here, it is not difficult to discern the Heideggerian concept of *Entzug*, which inspired these authors' *retrait*. Just as Being withdraws and is forgotten in the dispersion among entities, we can likewise speak of a repression of politics in that ontic sleep to which the existence of the age of technology is consigned. We must, therefore, return to the political – which has not disappeared or vanished forever – and follow its traces. The second meaning of *retrait* refers to *retracer*, or rather *re-tracer* – to trace, retrace and re-trace the political.[37] The motto is not, therefore, a call to seek escape routes or loopholes, but an invitation to deconstruct politics and rethink the political.[38]

However, the version that has had the most profound and lasting influence is the one developed by Lefort. What does it mean to rethink the political? This question runs through Lefort's programmatic 1983 essay 'La question de la démocratie'. 'If we are to reinterpret the political', he writes, 'we must break with scientific points of view in general and with the point of view that has come to dominate what are known as the political sciences and political sociology in particular.'[39] Lefort's polemic is targeted at those positivist and scientistic approaches which limit themselves to the empirically existing sphere of politics. This reduction has no methodological justification, nor is it dictated by chance. Rather, it must be understood in its political content. In words that were to become famous, this meant looking at the *forme* – the 'form' – of the *pólis*, and not at its *mise-en-forme*, its being 'given form', or even its *mise-en-sense*, 'given meaning', or *mise-en-scène*, its 'staging'.[40] Political philosophy must decisively distance itself from this 'fiction' dear to political science. It risks focusing on the established order, describing it in terms of its functionality, without considering the determining processes of its formation. This results in the domination of politics understood in terms of its institutional sphere, while the course followed by the institution itself remains beyond view, repressed and concealed. For Lefort, it is thus necessary to go beyond the objectified static character of politics in order to recover the underlying dynamics of the political. This alone makes it possible to reveal, together with the *mise-en-forme* itself, the contingency of the principles that led to this form's constitution-process. It is precisely this in-depth investigation – which gets to the bottom of the institutional structure that has been *mise-en-scène* – that provides the space in which to rethink the political.

Albeit with different emphases, the distinction between *la politique* and *le politique* reappeared in other authors following Lefort. I need only mention one of his early students, Pierre Rosanvallon. In his inaugural lecture at the Collège de France in 2001, Rosanvallon again took up this distinction, articulating it almost as a kind of manifesto:

> In speaking of 'the political' as a noun, I thus mean as much a modality of existence of life in common as a form of collective action that is implicitly distinct from the functioning of politics. To refer to 'the political' rather than to 'politics' is to speak of power and law, state and nation, equality and justice, identity and difference, citizenship and civility – in sum, of everything that constitutes political life beyond the immediate field of partisan competition for political power, everyday governmental action, and the ordinary function of institutions.[41]

To follow the trail of the political, and to re-trace it, does not mean separating oneself from politics, perhaps to the point of erasing it. Rather, it means suspending an adherence to politics as it imagines itself and purports to be understood and defined.[42] On the one hand there is the landscape of structures and institutions; on the other, the possibility of transgressing and overcoming them. Politics (*la politique*) is the politics of the 'Chinese emperors, of the Benin kings, of Louis XIV or of German social democracy'.[43] Today, it might be said to be the politics of calculation and governance, which administers things with a view to resolving problems that might arise. The sphere of the political (*le politique*) is the sphere of *questions* rather than of solutions. Here, it is the principles and foundations of the political form that are up for debate.

12. Terms such as *arché*, *eîdos*, *ousîa*, and *télos* are key concepts in Western metaphysics. They are metaphors not only of presence but also of the centre, which can be both outside and inside, origin and end. Among these, *arché*, which conveys the meaning of both principle and command, is the name *par excellence* for the foundation, the central hinge.

A politics constituted on the basis of metaphysics, arranging itself around the *arché*, can be called an archi-politics. Rancière rightly traces it back to Plato's *politeia*:

> Archipolitics, whose model is supplied by Plato, reveals in all its radicality the project of a community based on the complete realization of the *arkhe* of community, total awareness, replacing the democratic configuration of politics with nothing left over.[44]

Since its first appearance, political philosophy has been tempted by foundation, and by the archic gesture of arming the city with a key principle. The ideal model of Plato's *politeia* is that regime of community in which all expressions of the common life stem from the same principle. Moreover, this principle – philosophically founded and no longer questioned – ensures the suppression of politics.

Still, Rancière's considerations also need to be supplemented with some comments clarifying what archi-politics is, and making explicit its various meanings. At least three can be identified: 1) First of all, archi-politics defines a closed, saturated, and compact space, which is structured around an *arché*, a pillar. 2) In this space, there can only be this one, essential *arché*, which archi-politics constantly puts on display and continually refers back to. 3) The rigid limits of archic politics, in which contingency is removed, exclude every other possibility from the outset, and eliminate any other point around which the community might converge.

Only where the foundation gives way does the principle cease to appear as a principle. It is there that the *an-arché* characteristic of democracy sees the light of day. This does not mean the toleration of dissent within the suppressed space of archi-politics – as a ripple or a wrinkle on its surface. Rather, it means the fundamental absence of *any* commanding principle. Only where that Archimedean point becomes less crucial can the community once again decide its own fate; only there can politics get moving again.

Contrary to what might be believed, archi-politics remains at work in democracy, representing both its consolatory seduction and its threatening nightmare. The more rigid democracy gets, hardening around an *arché*, the more it self-destructs. The more democracy opens up an-archically, allowing itself to be surpassed, the more it self-preserves.

2

ANARCHAEOLOGY: A PHILOSOPHICAL EXCAVATION

1. There is perhaps no more monumental history than the commonly provided history of democracy. The more the present is gripped by crisis, the greater the attempt to draw on the monumentalized authority of the past. This should be taken in the sense of what Friedrich Nietzsche brought to light already in his second *Untimely Meditation*. He here referred back to Polybius, according to whom history is the true preparation for the exercise of politics (see *Histories*, I, i, 2). It is as if those who govern need to lean on a past that will provide them with models and teachers. At the root of this monumentalized vision is a belief in homogeneity and continuity – an unbroken chain that unwinds across the millennia. Such an appropriation of the past in the mode of apologia – viewed in terms of its everlasting classical status, its ever-repeatable grandeur – shines through in the image of dwarfs standing on the shoulders of giants. In its ambiguity, this image was destined to become the motto of the Renaissance and of the modern age.[1] Was it an admission of humility, or a declaration of arrogance? Are our contemporaries merely dwarfs compared to the ancients, or are they able to see further?

In his denunciation of monumental history, Nietzsche damned a generalizing approach that makes the dissimilar similar and puts everything on the same footing. In his words: 'how many differences must be overlooked, with what violence the individuality of what is past must be forced into a general form, its sharp edges and its lines broken in favor of … conformity'.[2] Monumental history deceives with its misleading analogies, spreading illusions through seductive similarities. The past itself is *damaged* by this: 'entire large parts of it are forgotten, scorned, and washed away as if by a gray, unremitting tide'.[3] What is left over are the embellished individual events, the names of rare personalities shrouded in a marvellous aura.

This does not mean there is not also an antiquarian history and a critical history of democracy, in the sense that Nietzsche gives these terms, i.e. a passion for detail and the veneration of relics, or the judicial-style interrogation and final verdict. But it is the monumental vision of history that predominates.

2. It is rare for a work devoted to democracy, especially among those published in recent decades, not to contain a reference to the Greek 'beginning' which, even as it stands out in its mythical distance, seems like the pledge of a solid foundation. Athens – the *pólis* where everything began, the birthplace of democracy – dominates the scene at the origin of Western civilization.

It is, therefore, customary to speak of the conquest, discovery, invention, or foundation of democracy as if it had been settled upon with barely a moment's thought, miraculously instituted with a stroke of the pen. The semi-fantastical image of a New Continent brought to light by a shrewd and sagacious discoverer emerges even in the words of such a judicious historian as Moses I. Finley:

> I am not concerned to deny the possibility that there were prior examples of democracy, so-called tribal democracies, for instance, or the democracies in early Mesopotamia that some Assyriologists believe they can trace. Whatever the facts may be about the latter, their impact on history, on later societies, was null. The Greeks, and only the Greeks, discovered democracy in that sense, precisely as Christopher Columbus, not some Viking seaman, discovered America.[4]

Such an edifying perspective inevitably runs the risk of abstraction – but it also suggests a certain connection in between the lines. For if Greece was an America *avant la lettre*, then America can and must be the latest version of Greece. Thus democracy reaches the rank of an exemplary model, an archetype *par excellence*, which stands above the ins and outs of history and political affairs. It is an idea and an ideal to be looked to as a point of comparison, a yardstick for modern democracies.

This desire for identification with ancient ancestors, even at the cost of trivializing their traits, was sharply criticized by Paul Veyne, a French archaeologist and historian close to Michel Foucault's thinking. In this telling, Veyne argues, it is as if the Greeks had invented the 'truth of politics' and discovered the very 'essence' of democracy, which – leaving aside the problem of slavery – ought to be imitated in its entirety.[5] For Veyne, this means considering only the tip of the iceberg, without bringing the hidden part into view. Such an absence alone would allow us to refer to an eternal democracy.

The myth of the 'Greek miracle' has not lost its place but rather become even more powerful in the twenty-first century, in the age of democracy understood as a civil religion.[6] The myth tells the story of the democratic constitution, which gave rise to politics, meaning a (not further specified) practice of good government. Having fallen from on high one fine day in ancient Greece – or rather in one city, Pericles' Athens – today it reveals itself like never before as the inescapable foundation of Western civilization.[7] The enchanted palace of democracy stands in the metaphysical sky between the two shores of the Atlantic. It is an ideal construction, an immobile archetype, a model sufficiently fantastical to itself be colonized by the 'true', i.e. modern, democracies.

3. This perspective, which leaps over all the ins and outs of the temporal world, neglects to notice the interruptions and crises and represses all trace of conflict. It is no wonder, then, that in this telling democratic Athens, seen as the first and last page of our history, appears itself devoid of history. This is, indeed, required by the metaphysical need for the archetype, the dream of an already perfected process, the myth of the legislator who in one fell swoop establishes a good society, a model city. Thus a state of affairs is described, a harmonious and stable picture, liable to serve as the *topos* of a long reflection, an inexhaustible reserve of clichés.

The tendency to dehistoricize Greece is not new. Suffice it to mention two illustrious names whose influence soon spread beyond German borders: Winckelmann, who identified democratic Athens as the cradle of classicism; and Hegel, who saw a beautiful totality in the Greek city.[8] If this idea of Greece was destined to become a necessary phase, later surpassed in the development of the Hegelian spirit, the imaginary projection of an organic community, almost inscribed in a natural order, would have significant effects not only in the *querelles* of the moderns but also in some twentieth-century interpretations.[9]

The metaphysics of the model, of the Athenian *arché* – the principle of true democracy and an eternal politics, following a divinely linear progression from the Greeks to us today – has brought about two mirror-image phenomena. On the one hand, the Greek *pólis* has been reduced to a monumental representation; on the other, it has become the archetype of Western democracy.

This Greece is spatially restricted to Athens, limited in time to the fifth century BCE, and coalesced around one name: Pericles. The archi-democracy, the foundation of the West, the model city, is Pericles' Athens. This is, moreover, how it is celebrated in Thucydides' unchallengeable account (II, 35–46).

No matter that the Athenian rupture with the Mycenaean world was much more limited than is generally believed, or that significant precedents for the democratic *pólis* can be identified from the ninth and eighth centuries onwards, in towns on the coast of Asia Minor or southern Italy. The latter, largely destinations for the second wave of colonization around 750, offer a particularly interesting chapter in philosophical and political terms, although the lack of documentary evidence hampers a properly historical examination. Unlike the Phoenician colonies and the later Roman ones – or those of the Jewish diaspora, where the new arrivals brought their own laws with them – the Greek colonies were the result of an experiment. Those who settled in them either created new laws or symbolically entrusted this task to a legislator. Cornelius Castoriadis sees in this a seed of democracy: 'The movement of self-institution therefore began as early as the eighth century, with colonization, which was like an early prototype of this self-posing of the political community.'[10] This leads him to hypothesize that the origin of the democratic *pólis* was contemporary with the poems of Homer, in the sense of dating back to the time of writing rather than the world of which the poet spoke.[11] Following the thread of the self-establishing political community, as found in the history of the colonies, Castoriadis arrives at the case of Lipari, in the Aeolian Islands. There, for about four years around 580, a sort of communist regime was established, which collectivized the land.[12]

What can we say about Sparta? Although it remained oligarchic in calling, and indeed in its structure, it was still part of Greece. This attachment cannot be dismissed just by citing a few of its more superficial traits. How much of Athens was there in Sparta and how much of Sparta was there in Athens? The symbolic opposition between oligarchic cities and democratic cities becomes less emphatic when they are both considered as part of a political world that revolved around *nómos* – the law that is the same for all and which all respect. This distinguished both from a world subject merely to the arbitrary whims of the despot. The Sparta of the seventh century BCE is remembered by the poets as an example of *eunomía*, the realm of *Díke*, the city of justice.[13] Paradoxically, a trace of incipient democracy can be found in Sparta's dark and controversial history. It appears in the so-called *Rhetra*, a document from the seventh century preserved by Plutarch in his *Life of Lycurgus*.

Obscure and partly altered, presented as an oracle of Delphi to the Spartans, and thus surrounded by an aura of sacredness, this text written in the Laconic dialect reads: *dámoi d'agorâi níkan kaí krátos*, 'to the people in the agora supremacy and power'.[14] There are also other versions, but all contain the two elements *dêmos* and *krátos*, which appear here together for the first time.

Archaeology, for its part, has served to raise doubts and shake prior certainties. The inscription from 570 BCE found on the island of Chios in Ionia offers at least some hints of democracy. It refers to a *dêmos keklеméno*, a 'people gathered together', and calls for a *bolè tèn demosíen*, a 'public council', a *boulé* elected by the people and called upon to decide.[15] Was this the dawn of democracy?

Perhaps these brief references are enough to give us a glimpse of what lies deep beneath the tip of the iceberg: an unknown history, destined to remain mostly unknown, but which cannot be ignored. This should lead us to question the established representation, the monumental vision that latches on to the so-called 'origin of ancient democracy' and confines it within fictitious and conventional schemas. Such stereotypes ultimately risk diminishing the Greek contribution and obscuring the concept of democracy itself.

The exaltation of Greek history as the dawn of democracy begins with the fall of the king and the end of 'Eastern despotism' – a polemical formula coined by Herodotus to emphasize the contrast between the Greek cities and the Empire. Such a reading remained extraordinarily widespread into modern times, with a long history of consequences that has not yet run its course.[16] The archic figure of the king who embodied religious, military, political, and economic functions in his own person, firmly entrenched in the palace of the Mycenaean civilization, was losing power. The previous sacralized version of sovereignty was being replaced by a different demythologized and enlightened form. This was the king of the *Odyssey*, Ulysses of Ithaca, the just legislator, the skilled strategist, who laboriously kept the nobles around him at arm's length. While the *basileús* was gradually reduced to a religious and ritual role, command passed into the hands of the aristocrats, from whose ranks came the bearers of public office. There was likewise a transition in architecture, from the palace to the *agorá*. This surge of political and institutional energies everywhere shook the *pólis*. Then came the seventh century BCE, which many have considered the century of reforms.[17] The aristocratic regimes entered into crisis, gradually being dismantled or overthrown. The first known case is that of Corinth in 657, when a new figure, the tyrant, appeared on the scene. But behind him the *dêmos* was already emerging. In Athens, after a period of tension and conflict, the archontate of

Solon began in 594–593, attempting to restore a balance between the city's different factions.

Was Solon the true founder of Athenian democracy? The *prôtos heuretés*, the first discoverer? Should its invention be attributed to this audacious leader? Behind the metaphysics of the model as if miraculously descended from heaven already complete, there emerge earlier beginnings of democracy – attempts and trials that were not always crowned with success. A history with many chapters starts to unfold. And behind the mask of Pericles, other characters peep out, other founders, who may have been the protagonists of change. Democracy – which was not yet called by this name – is here instead conceived as a slow and reassuring evolution, a constant and unstoppable process. After Solon's incipit and the interlude of the tyranny of Pisistratus and his sons, came the real turning point in that history, one linked to the name of Cleisthenes and his reforms. Here, then, is the place and date of birth of democracy: Athens in 508–507 BCE.

A goal achieved? Not quite. It was after the two Persian wars, from which the Greek cities emerged victorious, that the true golden era of democracy began, and not before. This was the age of Pericles, which lasted for over thirty-two years starting in 462. However, Ephialtes – the radical politician who dared to launch an unprecedented attack on the archontate, the ultimate seat of power in the *pólis*, and fell victim to assassination – has been passed over in silence. Was that, perhaps, democracy? A democracy that lasted only for the heartbeat of a collective passion, in a moment when the people, in a city without an *arché*, tasted the thrill of freedom? This quickly forgotten episode does not make it into the dominant schema, because it would cut the ground from underneath it.[18] It is easier to hark back to the subsequent compromise under Pericles – even if on closer inspection this cannot really be called a democracy, considering that even this war chief's contemporaries thought that he looked a lot like a tyrant. Thucydides himself – beyond any suspicion of partiality, given his wider praise for Pericles – defined him as a *prótos anér*, a sort of *princeps*, an exemplary figure who anticipated primacy and principality.[19]

What followed was a story of disasters (such as the Peloponnesian War of 431–404), political crises, oligarchic interludes, and attempts to restore democracy. Indeed, it seemed almost to flourish anew in the age of Demosthenes up till 322. However, the name 'democracy' had already been replaced by the more neutral *politeía*. How long did Athens remain democratic under Macedonian rule? And what about the other Greek cities? For Hans Vorländer, 'After the death of Alexander the Great, the classical era of Attic democracy came to an end.'[20] It is as difficult to establish a *terminus post quem* as it is to indicate a *terminus ante quem*. Questions remain about how long democracy lasted: from the eighth to the fourth century BCE? Throughout the fifth? Or much less, for only thirty years? Or even merely for that brief period in which the *arché* was deposed from the Areopagus, the time of radical democracy, of Ephialtes the incorruptible?

4. On closer inspection, the metaphysical construct crumbles; cracks and rifts emerge in the monumental narrative. The linear story does not hold up. While the end is not a conclusion, the starting point seems to splinter into a spatial and temporal multiplicity of beginnings. Intersecting and overlapping, they reveal different ideas, heterogeneous meanings, and unexplored potentials. The legitimate suspicion arises that 'democracy' can have many different expressions. This was already the case in the Greek scenario.

What happens next? If the idea of an eternal democracy, of its undying essence, is hollow and insubstantial, then so too would be the history that purports to reconstruct its uninterrupted evolution, its progressive fortunes, from its birth in Athens to its triumphant culmination in the 'true democracy' of the West – if only because democracy, historically, makes rare and distant appearances, showing its face and then fading away again. It can be glimpsed at best from a bird's-eye view. Over long periods, all traces of it are lost. In the Middle Ages, it was eclipsed and even the term itself vanished, absent from official acts and documents.[21] If we want to be precise, even across centuries of modernity the term 'democracy' remained part of an erudite language, a *topos* of philosophical and literary debate, following in the wake of readings of Aristotle. It was a sort of residue of the past, an inescapable corollary of mixed constitution, sometimes a degenerate form of *politeía*, sometimes an impracticable possibility, and, ultimately, a dangerous chimera. Only with the Enlightenment did it break out of scholarly discourse and burst into the public arena where, even while linking back to the Greek past, it presented itself as a new political concept.

This does not mean that during the long period in which the word was eclipsed, between the ancient and modern scenarios, forms of democracy did not spring up here and there: hints, opportunities, and genuine breakthroughs. In the European context, there were many and varied such cases: the pioneering experience of the Italian *comuni* over the twelfth and thirteenth centuries; the anti-royalist movement for the commons in seventeenth-century England; and the radical break of 1789 in France. These multiple beginnings were more or less direct echoes of the Greek ones so many centuries before.

But why limit our outlook to Europe, and why assume a Eurocentric perspective? More than one anthropologist has asked this question,[22] and with good reason. In a comparative study of the meaning of 'democracy', Marcel Detienne emphasizes the element of meeting in assemblies – 'the will to assemble together'. On this basis, he wondered whether the concept should not be extended to other times and places.[23] Democracy has not only multiple beginnings but also multiple 'sites of the political', as Marc Abélès called them, where histories distant from each other in both space and time may unfold.[24] These sites include, for example, the Ochollo people in the Gamo Mountains, who have inhabited southern Ethiopia since the nineteenth century; the Zaporozhian Cossacks in the fifteenth century; the Italian maritime republics that fought internally against noble forces and externally against Empire and the Church; and the towns of Magna Graecia that have been traced in the sand since the eighth century BCE. What are the similarities here?

The site of the political is not the fashionable distinction between friend and enemy, which Detienne passes wry judgement on. Rather, it is a 'provisional level' where the 'desire to come together to discuss common affairs' opens up the public space that the Greeks called *Héstia*, the common hearth of the *agorá*.[25] It is the site, and the time, of the assembly. 'Who wishes to speak?' This offering of a space for intervention – also chosen as the title for Detienne's study – echoes the phrase used by the herald who opened the assembly in the Greek *pólis*.[26]

5. The critique of the metaphysics of the model has identified two, mirrored, processes. The first lies in a strong tendency to dehistoricize and depoliticize, which has ended up imposing a monumental representation of Pericles' miraculous Athens. We will now turn to the second: the way in which that same Athens became the archetype of Western democracy.

Here it is worth looking at a brief, fleeting reference that Pierre Vidal-Naquet makes in the preface to his collection *Politics Ancient and Modern*. A similar reference appears – not by chance – in his short volume *The Atlantis Story: A Short History of Plato's Myth*, which, starting from Plato's dialogues, plunges into the dark depths of the sea and the endless distance of time in search of traces of the lost island, whose existence appears inseparable from that of an equally imaginary Athens.[27] The paths beaten by Vidal-Naquet, which trace a map of European culture, lead to modern nationalism and the use of myth in the Nazi Third Reich.

The path that led to Athens becoming the archetype of the liberal world is rather more peaceful. Still, it should not be overlooked that, from the outset, the city becomes a representation. It splits into a here and an elsewhere. This happens precisely with democracy. Athens is both the democratic city and the intellectual, or rather philosophical, 'elsewhere' of its critics – with Plato in the lead, followed by Aristotle. It is as if *Pólis* and *Allópolis* were two sides of the same Athens.[28] While there is no theory of democracy developed by its own lead actors, there is an implacable, at times fierce, critique coming from philosophers. This critique would have decisive repercussions; indeed, it was this view that predominated in the philosophical tradition.

The modern revolutionaries who sought reconnection with a past example of radical democracy found only these accounts offering merciless judgements and disparaging comments. It is no surprise, then, that Athens long represented not a political model deemed worthy of imitation, but rather an image of the power of culture. The radicalism perceived already in the practice of direct democracy, which was seen as a threat, meant that Athens became more of an anti-model from which modernity sought to distinguish itself.

The temptation to identify models runs throughout the Western tradition. In his seminar 'The City and the Laws', held in the mid-1980s as part of a series dedicated to ancient Greece, Cornelius Castoriadis drew on a key concept in his thinking – that of the 'imaginary' – to shed light on the moderns' attitude towards ancient democracy. There is no comprehensive work reconstructing all the stages of this process. Still, it is necessary to examine the tendency that emerged and became consolidated in modernity: that of making the Greek *pólis* the object of 'an investment, a projection, [which] if not purely and simply phantasmal, [is] at least ideological-phantasmal'.[29] Made into a rigid structure and reduced to a metaphysical projection screen, Athens is taken for a model or an anti-model.[30] Although indicators and evidence can be found also in earlier periods, it was from the Renaissance onwards that this tendency took on ever-sharper contours. Greco-Roman antiquity was taken up as a weapon in the struggle against the regimes of the time, both monarchy and ecclesiastical-feudal power. Machiavelli offers the most eminent example of this attitude. Still later, albeit less visibly, the ancient world continued to be invoked – although in truth this meant Rome more than Athens. While in the modern context Baruch Spinoza and Jean-Jacques Rousseau were exceptions, each in their own way – not least due to the attention they paid to important aspects that risked being overlooked – the constitutions of the past generally served as a screen on which to project the ideological requirements of the present. The temptation to use models reached its peak with the French Revolution of 1789, when the ideological spectres of three cities contended on the political scene: Athens, Sparta, and Rome. If Rome ultimately prevailed, the Montagnards' complete identification with Sparta – a source of almost millenarian inspiration – ought not to be forgotten.[31]

But the real turning point, destined to have a profound and lasting influence on the moderns' attitude towards the ancient model, came with the age of Restoration. The call for democracy had played a significant role in the revolutionary period, not only in the struggle against monarchy, but also in the defence of citizens' rights. But it took an unprecedented turn with the emergence of an individualistic liberalism. Stepping forward to the centre of the modern scenario was the individual owner who, empowered by his inalienable rights, agreed to cede part of his sovereignty only under certain conditions, so as to establish an order from which he could withdraw at any time.

The significance of this turning point is clearly illustrated in Nicole Loraux and Pierre Vidal-Naquet's essay 'The Formation of Bourgeois Athens'.[32] Drawing on a wealth of detail, the authors reconstruct a century-long process with identifiable starting and end points: namely the *Tableau philosophique des progrès successifs de l'esprit humain*, presented by the young Jacques Turgot at the Sorbonne in 1750, and the *Histoire grecque*, published in its first edition in 1851 by the obscure *lycée* teacher Victor Duruy – a work destined to have an influence beyond France. The authors focus on what happened immediately before and after the revolutionary crisis in France, when the so-called *idéologues* – writers, politicians, intellectuals, and philosophers – engaged in a restoration project that included a revision of the ancient history that had inspired the Jacobins. Athens did not become merely a *topos* for reflection on France, or an instrument for keeping the France of the day at a critical distance, as in Chateaubriand. Rather, in an ideological shift, Athens 'became the model of a liberal and bourgeois society and even, in the last analysis, of a "civil society" detached from political society but nevertheless possessing a history with a beginning, a climax and a decline'.[33]

Although it is possible to identify important precedents, the protagonist in this shift was undoubtedly Benjamin Constant. The ideologue of modern liberalism, Constant was determined to keep antiquity at a safe distance. In a lecture given at the Athénée Royal in Paris in February 1819, entitled 'The Liberty of Ancients Compared with that of Moderns', he revived the traditional *querelle* that had, especially in the seventeenth century, animated the disputes over the primacy of the ancients or the moderns. The novelty of the lecture, however, lies in its theme of freedom, the pivot around which

Constant's thirty famous pages revolve. The basic thesis is easily summarized: the liberty of moderns is characterized by the personal autonomy of the individual and the protection of their individual rights; the liberty of ancients, on the other hand, aimed at the active participation of all, at the common exercise of sovereignty:

> The aim of the ancients was the sharing of social power among the citizens of the same fatherland: this is what they called liberty. The aim of the moderns is the enjoyment of security in private pleasures; and they call liberty the guarantees accorded by institutions to these pleasures.[34]

Whatever care Constant tries to take in distinguishing the more liberal Athens from Sparta and Rome, he nonetheless arrives at categorical judgements: the ancients accepted 'the complete subjection of the individual to the authority of the community'; '[n]o importance was given to individual independence'; '[a]ll private actions were submitted to a severe surveillance'.[35] In this hardly edifying picture of the ancient *pólis*, presented – in words similar to those of his contemporary Hegel – as a beautiful (disturbing) totality, Constant cast a spectral shadow over Greek democracy. This shadow would long endure, and over time would thicken, threatening to envelop this democracy in the thick fog of a totalitarian universe. The participation of all citizens proves to be a mistake, and collective sovereignty a danger; freedom turns into slavery. This is even more true since this form of direct self-government, feasible in small ancient cities, cannot be replicated in large modern states. As Constant observes: 'This compensation no longer exists for us today. Lost in the multitude, the individual can almost never perceive the influence he exercises.'[36] He thus sings the praises of the liberty of the moderns, which – consisting in the peaceful enjoyment of private independence – must not be sacrificed. What counts is the private sphere, which has to be protected from all political interference. The pillar of the modern world is the individual *qua* self-legislator; his individual and proprietary rights reduce whatever is common – but also whatever is political – almost to a superfluous residue.

The contrast between the ancients and the moderns is sharper than it seems, and goes far beyond a neutral weighing up of strengths and weaknesses. Athens can become the ideological locus of liberalism only insofar as it may serve as an anti-model of democracy, a screen onto which the gloomy spectres of modern anxieties can be projected. The *querelle* is not simply between past and present. Nor does it remain within the limits of the antithesis between direct democracy and representative democracy. Between these two poles, it is already possible to glimpse the questions – of freedom or equality, participation or security – that trouble contemporary debate.

Constant's great inversion of the question also had repercussions for historiography; indeed, after Duruy, this shift would truly be enshrined in Fustel de Coulanges' *The Ancient City*. Published in 1864, this work enjoyed broad prestige. The subtitle could have been: 'Stop imitating the ancients'.[37] Drawing much clearer conclusions than Constant, and taking an even more drastic approach, Coulanges describes the individual in ancient democracy as completely subjugated to the community. Referring to the omnipotence of the state, he repeatedly oversteps the mark in reducing the *pólis* to modern categories. Although Coulanges has often been criticized, and his work has been largely superseded by developments in historical and philological studies, his antithetical schema and his vision of the ancient city remain almost unchallenged in philosophical-political thought.[38] Perhaps it is no accident that, after a long period in which the ancient *pólis* was a subject only of specialist studies, a new interest arose in the aftermath of the totalitarian experience, thanks to the rediscovery of the political.[39]

6. The monumental representation has maintained an almost unchallenged dominance. It has done so despite the archaeology which has sporadically made discoveries which do not fit into the ideal model, instead revealing cracks and raising questions. Given this monumentality, we can properly speak of the 'constitution' of democracy, or of democracy as a 'constitution'. By this I mean the establishment and consolidation of a tradition which – filling in the blank spaces of the texts and bridging the gaps in the crumbling ground around the monuments – has been happy to retrace the path from beginning to end, from the *arché* to the *télos*, or rather, from the *télos* to the *arché*.

This archic teleology traces a path back from the ultimate aim of 'good government' to the original political system. This is an almost immobile history, one that heads along a gentle slope. It presents itself as a process of constant refinement, a steadily growing rationality; it remembers, it acquires, it progresses. But as this teleology endlessly harks back to the beginning, it does nothing more than insist on the greatness of the eventual outcome. It is as if the solemn ghost of the precursor served to legitimize the epigones. The foundation is perpetuated, the traces multiply, the connections become saturated. The description of obscure continuities, the reconstruction of a linear path of development, struggle to conceal the totalizing trend. Thus the monumental history of democracy seems to resemble a history of ideas, that 'discipline of beginnings and ends' which, according to Foucault, reproduces in its methods and requirements a 'rather shop-soiled' image of history.[40] In the case of democracy, however, this approach seems all the more forced and paradoxical. For democracy, as we shall see, emerges where the *arché* fades, and thus escapes any archic capture; as long as it is democracy, it remains resistant to any totalizing end.

To interrogate the meaning of democracy and its emergence is to confront the powerful tradition of an established historiography. Far removed from Nietzsche's 'effective history', this tradition does not merely indicate a path of interpretation, but sets itself up as the guardian of what is handed down, reduced to the self-evidence of the already understood and already elucidated. It would then seem that any further hermeneutic excavation is superfluous. Herein lies the power of a rigid tradition, capable – as Heidegger wrote – of making us forget its own origin.[41] Access to the sources is not so much blocked as covered up. Any attempt at going back, at retreating into the past, can only appear futile and unrealistic.

We can thus speak of an 'archive' of democracy, which modernity has decisively contributed to preparing and consolidating. Alongside the corpus that brings together documents and testimonies, the archive is not only a site of collection and preservation, but also one where the hermeneutic authority of the past and the ancient is established. It is worth repeating the words of Foucault, who saw in the archive a question of power rather than knowledge. For him, 'The archive is first the law of what can be said, the system that governs the appearance of statements as unique events.'[42] The documents that are handed down do not fit into a linear and smooth sequence, nor do they appear in an amorphous multitude. The archive is the site that orders and composes these documents, from the moment of their emergence, the one that regulates their formation and shapes its transformations. It would be misleading to think of the archive in terms of the dust on the shelves or the preservation of treasures. The archive is a device that varies across historical periods, between tradition and oblivion. We can then understand why, in the delicate balance between past and present, it can be the privileged site for a diagnosis of today's world.

This is all the more true when it comes to democracy. Once it is reduced to an archic teleology of 'good government', a neutral constitution, a metaphysical archetype of politics, democracy risks being definitively archived. This means consigning the most peculiar germ of democracy to oblivion, as its most unprecedented potential is stifled.

7. This raises a decisive question of method. What method is most appropriate for an investigation that heads into the archive of democracy – one that does not seek to retread the path already beaten by monumental history, or to follow the traces of a linear chronology leading from miraculous beginning to ultimate outcome? That would mean yet another metaphysical quest in search of the immutable form of democracy, its pure idea, its essence preserved from all (mis)adventures and change. This is ultimately the plan more or less implicit in numerous introductory essays and manuals, but also in many exercises in historical reconstruction and specialist articles, which, even in their titles, promise to go back to the birth, to trace the origins, to find their way to the foundational beginning. It is as if, beyond the usual stages connected in a unified sequence in a repeated narrative, it were possible – by establishing a foothold outside of time – to reach beyond history towards the *arché*.

But here we cannot fail to recall Nietzsche's radical critique, which detects behind each thing something completely different. Behind the supposedly timeless principle, it unmasks the really historical character of the beginning, in its many-coloured pattern of development. This critique is taken up by Foucault in order to dispel the 'chimeras of the origin' that hang over all historical research.[43] It would be futile, and risky, to look towards the solemn foundational beginning upon high, for all the emergences of history arise from below. This demands that we survey the depths, without hesitation and without fear of encountering unexorcized ghosts, repressed shadows that continue to disturb.

It thus seems necessary to deconstruct the dominant tradition which has become more entrenched and more rigid in recent decades. It is as if the monumental vision of democracy has led to its near-canonization, conditioning access to documentary sources and, above all, feeding the habitual narrative, the history that proceeds from self-perpetuating foundations. The path that opens up to such a deconstruction is 'philosophical archaeology', in the sense outlined by Agamben, developing intellectual cues and thoughts from Kant, Nietzsche and Foucault:

> We could provisionally call 'archaeology' the practice which, within any historical investigation, has to do, not with the origin, but with the question of the point from which the phenomenon takes its source, and must therefore confront itself anew with the sources and with the tradition.[44]

This is the move against the grain which Heidegger already identified as *Rückgang*: a retreat into the past, a backward step, which allows us to revisit established paradigms and deconstruct cohesive interpretative frameworks, even before we get into rereading the sources. But the key term in Agamben's argument is 'point of emergence', an expression with which Foucault translates the meaning of *Entstehung* in Nietzsche's genealogy.[45] What does emergence mean? In what way does the 'source' understood as a point of emergence not coincide with the documents of the tradition? Agamben follows a cue from the theologian Franz Overbeck, Nietzsche's faithful friend, who speaks of *Urgeschichte* or even *Entstehungsgeschichte*, 'prehistory' or 'history of the emergence'.[46] There is a fundamental discrepancy at the heart of any history, an unavoidable heterogeneity between what has emerged and what has not, or still has not, and which has remained latent – not in a remote past or even in a meta-historical structure, but rather in a 'fringe of ultra-history'.[47] As linguists studying Indo-European words teach, this is a tendency which – while originating in the past – continues to operate in the present, conditioning the development of historical languages over time. In other words, a fault line divides every historical phenomenon into that which has remained at its source and that which has translated into facticity. The point of emergence lies on this fault line.

It is easy to understand the need for an investigation that goes against the grain of tradition, for an archaeology that does not follow the continuous transition, the all too obvious connection, but delves into the cracks of history, between fissures and composite layers, where the shocks make history unstable. What had appeared immobile and static instead fragments; what had presented itself as self-identical and consistent now crumbles, revealing its underlying heterogeneity. The identity preserved at the origin is nothing more than the discord of the disparate.

It is ultimately, for Foucault, the task of the researcher to maintain a delicate balance between a critique of the archive and a diagnosis of the present world. It straddles a dual perspective, archaeological and genealogical, depending on whether one looks at the starting point of a phenomenon or at the turn taken by its outcome.[48]

8. This poses the need for a philosophical archaeology of democracy. Such an investigation has not been carried out to date, surprising as that may be. But it responds to the most pressing need and deepest concern of the radical perspective. At stake is the future perfect of democracy.

The retreat into archaeology, as a philosophical excavation going against the grain of history, aims to get to the fault line where the lived and the unlived, the realized and the potential, the preserved and the repressed, combine and separate. Its attention is thus focused not on the origin, but on the emergence.

Thus its concern is not to gain access to an atemporal, meta-historical principle, or to head back into a nebulous distant past. To steer clear of the chimera of the origin means, rather, to deconstruct the archic image that democracy tries to give of itself by way of monumental history. It is as if its own an-archic source were a cause of embarrassment and discomfort, to the point that it instead presents itself as *arché*. To evade censure, avoid harsh judgement, and escape the condemnation that has weighed on it since its inception, democracy pretends that it was not an-archic. But what is repressed still remains latent. Anarchy ultimately reveals itself as the *pudenda origo* (Nietzsche's idea of the 'shameful origin') of democracy. Hidden away because it is reputed inadmissible, concealed because it is considered heterogeneous and other, anarchy is relegated to the margins where no democratic regime can keep it under guard. So, anarchy remains latent, as if, still working away, it were about to explode with its full subversive force.

Philosophical archaeology captures democracy at its point of emergence, catching it by surprise at the point where it arises. In this sense, such research does not establish foundations, but rather destabilizes and disturbs. It follows the irruption of democracy, its leap onto the stage of history, without ever losing sight of what is happening behind the scenes. Precisely because it takes shape on a stage, the emergence refers not so much to a point as to a site of confrontation, or rather to an empty space, which is the opposition of forces as such. It is a void through which threats are exchanged and commitments are made; it is the distance of the struggle, as forces confront and prevail over each other. This is why, in thinking about the point of emergence, we should not imagine a single event – the fundamental reform, the decisive treaty, the crucial battle – that sets in motion a continuous chronology, as if dissolving into a teleological movement. Examining the pattern of history – the tangle of intersecting accounts in its distinct and juxtaposed passages, its sequences rebelling against any single law – the gaze that digs down and draws distinctions seeks to grasp the event in its unique and specific character. It does not look up high, where the memorable events are meant to be gathered, but scrutinizes the depths and the margins. For it is there that an unknown word will enter the scene, domination will be unmasked, a balance of power will be reversed, and an indistinct mass will take on a new profile.

Philosophical archaeology is a counter-memory of democracy. However, it does not nostalgically yearn for some phantom origin. Rather, it pulls back into a past that 'did not happen' but which *could have been* and perhaps *still can be*.[49] This is a heterogeneous past, but one not unconnected to what has come to be; it is a past that remains in a latent phase and is thus still operative in the present. Philosophical archaeology recovers what has been repressed; it summons up the ghost of the past, not in order to restore it but rather to glimpse its imminence in the present. Only in this way does the past that did not happen reveal itself as an indispensable source, a means of access to the present.[50] Moreover, precisely because it *could have been* and *could be*, it is the past that *will have been* once philosophical archaeology has deconstructed the monumental tradition and flushed out the ghosts. In this past in the future, in this future perfect, the archaeological investigation is condensed. The an-archic past that will have been is the future perfect of democracy.

9. It is called archaeology, but it should not be mistaken for the *lógos* on the *arché* or of the *arché*. Here lies both the most banal and the most serious misunderstanding. Any archaeological excavation or genealogical investigation runs the risk of reifying the *arché*. The researcher heads back and delves deep until they seem to arrive at a clear beginning, a solid foundation, as if it were possible to reach – beyond tradition, over the top of history – an indestructible *arché*, an ontological anchor, a metaphysical remnant.

Derrida warns against this danger on several occasions, from *Of Grammatology* to *Resistances of Psychoanalysis*. Even in the most patient and careful work of deconstruction, there is always the risk of producing an excess of origin. 'It is always a matter of undoing, desedimenting, decomposing, deconstituting sediments, artefacta, presuppositions, institutions.'[51] However, it is not enough to deconstruct; it is necessary to guard against both the possibility of and the desire for the origin and the original. The concern to ward off this spectre is exemplified in 'archi-writing', where traces of the *arché* are preserved without any attempt to erase them or, even less, to reappropriate them.[52]

Archaeology is not the *lógos* on the *arché*, but rather a *lógos* that deconstructs the *arché*. It undermines it, erodes it, puts it into doubt. In so doing, it goes back to the point of origin which, far from being identified with the *arché*, is instead the fault line where history becomes accessible. Hence the close link between archaeology and history, which only becomes clear when considered from this perspective. The *arché* does not remain an 'operative force', in the sense that Agamben ultimately seems to understand it.[53] Rather, it emerges, in its spectral appearances, as an archic paradigm.

We can speak of an 'an-archaeology', to refer to that work of digging that does not stop at picking apart principles or criticizing assumptions. The *an-* has not so much a negative value as a privative one. The expression is found in Foucault's lectures at the Collège de France in 1979–80, in which he rethinks classical anarchism's naive claim of situating itself beyond power – a pretence born of its vain hope of transcending state domination. 'So I will say that what I am proposing is rather a sort of anarcheology.'[54] Foucault is not seeking to reject anarchy, but to review its tacit metaphysical premises, its archic residues.[55] Anarchaeology, which he briefly mentions, points in this direction. For Foucault 'it is not a question of saying all power is bad, but of starting from the point that no power whatsoever is acceptable by right and absolutely and definitively inevitable'.[56] The question lies in the 'non-necessity of power' – at the start of its work and not only once it has concluded its endeavours. No power is self-evident, no power can be taken for granted. It can thus be said that anarchaeology is that investigation which, having neither foundations nor teleological purposes, proceeds from non-power, from *an-arché*.

10. 'The way that most men deal with traditions, even traditions of their own country, is to receive them all alike as they are delivered, without applying any critical test whatever' (I, 20, 1).[57] With these words the great historian Thucydides bewailed the lack of a critical spirit, a lack that gradually leads to an accumulation of misconceptions, unconfirmed claims, and misleading judgements. He is indicting his contemporaries, the Athenians, and gives numerous examples in this regard. Can it be that they have accepted tradition as a higher authority? 'So little pains do the vulgar take in the investigation of truth, accepting readily the first story that comes to hand' (I, 20, 3). The path to *alétheia* is arduous. Thucydides turns back to take a final brief view of it from the summit he has reached. His words are steeped in the effort, the anxiety, and the difficulty of a historian's investigative work. Unlike others, historians do not put their faith in what is handed down by tradition; rather, they dig behind the facade of convention, scrutinize facts that others take for granted, and raise questions.

Thus concludes the famous *Archaeology*, the name given to the research into the past contained in the first twenty chapters of Book I of the *Histories* (I, 2–19). At the centre of attention in the opening section is the Peloponnesian War, the 'greatest movement', *meghíste kínesis*, not only in Greek history but in the history of humanity (I, 1, 2). The two superpowers, Sparta and Athens, clash 'at the height of their power', dividing the world between them. This is the theme

Thucydides plans to address, and the reason why he wants to leave a complete account for posterity. From the outset, he has gathered the first clues, the useful facts of the matter, sensing that this would be an unprecedented event, *axiologôtaton*, the most memorable. Hence, Thucydides' investigation takes place in the present, within the limits of contemporary history.

But what does this have to do with the past, the prior events, and those even further back? Passing a judgement on the war would seem to require a comparison with what came before it.[58] Thucydides then pauses for an archaeological *excursus*, in which he attempts a 'quite remarkable experiment in non-narrative history', a 'strange history/non-history', broadly outlining that distant and nebulous age.[59] It is a picture of what he believes he knows on the basis of the clues and signs gathered, the *tekmḗria* and *semeîa*. But for a historian like Thucydides is it really possible to know the past? The appearance of the term *adúnaton* in the first lines (I, 1, 3) would suggest that it is impossible. The gaze, however, extends ever further back, and the historian, returning from those remote recesses, outlines coordinates, selects data, and gathers traces, in a difficult yet tireless endeavour. These are *ónta anexélenkta*, facts that cannot be verified, as the facts of the present may be (I, 21, 1); this does not, however, condemn the historian to silence. Clarity, *saphḗs*, is lost with the passage of time: the contours of events become blurred, confused, and here and there vanish outright. Yet it remains possible and necessary *heureîn* (I, 20, 1), that is, to discover, find, and comprehend.[60] Archaeology is a hermeneutics of the past that does not report or recount the facts as the present can. It proceeds not only through time – the passing of the years which dulls the memory – but also through the tradition which encrusts and ossifies all that it passes down, thus reducing it to a mostly uncritical acceptance. The historian is an interpreter insofar as they get in the way of things, break with traditions, make distinctions and choose signs, reorder the universe of clues, and thus transform the vision of the past. Archaeology is not a naive bid to get back to the origins, to be contrasted with the facile versions embellished by the poets and sugar-coated by logographers as the custodians of memory (cf. I, 21, 1). To make use of *élenchos*, to sift through and refute, is to cut a path through the archic space itself, retracing that tradition which is its only kaleidoscope, its only distorted image.

Knowledge of the past cannot be the same as knowledge of the present: it loses clarity and seems less comprehensible. So, according to Thucydides, the historian must refrain from giving details, limiting himself to broad strokes, not in the spirit of continuity, but by way of analogy. This seems to be the aim of his own research. Why else would he set out to narrate the Peloponnesian War, if not for those who come after him? The fear arises that this tumult in human affairs is not separate from the subsequent history. Therefore, Thucydides says that his narrative was composed not for *agónisma es tò para-chrêma*, 'momentary entertainment', but as *ktêmá te es aieí*, a 'possession for ever' (I, 22, 4). In what he has lived through, he sees the seeds of what others may experience in the future.

11. It was through rereading Thucydides, and more specifically his pages on historiography, that Castoriadis was inspired to look closer at Greek democracy.[61] Hannah Arendt had already set out on a similar course just a few years earlier. This dovetailing interest is hardly surprising. Notwithstanding these authors' differences of approach and perspective, the similarities are clear. After experiencing totalitarianism – of which they were, each in their own way, direct witnesses (and in part victims), fierce opponents, and deeply insightful interpreters – each felt the urgent need to radically rethink politics. Yet, this endeavour did not allow them to pursue the fuller realization of modernity, which had in the meantime taken on the contours of liberal capitalism. For the totalitarian catastrophe was but the culmination of the modern tradition, whose most disturbing and monstrous face had thus been revealed. This also gave rise to a critique of orthodox Marxism: of the dialectic through which a deterministic foundation and a transcendent norm were reintroduced by the back door, by means of the laws of history. The protest movements of the 1960s, which both so enthusiastically supported, prompted them to recover what Arendt considered the lost treasure of political action.[62] From the Budapest Uprising to the Paris Commune to the democratic revolutions of the eighteenth century – such are the periods in which autonomy and political creativity make themselves felt, while history seems condensed.[63]

The Greek *pólis* has a special place among these most prominent moments. But what does it mean to head back to the source of democracy? For both Arendt and Castoriadis, it is not a return, but rather a recourse to that Greek experience which, in addition to inaugurating the space of the *pólis*, left its mark on philosophy. Historical reflection becomes the arena for political self-reflection. Their paths would diverge, and in the 1980s Castoriadis distanced himself from Arendt in a sharp engagement. Up to that point, however, the convergence lay in their strong opposition to the metaphysics of the model, of the beautiful totality deemed necessary but outdated in the supposed progress of the moderns over the ancients. This is not a distant model, an abstract paradigm, according to the canons of the dominant interpretation. Arendt writes: 'The Greek pólis will continue to exist at the bottom of our political existence – that is, at the bottom of the sea – for as long as we use the word "politics."'[64] Here we have the image of the source which would be so crucial for radical-democratic currents. Suffice it to mention Abensour's 'insurgent democracy'. We should understand this not only in the sense of an 'insurgent' movement but also in the simple sense of 'to surge': to spring forth, to be born.[65] It should not be imagined as an initial and spontaneous phase of democracy, for that would be to fall back into the archic paradigm. Arendt herself, in a particularly evocative passage in her essay 'What is Freedom?', refers to the 'secret source', the 'spring' which may remain hidden yet continues to flow, managing to survive even in those 'epochs of petrification' of political life.[66] Only when it finally re-emerges does freedom become tangible.

Castoriadis, in turn, uses the term 'source' here and there to refer to political reflection that moves beyond a historical and philological exegesis.[67] The emphasis here is on the contingency of the *nómos* – of laws and institutions – which, by allowing the very possibility of action, opened the way through the *pólis* to a democratic exercise of power.[68] But it is precisely the importance that Castoriadis attaches to the self-instituent process that prompts him to speak of Greek democracy in terms of a 'germ':

> Greece is the socio-historical *locus* where democracy and philosophy were created and where, consequently, our origins lie. Until the meaning and power of this creation are exhausted – and I am deeply convinced that they have not been – Greece will be a germ for us: neither a 'model' nor an example among others, but a germ.[69]

Castoriadis justifies the use of this word in numerous passages, largely with the aim of emphasizing the antithesis between germ and model: 'I have repeated many times that I am not talking about ancient Greece as a model, but as a germ'; 'I will insist on this word, in opposition to "model"'; 'I am not proposing Athenian democracy as a model at all; I am saying rather that there is a germ there for us.'[70] His critique is directed at the attempt to reduce that historical experience to an abstract concept within a *tradition* – even turning it into a norm. Athens cannot be held up as a model, nor as an anti-model, because in its singularity, in its strangeness, in its unexpected extraordinariness, it eludes all imitation. Nor is there any project to reproduce it that would make sense.

Still, it would also be misleading to imagine Athens as the genesis of modern democracy, as per that approach, widespread in the history of ideas, which emphasizes the dimension of continuity. This is not what Castoriadis means when he refers to a 'germ', which is instead interpreted as 'an indication of possibility'.[71] The latter is perhaps the most precise definition among those that appear in his pages. The germ refers to possibilities that – being already in part fulfilled, virtual, and repressed – are capable of resurfacing in history, of becoming realized in their fruitful productivity. Precisely because the germ is an index, one that marks a direction, the past is also of interest for the future. Thucydides had the same insight when he wrote of 'archaeology'. Athenian democracy is thus a germ, in the sense not of a founding origin, but of an origin inscribed in the becoming and passing of what is born.

Perhaps no one was better able to grasp the connection between past and future than Walter Benjamin, indeed already in the early years of his reflection. We can assume that his attention to language and to the development of languages, latent in their structure, contributed to this. This is evidenced by his 1922 essay 'Aufgabe des Übersetzers', which refers to the 'after-ripening' of words.[72] However, it is in a memorable page of the 'Gnoseological Preface', which opens his 1925 work *Origin of the German Trauerspiel*, that Benjamin sees the link between 'Vor- und Nachgeschichte', pre-history and post-history.[73] The recovery of the term 'origin', revived also in the title, is not aloof to Nietzsche's critique, which had also resonated in Heidegger's considerations in this same period.[74] Following the etymological path, *Ursprung* is linked back to the verb *entspringen*, meaning to spring or gush forth like a jet of water bursting out of the ground. It gives us an origin in the sense of a source, a wellspring, not in the sense of genesis. In other words, origin is not a 'becoming of the already born'. It should thus be taken for a historical rather than a logical category. And Benjamin considers it historically:

> The origin stands as an eddy in the stream of becoming and vigorously draws the emerging material into its rhythm. In the naked, manifest existence of the factual, the original never allows itself to be recognized ... The origin, then, does not arise from the facts attested but concerns their fore- and after-history.[75]

The factual does not exhaust the origin, which remains as a source of unrealized possibilities. Precisely for this reason, while the origin must be seen in its incompleteness, it must also be recognized as recovery and redemption. The collection of finds, the *Befund*, is also a *Wiederherstellung*, a restoration, or rather, a redemption. This word, which recurs here, would have an earth-shattering meaning for Benjamin's messianic reading of history.

Between the factual and the possible, the origin is thus traced back to what Foucault and Agamben called the point of emergence. Benjamin is to be credited for having situated it between pre-history and post-history, in that dynamic intertwining, the bond of a future-present, the profound archaeological nexus that philosophy is called upon to scrutinize.

12. The unavoidable question that must finally be addressed concerns the relationship with the Greek past that is said to stand out in the future. These are voices from another time, said to serve as bearings for orienting ourselves in the present. Do we really need the Greeks in order to rethink democracy? Do we need them – more generally – for thought?

It is thus worth questioning the meaning of this recourse to Greek experience, which is not merely a return to the past. The discussion here revolves around conceptions of the relationship with the past in which tradition and, ultimately, history are considered. Liberal modernity has been built on an increasingly intransigent opposition between 'them' and 'us', 'ancients' and 'moderns'. We look down on the Greeks from the heights of a historical evolution considered to represent progress, with the superiority of those who believe they possess an enormously more refined political system. Any comparison only serves to strengthen a reassuring sense of distance which, on closer inspection, proves to be an outright separation. Greece stands out in an archic distance, in a past that is complete and by now surpassed.

This seems to pose an alternative between the meticulous preservation of the past and its hasty dismissal. In the first case, that of the historicist perspective, what matters is fidelity to a legacy that must be handed down to posterity as it is: what counts is an authentic memory, accurate down to the smallest detail. The cult of the past, so dispassionate that it lays claim to objectivity, is linked to a disengaged vision in which the present vanishes, while philosophy looms only as the threat of an intolerable anachronism. This also applies – indeed, especially so – to that historical reconstruction that retraces the stages of thought, that is, to the history of philosophy, which is most often reduced to the non-philosophical repetition of the words of philosophers. Studying Plato, in this approach, would mean reconstructing 'what he really said', without interposing oneself, without betraying him, regardless of one's own point of view. At the root of this historicist attitude is, ultimately, a clear rejection of any dialogue with the Greeks. The opposite position is that which characterizes analytical thinking – open about its forgetting of the past, and thus allowing a timeless present to dominate. Here the history of philosophy is viewed in the same light as the history of science. In such an approach, we can easily do without Greek philosophy – and the undoubted accretion of progress would only serve as confirmation. If it were necessary to engage with them, then the Greek philosophers might simply be taken as colleagues, and their pages could be read as if they had been published in the latest issue of *Mind*.[76] To study Aristotle would not mean reconstructing what he truly said, but evaluating whether what he said is true. In this ahistorical position, where the past is judged in light of present-day truths, the rejection of dialogue is equally clear.

A different path is opened up by philosophical hermeneutics, which, starting with Heidegger, has been conceived as the unfolding and deeper exploration of a radical question addressed to Greek philosophy. Here, a relationship of circularity emerges: in undermining the linear scheme, it also undermines the opposition between 'them' and 'us', 'ancients' and 'moderns'. The demand of phenomenology – which requires us to free ourselves from the shackles of a narrow historical erudition in order to retrain the philosophical gaze – is combined with Nietzsche's powerful critique. But what does this radical question mean?

Retracing the course of philosophy means listening more closely to words such as *phúsis* and *alétheia*, in which the original experiences of thought seem to be condensed. It is thus first necessary to destroy the overlapping layers of tradition, to remove the petrified language of metaphysics. Even when he spoke of 'destruction', however, Heidegger was well aware of the tragedy of the dialogue with the Greeks.[77] Who could ever imagine arriving at that experience, reaching that 'initial Greek', without the filter of the present by which our vision is fixed and predetermined? Nonetheless, this does not exempt us from the radical question, which is justified insofar as it does not spring from a completely external, completely disconnected horizon. The artificial separation between 'them' and 'us' disappears. How much of the Greek past is always already present in the constellation of the present? Language itself bears such traces, because it is the posthumous life of the past in the present. Hence the need, *alongside* destruction, for the hermeneutic path indicated by translation.[78] Dialogue with the Greeks does not mean returning to an archic remoteness outside the present. Rather, it means listening from afar to a word that has never been lost to the present. However, it would be misleading to reduce the exercise in translation to a mere gesture of appropriation. Dialogue begins where the illusion of familiarity is dispelled. What at first seemed self-evident is no longer so. Only in this sudden distance, even when a proximal one, and only in this difference, does the word reveal its forgotten, repressed depths, which emerge in all their strangeness. It is here that the radical question is posed. The source can prove fruitful; and yet, this is a twofold movement, a coming-and-going from future to past and from past to future. Nietzsche writes: 'The voice of the past is always the voice of an oracle; only if you are architects of the future and are familiar with the present will you understand the oracular voice of the past.'[79]

To interpellate the Greeks by starting from the demands of the present, in order to then return to these questions burdened with ancient problems, is a legitimate and indeed necessary exercise in historical anachronism.[80] To accept the challenge that comes from the past is to understand the present in a new light. The modern aspects of Greek democracy are too often emphasized, to the point of trivializing them. The *Greek questions posed to modern democracy* will instead offer more promising cues to reflection.

3

THE SPECTRE OF ANARCHY

1. In the monumental history of democracy there is a deeply repressed element: anarchy. As we said in the Preface, layer upon layer of diligently written histories and dusty old traditions have stashed anarchy away in the oblivion of the archives, the institutional seat of the *arché*. This is the domicile of the *archeîon*, where the archons who surveil and interpret reside, guarding the repository of documents and calling upon the powers of the established exegesis. Thus, the titles and qualifications of archontic primacy, and the authority of archic command, have been able to fuse into a landscape of institutional domination. Perhaps today democracy suffers from an 'archive fever' – that impulse for conservation that turns into a destructive force.[1] But it is also well known that every archive is haunted by disturbing shadows, ghosts that reappear, spectres that remain disguised and forbidden, but which no one has managed to expel.

I have spoken of a philosophical archaeology of democracy, reaching back to the dawn of history. This appears as a regression which – to borrow a suggestion of Melandri's – could be described as 'Dionysian', in Nietzsche's most misunderstood sense.[2] It eludes all forms of rationalization and remains a subliminal hermeneutic. However, it is distinguished precisely by 'the recovery of the alienated, the excluded, the repressed'.[3] But what does 'recovery' mean here? It may seem ambiguous. It does not mean summoning up the historical repressed, bringing it back for conscious reflection. Nor is it a question of reconstructing the process of exclusion itself, as a history of the defeated would do. Rather, it means going back to what made it so, to what consigned it to the archives. This requires a closer examination of the anarchic sources of democracy.

2. Of the three political forms that emerged in the ancient world, democracy alone does not designate a sovereign in the supreme role of command. Mon-archy attributes this role to one person, whereas olig-archy attributes it to a select few. When the word democracy broke through at the dawn of the *pólis* it seemed clear that its subversive, disruptive force pointed to two related events. It referred to both the entry of the *dêmos* onto the stage of history and, at the same time, to the annulment of all sovereignty, the absence of all *archía*. It surely *might* have been called *demarchía*.[4] And yet, in the new compound, the verb *krateîn* is used instead, aimed at revoking and disavowing sovereign power. Demo-cracy is an an-archy.

In the strict sense, the term democracy is distinct from, or rather opposed to, monarchy and oligarchy, because it radically departs from the principle of *arché*. This should raise doubts about whether it may even be counted among that set of political forms which – because they more or less pivot on the *arché* – are indeed archic forms, standing on a sovereign foundation. The exceptional nature of democracy, interrupting and overwhelming this order that had been in place since the beginning, is cause to believe that it is not just one form to be classed among the rest. It may not be a simple political form at all. Insofar as it has traditionally been considered as such, this is only because of an oft-repeated simplification – and, before that, of a tacit bid to domesticate democracy, trivialize it, and make it submit to the codes of the archic order.

It might more aptly be said that democracy can emerge precisely insofar as all *arché*, that power which boasts of its original status, is thrown into doubt. The principle of command – the command of the principle – is thus interrupted. Even in its very name, democracy speaks of this revolutionary interruption, referring to the anarchic dissolution of every *arché*. It does so also as an appeal directed towards the future. Should this appeal be disregarded or circumvented, it would mean a slide back into an archic regime.

Democracy's point of emergence is anarchic. To bring this repressed element back to light, allowing it to re-emerge, is to look beyond the disruptive action itself and to probe deeply into democracy's connection with anarchy. This is an ontological question even before it is a political one. A continuous passage from ontology to politics, and vice versa, is needed to avoid both taking democracy as a mere force of revolt and dissent and ignoring the political repercussions of that liberation from the *arché*. Scrutinized at its roots, democracy reveals its indissoluble link with anarchy. With this, all the adjectives used to evoke turmoil and conflict and to guarantee an inexhaustible reserve of disorder are themselves swept away. For the ground is cut from underneath them by that one adjective which, instead of making democracy determinate, allows its fundamental indeterminacy to emerge. Is democracy wild, indomitable, insurgent, or emergent? At heart, it is anarchic.

To get a measure of democracy's exceptional nature and grasp its connection to anarchy, we need only look back to its birth in Greece. This birth would, over history, bring other births and rebirths, further ruptures and new interruptions. But it was there in Greece, where an unprecedented and unheard-of word arose to overthrow the project of a city ordered according to the *arché*, that this connection revealed itself in all its radical force. *Demokratía* unhesitatingly reveals its an-archic foundation, exposing its underlying *anarchía*.

Which makes it all the more remarkable that this connection has never been investigated, let alone deeply discussed. There is no shortage of valuable ideas, deep insights, thoughts, and analyses capable of opening up crucial avenues into the problem. However, neither historians working against the grain, nor scrupulous philologists, nor far-sighted anthropologists, have dwelt on the bond that fundamentally links anarchy and democracy. The same is true of philosophy: exponents of radical thought prefer to reread the political tradition of modernity, and end up neglecting this Greek source. There are important exceptions, from brief references in Abensour, to Rancière's dense pages on Plato's *Republic*. It is striking, however, that even a historian and Hellenist such as Nicole Loraux, who cast an implacable gaze on the divided city, lost sight of the anarchic emergence of democracy.[5] A case apart is Jacqueline de Romilly. Having examined the blindness of the people, she addresses the problem of democratic anarchy – only to reiterate the traditional view that goes no further than condemning the impending disorder.[6]

The spectre of anarchy already haunted the earliest documents, in the texts of poets and historians, philosophers and tragedians. Even when the connection with anarchy is concealed it bursts forth between the lines. But Plato spoke clearly, denouncing the subversive alliance: *demokratía* is *ánarchos* and *poikíle*, 'anarchic and variegated' (*Republic*, 558c 5). It is a constitution that contains all constitutions and no constitution, a non-constitution, a non-regime – an epochal upheaval. Plato sounded the alarm: the city's very existence was under threat. For the truer democracy is to itself, the more it borders on anarchy.

Plato's accusation gave rise to a reticence that would last for centuries, an ironclad aversion. It would seem that anarchy is the inseparable shadow of democracy: at once the spectre that haunts it, tarnishing its name with the threat of collapse and disintegration, and the inspiration that preserves its absence of principle, the impossibility of command, the temperament that delegitimizes any *arché*.

3. What does *anarchía* mean? The Greek noun is composed of the privative alpha and the verb *árcho*, which means 'to command'. It means a lack of command, an absence of government, a missing order. This may have different, if not outright opposite, causes: whether the inefficiency of those meant to be exercising authority, or the non-compliance of those who skirt around the laws, creating turmoil.

Anarchía is attested since at least the mid-fifth century BCE, and may be even older, like many similar compounds. It was preceded by the adjective *ánarchos*, which means without a leader, without a master – and thus also free. Already in the *Iliad*, *ánarchoi* appears to refer to those who are part of some sort of leaderless association (II, 703, 726). The semantic latitude of the term, referring to any absence of domination, must have quickly extended from the military to the political sphere to refer above all to the disappearance of the *árchontes*, the supreme offices, the archons installed in the *archeîon*, the palace of command, the seat of the *arché*. '[B]ecause of party strife [*stásis*] they did not appoint an archon, and again in the fifth year after that they enacted a suspension of the archonship [*anarchía*] for the same cause.'[7] The climax was reached with the abolition of the Areopagus in Athens.[8]

But it is at sea, amid the disorder of restless waves and boundless open spaces, that anarchy has wind in its sails. Its emblem is the sailors, common people with no family tradition, lacking discipline and respect for their leaders, ready to flee and retreat, even to abandon their weapons – to desert. They have nothing in common with the solidity of the infantrymen, the compact ranks of the hoplites, the pride of the Spartan phalanx. Yet it is they, the sailors of the Athenian fleet, who have often prevailed with their ready manoeuvres and spontaneous pirouettes, without waiting for orders or instructions. Once back on shore, however, they prove impulsive and immoderate to the point of impertinence – particularly with women. Euripides allows Hecuba to express her full apprehension: what frightens her more than the 'mob' is the *nautiké anarchía*, literally 'seafaring anarchy' (*Hecuba*, 607).[9] A similar expression appears in another of Euripides' tragedies, where Clytemnestra says: 'I, a woman, have come, as you see, to a camp of lawless sailor-folk [*nautikòn … ánarchon*], bold in evil's cause, though useful when they wish' (*Iphigenia in Aulis*, 915).[10]

Echoes of this reputation, traces of this reproach, can be found in both contemporary and later texts by traditionalist authors, the intransigent defenders of oligarchy. Already in the first lines of the pamphlet by the Anonymous Athenian, the Pseudo-Xenophon or Old Oligarch, unsparing in his criticism of the people's democratic aspirations, the finger is pointed at rowers, helmsmen, manoeuvrers, carpenters – in short, the rabble of the fleet, to whom the city entrusts its strength. And it does this instead of relying on the hoplites, the nobles, the respectable! No wonder, when public posts are open to all and anyone can speak in the assembly (*On The Athenian State*, I, 2). While indiscipline, *ataxía*, spreads, insolence, *akolasía*, also infects slaves and metics. Just look at what happens in the streets and squares, where these individuals do not stand aside, do not give way to their superiors. The unprecedented upheavals are evident in every corner: 'where there is naval power ... men must be slaves of their slaves' (I, 10).[11]

Plato offers considerations of a similar tenor. For him, it would be better for a city not to be built near the sea – a source of trade and traffic and political instability, which is bound to induce dishonest and fickle customs (cf. *Laws*, 705b). Furthermore, sailors – so used to constantly disembarking and then fleeing again on the waves – should not be chosen in place of hoplites. Not to mention that this would mean having to honour men of low birth and unsavoury character (cf. *Laws*, 706c–707b).

The speed with which military indiscipline leads to a loss of restraint should not be discounted. The historians are clear about this connection. The lack of a leader, referred to by Herodotus, and the disorderly anarchy condemned by Thucydides, already hint at the further meaning: the *ánarchos*, who does not follow a leader, is *atáktos*, disorderly, unaligned, not in his rightful place.[12]

This is how *anarchía*, while maintaining its privative character, also takes on broader, more figurative meanings: from the absence of command to growing disorder and explicit disobedience. Perhaps an expression such as that found in Aeschylus' *Agamemnon* can rightly be applied to the disobedient: *demóthrous anarchía*, anarchy accompanied by the clamour of the people (883). Restlessness and unrest take hold. Thus emerge the two mirrored meanings of anarchy: both an absence of command, a failure to exercise power, and, at the same time, transgression, disobedience, and revolt.

The second sense clearly shines through in the description of those who behave in an anarchic manner. As the historian of anarchism Max Nettlau wrote: 'The Greek term anarchía refers to individuals who consciously spurned authority and rejected government; only when they began to be opposed and persecuted did the name come to refer to those dangerous rebels who jeopardized order itself.'[13]

4. Decisive, in this regard, is the outbreak of anarchy in the *pólis*. Terrible and ominous spectres disturb the city, instilling fear. They proceed hand in hand with the struggles of the people, their successes and their conquests, which are at once both unimaginable and disturbing. And so even the Areopagus – the last bastion of archic power – is overthrown. Even Aeschylus, who had celebrated democracy, retreats in terror. His enthusiasm fades and he moderates his position. The *Oresteia* trilogy ends with a verse that both encapsulates and anticipates a political theory destined for many future developments. For Aeschylus, it is necessary to respect moderation and firmly avoid excesses. 'Neither anarchy nor tyranny – this I counsel my citizens to support and respect' (*Eumenides*, 525, 696).[14] This meant spurning excess and praising a form of life, *bíos*, that would be neither *ánarktos*, or *ánarchos*, nor *despotoúmenos*. Here emerges the dichotomy, later intensified, between the opposite poles of anarchy and tyranny, two threats looming over the *pólis*. The real danger, however, is anarchy, which, given its connection to the indiscipline of the people, seems to increase where democracy is strongest. Is this perhaps democracy's fatal illness, its relentless scourge? Does democracy bring anarchy along with it?

Sophocles' theatre gives vent to new concerns, as the warning 'neither anarchy nor tyranny' takes the form of a dilemma represented by different characters and the ups and downs of their confrontations. One such example is *Ajax*, in which even the danger of lawlessness does not prevent Sophocles from depicting the bearers of power in less than edifying terms. But it is in *Antigone* that the dilemma becomes a real conflict: on the one hand there is Creon, whose rigid adherence to the law and obtuse devotion border on a will to tyranny; on the other there is Antigone, whose sacred transgression tears open a sky clouded by a law which stands far from justice.

Creon defends his edict and demands obedience. The words he utters are reminiscent of those in circulation at the time of the play, including his use of military metaphor (*Antigone*, 667–77):

> But if anyone oversteps and does violence to the laws, or thinks to dictate to those in power [*árchein … árchesthai*], such a one will never win praise from me. No, whomever the city may appoint, that man must be obeyed in matters small and great and in matters just and unjust … But there is no evil worse than disobedience [*anarchías dè meizon ouk éstin kakón*]: This destroys cities; this overturns homes; this breaks the ranks of allied spears into headlong rout. But the lives of men who prosper upright, of these obedience has saved the greatest part.

> Therefore we must defend those who respect order, and in no way can we let a woman defeat us.[15]

She is an open rebel, who behaves like a stranger in her own home. Instead of remaining submissive, this woman contravenes the order, challenges the chief, undermines his authority. The verses resound with the most threatening subversion: not a mere act of insubordination, but a gesture that strikes at the heart of things, and which risks overturning those two verbs – *árchein* and *árchesthai*, to command and to be commanded – that govern the *pólis*. It would be a mistake to take this for indiscipline. It has a name, which Creon is himself ready to pronounce: *anarchy*. This is the plague that hangs over the city, all the more serious because its origin is obscure. Does it come from outside or from within? Antigone disobeys the decree in order to honour the ties of family, meaning her unburied brother. But this is an anarchic disobedience, confirmed both in the words used in accusation against her, and in those she offers in her defence.[16] Notwithstanding the intricacies of the tragedy, Antigone's final intervention expresses the full force of the gesture with which she ousts power from its throne. While the chorus, hesitant, seems to go along with the despot, Haemon – Creon's son and Antigone's soon-to-be husband – intervenes with a call for calm reflection. Within the limits of filial respect, he turns to his father to emphasize the dangers of despotism: one must not be stubborn, obstinate, closed in on 'one mood only' (705). For this would mean acting like a helmsman who fails to ease the tension in the sails: not knowing how to yield to the winds, he ends up capsizing the ship (cf. 715–17). After all, '[t]hat is no city, which belongs to one man' (737).

As Antigone prepares to speak, the atmosphere seems to shift. Even the chorus, moved by pity, cannot hide a certain sympathy for this young woman who is ready to die in order to remain true to her convictions. The dilemma remains: 'neither anarchy nor despotism'; but disobedience, far from being frowned upon, has now crept into the city. This is one of the most famous passages in Greek tragedy. Creon: 'you dared overstep that law?' Antigone: 'Yes, since it was not Zeus that published me that edict' (449–51). But her gesture does not only seek the protection of higher, unwritten laws, it also uses them to unmask the *nómoi* issued by Creon. These are only precarious decrees, lacking legitimacy and foundation – decrees without *arché*. In this lies Antigone's an-archic act of destitution.

5. Historically, it has often been the detractors who shed light on realities that would otherwise remain unseen, even if they cast them in the harshest terms. This is how the ontological-political

link between anarchy and democracy comes to the surface in the pages of Plato and Aristotle. Each, in his own way, is an opponent of that bizarre form of government by the people which, on closer inspection, is a non-government, an epochal disorder capable of jeopardizing the very existence of the city. However, such polemical distortions and intentional misrepresentations reflect a gradually clearer and more perceptive picture. Far from representing an accidental aspect of democracy, its drift to the extremes, anarchy constitutes its very essence.

Anarchy is at once both political chaos and ethical disorder. It is capable of insinuating itself into the life of the city as well as that of the individual, spreading the seeds of insubordination. It presents itself with the seductive face of freedom in Book VIII of *The Republic*. These are pages of decisive importance in Plato – not a historical testimony bearing witness to the past, but a philosophical diagnosis of the present.

Freedom, *eleutheria*: what word could be more widely shared, more unanimously accepted? Plato seems almost to be giving a eulogy, punctuated by the pressing and lively rhythm of *eleutheria*: freedom of speech, freedom of action, above all the freedom to organize one's life as one pleases. In relation to the latter, however, the recurrent term is licence, *exousía*, which also means boldness, insolence. Everyone behaves as they wish, while the city, full of these different customs, enlivened by multiple characters, reveals itself to be *poikíle*, colourful, like 'a garment of many colors, embroidered with all kinds of hues' (*Republic*, 557c 1).[17] Does it not appear *kallíste*, beautiful? Perhaps to those who are content to look at it with the eyes of women and children. The amused tone begins to soften, and the irony becomes more biting, as Plato considers the licence which, throwing off all restraints, translates into the absence of the obligation to command, *árchein*, and to be commanded, *árchesthai* (557e 3). What now comes to the fore is a violent irritation. For this is not, as many believe, simply a condemnation of the arbitrariness of the individual, of lawlessness or disorder. Plato knows full well that the city he is describing is not merely one in which individuals do as they please, but one in which the disease of anarchy has struck at the heart of things, corroding the *arché* itself. This is the real subversion. If no one is forced to obey any more, it is because every principle of authority, all respect for command, has broken down. Such *eleutheria* has a ruinous effect, which Plato sums up as follows: 'it commends and honors in public and private rulers who resemble subjects and subjects who are like rulers [*árchontas archoménois*]' (562d 7–8). This is anarchy, a swapping of roles, indeed a continuous reversal, which ultimately ends up abrogating the *arché*. There is no need for its ostentatious rejection, in a violent clash or open conflict, for the *arché* can be undermined in other ways. Plato sees the danger and warns that this is exactly how 'this anarchical temper … must penetrate into private homes and finally enter into the very animals' (562e 4–5).

What does it mean to not tolerate even the slightest subjection, to have no one above you, to be without leaders and without masters? How does anarchy come about? The answer appears in a famous passage from *The Republic* (562e 7–563d 1):

> the father habitually tries to resemble the child and is afraid of his sons, and the son likens himself to the father and feels no awe or fear of his parents, so that he may be forsooth a free man. And the resident alien feels himself equal to the citizen and the citizen to him, and the foreigner likewise … and such other trifles as these. The teacher in such case fears and fawns upon the pupils, and the pupils pay no heed to the teacher or to their overseers either. And in general the young ape their elders and vie with them in speech and action, while the old, accommodating themselves to the young, are full of pleasantry and graciousness, imitating the young for fear they may be thought disagreeable and authoritative … [T]he climax of popular liberty [*eleuthería*], my friend, … is attained in such a city when the [*plêthos* of] purchased slaves, male and female, are no less free than the owners who paid for them. And I almost forgot to mention the spirit of freedom and equal rights [*isonomía*] in the relation of men to women and women to men … Without experience of it no one would believe how much freer the very beasts subject to men are in such a city than elsewhere. The dogs literally verify the adage and 'like their mistresses become.' And likewise the horses and asses are wont to hold on their way with the utmost freedom and dignity, bumping into everyone who meets them and who does not step aside. And so all things everywhere are just bursting with the spirit of liberty.

Here Plato offers harsh condemnation, in a vivid fresco depicting the darkest and most appalling of scenarios. Everyone has been made equal: fathers and sons, citizens and foreigners, teachers and students, old and young, slaves and free men, even men and women! It is no wonder that even the animals sense this freedom, and now donkeys rule the streets. A sort of waking nightmare has materialized. Everything is upside down. Natural relationships are turned on their head. The *arché* of fathers, the propertied, the autochthonous, the heirs, has been deeply undermined and stripped of legitimacy. As we saw in the Preface, this is the abolition of the principle of birth that orders and arranges, of natural authority, of the line of descent, of patriarchal power, of the transmission of property, of ties of blood and soil, of the code of autochthony, of the right of inheritance. In short, it has torn down the *archic* form of the community, leading to chaos in the streets and squares occupied by shameless women, insolent children, and stubborn donkeys. Plato cries scandal.

But what is he really talking about? Which *pólis* is this? What Plato describes so colourfully is not so much anarchy as democracy. But the boundaries are blurred – the one leads into the other. For Plato, anarchy is democracy's inseparable shadow, the perennial nightmare of it leading to ruin. In fact, the terms he uses just a few lines earlier to describe this singular *politeía* leave no room for doubt. This is not a form of government, nor a constitution, nor even a bazaar of constitutions, because it lacks even an *arché*. What to call it?

> These and qualities akin to these democracy would exhibit, and it would, it seems, be a delightful form of government, anarchic [*ánarchos*] and motley [*poikíle*], assigning a kind of equality indiscriminately to equals and unequals alike! (558c 3–6)

Democracy is intricate and ever-changing, because it knows neither order (*táxis*) nor necessity (*ánanke*). It cannot remain standing, any more than an army without leaders could (560e 3). But what does this really mean? When Plato introduces the formula *anarchía kaí ano mía* (575a 1), he does not merely echo the tragic poets, who had condemned whoever disregarded the law, but introduces a theme that was destined to have many further echoes. For here he refers to something that democracy and tyranny have in common. If an excess of freedom can easily turn into an excess of slavery, it is easy to see why tyranny develops out of democracy, and indeed is its opposite extreme. While for Plato it has many more virtues, it retains the same disease as democracy, with the difference that it is now concentrated in the sovereign *eros* of the tyrant who breaks every law (575a 1). Thus, tyranny is an archic reaction against democracy, a powerful revival of the *arché* in the face of anarchic ruin – a response, however, that is futile and harmful, because it is marred by the same flaw.

What Plato is ultimately lamenting, in his indictment of democracy, is the disappearance of *arché* – in the *pólis*, as in the *bíos* of each individual. Hence the repeated warnings scattered throughout the text of the *Laws*. Sophocles' words are echoed almost verbatim: 'any social institution whatsoever … naturally has a commander (639c

1–2).[18] This imperative applies not only to the ties of community, but also to the existence of the individual: 'nobody, male or female, should ever be left without control [*ánarchon*]'. The individual should, 'both in war and peace, [keep] his eyes fixed constantly on his commander and [follow] his lead; and he should be guided by him even in the smallest detail of his actions' (942a–b). Plato lays repeated emphasis on the need for an archic form capable of impressing itself on the citizen's inner *psuché*, thereby educating them and making them accustomed to this. It is therefore necessary to 'train children, in times of peace, to command and be commanded [*árchein te állon árchesthai*]'. Only in this way can the seed of insubordination and rebelliousness that creeps in everywhere be eradicated: 'Anarchy [*anarchía*] must be utterly removed from the lives of all mankind, and of the beasts also that are subject to man' (942c–d).

But if democracy were nothing more than one of the many forms of bad government, the threat would soon be averted. With all this talk of stubborn donkeys, insolent children, and shameless women, there is something more than a mere reversal of relationships. In a passage in the *Laws* (690a–c) Plato clarifies what the fresco offered in *The Republic* had left in the shadows.

What are the *archaí*, the principles, the titles to exercise command, which this reversal disregards and violates? Plato lists seven, four of which are the traditional ones based on birth: those who are born earlier, to better families, are in command. This justifies the power of parents over their children, of the elderly over the young, of masters over slaves, of those of noble origin over those of obscure origin. The next two titles, although not related to birth as such, are still based on nature. The fifth is, in fact, the law of nature *par excellence*, consisting in the power of the strong over the weak. Celebrated by the ancients, starting with Pindar, it appeared to Plato as obvious and irrefutable as it was controversial. Who is the strongest, and how is this determined? The sixth title is almost an answer to this question, because it identifies strength with the virtue of the bearers of knowledge; that is, the authority of the wise over the ignorant. For Plato, moreover, this is the only legitimate authority. In short, while the first four titles outline an order in the *pólis* based on lineage, the fifth and sixth, which evoke the superiority of strength or the authority of wisdom, demand that it is not the firstborn or the most noble who commands but the best. Hence, birth is no longer the key qualification for command, and order in the *pólis* no longer corresponds to lineage (*Laws*, 690c).

This succession of different qualifications veers away from the law of origin and of the tribe.[19] But the decisive break comes with the seventh title, that *arché*, that principle 'dear to the gods', which is the drawing of lots, *klêros*, whereby 'if [a man] gains the lot he will most justly be ruler, but if he fails he shall take his place among the ruled' – *árchein, árchesthai* (*Laws*, 690c).

This temporary distribution of ranks, which breaks the chain of family descent and disrupts the order of the *pólis*, does not correspond to qualifications based on nature or superiority. Indeed, it does not correspond to any such title. The seventh title is the manifest absence of qualifications. Those who have no title to govern, do govern: this is democracy. As such, it is the scandal for those who presume to have qualifications of birth, seniority, wealth, virtue, and competence. The unheard-of subversion is the power of the *dêmos*: the command of those who have no qualifications to exercise the power of the *arché*. However, it is not just a matter of overturning and reversing. Democracy does not simply mean the power of children, women, servants, or animals. The roll of the dice is a much deeper subversion. For it is a principle that is not a principle; even as it is affirmed and proclaimed, the principle is denied and revoked.

This non-principle renders *arché* impossible. With this seventh means of selection, what collapses is the archic structure on which the *pólis* had believed itself founded. The closed circle made up of the pair of beginning and command is now interrupted. The seventh qualification – the absence of all titles to command, the prerequisite of anarchy – establishes the beginning without beginning, the command of those who do not command. Plato senses that the anarchy of democracy implies not just simple disorder but the contingent nature of all government.

6. Many passages in Aristotle revolve around the *arché*, the principle, the command. But one in particular seems emblematic, both for its military context and for the metaphysical and metapolitical transition realized therein. It describes a retreating army, a disorderly crowd of men without leadership, who have broken ranks and abandoned their posts. The adjective *ánarchoi* would be well suited to such men. However, Aristotle avoids it and instead describes how everything is brought back within the remit of *arché*: 'when one side gives way in battle, if a single man [should] rally, another rallies also and then a third, until the original order [*arché*] has been restored' (*Posterior Analytics* II, 100a 12–14).[20]

Especially striking in this passage is the recurrence of the verb *hístemi* – to stand – alongside *héteron* – other. One man rallies and takes a stand – and then another and yet another. The soldiers suddenly halt, overcome their fear, turn their gaze back towards the enemy, regain their courage and obey orders. In describing this,

Aristotle draws on the semantic ambiguity of the word *tropé*, which means 'fleeing', or a 'rout', but also 'change'. Suddenly, things turn around and are straightened out again. Having been scattered and dispersed, the soldiers now instead return to the starting point, *epì archèn*, to the beginning of the command, to the initial command, to the leader. This passage from the *Analytics* serves to illustrate that process within the *psuché*, the soul, whereby one sensation after another stops, until suddenly *kathólou*, the universal, presents itself. Without that arrest, speculative activity would be impossible. However, Aristotle's military metaphor, which has drawn the attention of more than one interpreter,[21] has an exemplary value that extends beyond the cognitive sphere alone.

Indeed, it is not difficult to imagine how this principle of unifying men under the sovereign might operate in other contexts. What may be legitimately be discerned in this is the connecting thread that links speculative philosophy to practical philosophy: the multiple is referred back to and reduced to the one, *pros hen*, to the First, which gives sense and direction. The political significance of this relationship, as emphasized by several commentators, is striking. Reiner Schürmann writes in this regard: 'Aristotle views command (*arché*) imposing its order on the runaways just as he views substance, as *arché*, imposing its unity upon the accidents.'[22] This establishes a 'substantialist framework' which – taken up by metaphysics, and even before that by physics – is projected onto politics.[23] It is suggested that the same logic may operate in both cases, i.e. one which makes the multiple rely on an archic unity. For Aristotle, this unity is both the first cause and the commanding principle. Political life is not only reduced to the logic of natural phenomena, but also read through the prism of external ontological criteria.[24] This undue transposition would long preclude any other perspective on human action, as the Western political tradition remained captive to Aristotle's *Physics*, his *Grundbuch*.

Schürmann is forthright in saying that while Aristotle can be credited with a critique of Plato's rigorous utopianism, i.e. his conception of an abstract and universal *pólis*, Aristotle himself betrayed politics by bending it into rigid schemas. He therefore made Socrates speak with the language of the physicist. Schürmann indicts the repeated imposition of the *pros hen*, meaning the dovetailing of the many parts into the one; he stridently denounces its political effect through its 'totalitarian sweep'.[25] Thus, individuals are subordinated to those who command, and their actions will find their meaning in the actions of the city as a whole. It is as if everything had to be directed towards a higher end, towards the good of the *pólis* – in *Politics*, the perfect *politeía*, and in the

Ethics, happiness. Substantialism turns towards the end: the *télos* reigns, and commands, exercising the function of *arché*. In this way, Aristotle arrives at a strange identification of the *arché* with the *télos*. Schürmann thus speaks of a 'teleocracy'.[26] But if this logic applies to architecture – the paradigmatic art in which the stipulated end guides the action that leads to it – it can hardly be applied to politics. Yet Aristotle considers politics as a subdomain of architecture, as if rulers could remould the city because they are themselves moved by the idea of its end goal. In Schürmann's view, teleocracy thus reveals itself as that total domination of the end goal (the *télos*) that would extend its grip over politics for centuries. This gives rise not only to many common stereotypes, but also to the foundationalist-normative approach that still prevails today.

One can only agree with Schürmann's analysis when he sees a shift in Aristotle from *arché* to *télos* – a move that ultimately turns politics into a teleocratic architecture. However, this analysis overlooks both the context in which it emerged and the reasons that led Aristotle to make such a shift. These are far from negligible historical details. They could help shed light on the origin of the teleocratic concept of *arché*. Why did Aristotle feel the need for it? And why did that model remain dominant so long? Oddly enough, Schürmann does not address Aristotle's reaction against democracy, his fear of it and opposition to it. The move towards teleocracy – perhaps telearchy would be a better term – happens because democracy has undermined the *arché*. Aristotle intervenes with a retrospective judgement that is anything but favourable. Having already glimpsed the full anarchic potential of democracy, he prefers to pass over it in silence whenever possible. Since democracy had shattered the substratum of politics, revealing its contingency and lack of any foundation, it was necessary to restore the *arché*. But the post-democratic city no longer held together in its archic structure, whose axis had been thrown off its hinges. Aristotle's move, then, is to project the *arché* onto the *télos*: the crumbled foundation is reconstituted through its crystallization in an end goal. In other words, if the archic paradigm can no longer rely on the substratum of the past, its restoration becomes a re-foundation dependent on the *télos*. This is a telic and normative foundationalism. The transition to telearchy is accomplished by way of democratic anarchy. Believing that he is putting up a barrier to anarchy, it is here that Aristotle betrays politics, because he reduces it to an architecture dominated by the end, the *pros hen*, the ultimate centre of reference.

It is easy to understand the success that Aristotle's work has enjoyed in that long tradition of political thought which – precisely in the name of Aristotelianism – has never taken democracy as its point of reference and has instead steered well clear of it. This is an attitude built on reluctance and resistance. It should be attributed not so much to the idea that there is only a relative distinction between the family unit and the political community, which thereby justifies a patriarchal conception of power, as to the reassurance that the teleocratic paradigm may offer. This finds confirmation in the rather softer and more conciliatory late twentieth-century versions of Aristotelianism, which nonetheless do little to hide their normative traits. These range from the rehabilitation of practical philosophy (Hans-Georg Gadamer and Joachim Ritter) to US communitarianism (Alasdair MacIntyre, Michael Sandel, Charles Taylor, and Michael Walzer), to liberal adaptations of Aristotelianism such as that undertaken by Martha C. Nussbaum.

The question that needs asking, however – and it is one that Schürmann avoids confronting – is whether reflections and further repercussions of teleocracy can be found in Aristotle's political analysis. The answer lies in his use of the word *politeía*. Times of revolution now lie in the past. The city has stabilized, and democracy has lost much of its disruptive novelty and utopian charge. Yet, a subversive echo remains, in the *krátos* that *demokratía* still holds in store. Hence the techniques of circumvention, the strategies of substitution, and the attempts to establish distinctions between well-regulated and ill-governed democracies. The aim is to water down democracy itself. Aristotle's proposal stands out in this regard: in *Politics*, he calls *politeía* the best regime in his view, despite its obvious similarities with democracy. It is better to use the term 'constitution' than to invoke a name associated with revolution.[27] Moreover, *politeía* also has the advantage of referring to the citizens as a whole, even before it identifies any particular political order; and it thus removes the *dêmos* from the equation. As power flows back into the stabilized city, spared from divisions and upheavals, organizational concerns and institutional aims prevail.

The keystone becomes the *méson*, the centre where the *arché politiké* is to be restored. This is the operation carried out by Aristotle, which it is worth examining in order to avoid misunderstandings and misinterpretations. The meaning of the *méson* had already been extended from that of a geometric place to that of a political space, and it thereby became a focus of disputes and disagreements. This was all the more true since the *arché* had been placed at the centre – simultaneously toppled from its perch and placed in the hands of citizens. Such had been the democratic upheaval – on closer inspection, an *an-archy* – which also had repercussions on the centre, destabilizing it and emptying it. Aristotle starts from here in his effort at restoration. It is necessary to recognize the victory, *krátos*, of the *méson* – that happy medium which stands out for its superiority. In a single move, at least two objectives are achieved. First of all, the *dêmos* – which has been pushed away from all *krateîn*, from all its conquests, of which it no longer seems worthy – is stripped of power, marginalized from the centre of the city, pushed out to the extremes, to the *ánarchon* of anger and disorder. While the link between *dêmos* and *krátos* is thus broken, overcoming the democratic interlude, an attempt is made to re-establish *arché* in the *méson*, presenting it as the golden mean, the indispensable irenic centre, the necessary bulwark of the *pólis*. The only remedy against the devastating anarchy that is democracy has to be a rehabilitated *arché*, able to regain its central position in a politics without upheavals, in the geometric centre of the city's architecture.[28] All this, it goes without saying, is done in the name of the good of the *pólis*, its reconciliation and its unity. The *krátos*, brought back to the *arché* of the golden mean, can be neutralized and consigned to oblivion. With a wipe of the sponge, the power of the people is thus erased. What makes this possible is the archic paradigm, whose restoration relies on the *méson*, the golden mean, the middle class, the people of the centre, who had in any case maintained a tight grip on power. But the *arché* is no longer what it once was, the axis is irreparably cracked, and the fulcrum unsettled. It is no longer possible to speak of firm underpinnings. All that remains is to project the *arché* towards the *télos*, making the *méson* the norm of the best form of government, the end goal of political and ethical action. The postulate of the golden mean would become the normative path most taken in order to neutralize democracy.

Politeía encapsulates all this, because it is but the moderate constitution of the *méson*, the best and only legitimate form of government. Compared to *politeía*, democracy turns out to be a huge danger, an outright deviation.[29] This is corroborated by the way in which Aristotle distinguishes between just constitutions, meaning those that look to the common good, and degenerate constitutions, which instead aim solely at the interests of the rulers (cf. *Politics*, 1279a 17–21). The former are classified according to *number*: these are monarchy, when power is held by just one person; the aristocracy, when a few rule; and the *politeía*, when many govern. Aristotle admits his reliance on a *koinón ónoma*, a common word, a term shared by all constitutions, *tôn politeiôn*, the common name: *politeía*, constitution (1279a 39). It is better to take a cautious distance from a word that is so stigmatized. But this is not only a linguistic problem. The deviant forms of government include tyranny, a perversion of the kingdom; oligarchy, a deterioration of aristocracy; and democracy, a degeneration of *politeía*. Immediately after this, however, Aristotle replaces the traditional criterion of the *number* of rulers with the newer criterion of property ownership: here, the alternative is between oligarchy, a government by the rich, which seeks their own advantage alone, and democracy, a government by the poor, which pursues only their interests. Both are degenerate because they pursue a partial idea of justice: oligarchy understands justice as equality in wealth, democracy as equality in freedom, whereby all free people, no longer slaves, are in power. Both of these constitutions (and this is Aristotle's critique), in their assumption that the purpose of the *pólis* is simply to live, forget that the supreme end is to live well. This perfect life requires, in addition to wealth and freedom, above all *virtue*. These constitutions' partiality also drives them to use force and violence, whereby they slide into tyranny, from which they do not differ in principle. They can therefore be considered, respectively, as the tyranny of the rich and the tyranny of the poor.

This opens the way towards an alternative – the *politeía* – which is a synthesis of the two (cf. *Politics*, 1294a 30–6). There are three criteria for reaching this end goal. One is the mixing of the laws of one and the other, for example a fine for the rich if they do not want to be judges, but no reward for the poor if they do want to be judges. The next is the embrace of the *méson*, the middle ground between what the two constitutions prescribe, for example by establishing a property requirement for participation in the assembly that is neither too high nor too low. The last is to take some features from both, for example the election of officials, as is customary in an oligarchy, but admitting those who do not meet a property threshold – without thereby allocating offices by lot, as is the custom in a democracy (cf. *Politics*, 1294a 36–1294b 14).

In this respect, *politeía* is the best possible constitution, in the sense of *téleios*: the one consistent with the best kind of life. In characterizing this constitution, Aristotle refers to *mesótes*, the middle ground between extremes, in which alone virtue resides, as already celebrated in the *Nicomachean Ethics* (cf. *Eth. Nic.*, 1101a 14–16; 1153b 9–21). This translates politically into a government made up of those who are in the middle, in between rich and poor, and who are therefore called *hoi mésoi*. The middle constitution, the *politeía*, is thus based on the middle class, the people of the centre, the stable foundation, and is at the same time the one that best conforms to the end – the *télos* – that amounts to perfection.[30]

Aristotle's condemnation of democracy leaves no room for doubt. But what role could anarchy play here, given that it does not even appear to be mentioned? In *Politics*, the different forms of democracy are classified into two variants, the one based on a political-legal criterion, and the other on a socio-economic criterion.[31] From both, there emerges a third and final form which, compared to the others, is not a degeneration of democracy but its radicalization, to the point that the law, *nómos*, is suspended, and offices, *archaí*, cease to exist. In describing this situation – which exceeds each of the others – Aristotle does not explicitly refer to *anomía* or to *anarchía*. It is almost as if he preferred not to call the spectre lurking behind this form of democracy by its name. However, he cannot help but wonder where sovereignty has gone if it is no longer recognized either in laws or in offices. The answer is that in such a case sovereign power goes to the people: the *kúrios* is the *plêthos* (cf. *Politics*, 1292a 3–4). Aristotle does not use this pejorative term by accident; indeed, it also recurs a little later on when he discusses the socio-economic criterion: the poor multitude becomes the sovereign of the constitution, *tò tôn apóron plêthos kúrion tês politeías* (1293a 10–11).

The tone harshens and Aristotle has no qualms about criticizing a 'democracy of this kind', where the best citizens are marginalized while the people, prey to demagogues, rises up as a monarch and ultimately exercises a despotic power. Such is the other side of this democracy: tyranny. Everything comes full circle – and Aeschylus' warning against both *ánarchos* and *despotoúmenos* echoes here, just as tradition decrees. Aristotle's condemnation of democracy, his indignant judgement against it, surfaces everywhere. It is condensed into a few images, for example, in his denunciations: 'the power of the Council is weakened in democracies of the sort in which the people in assembly deals with everything itself' (1299b 39–1300a 2). Even the *dúnamis* of the *boulé* will fail, where the *dêmos*, the people, *sunión*, gathered together, *chrematízei*, discuss, deliberate, and conduct their own affairs. Contrary to what might be imagined, this is not simply a problem of abuses of power or of the weakening of institutions. The issue seems rather more serious than that – and to run deeper. This is confirmed by a decisive passage in which Aristotle returns to Plato's remarks in the *Republic* about an 'anarchic and motley' democracy, a constitution that contains all and none, a non-constitution (558c). It is a 'reasonable criticism', says Aristotle. He reiterates this twice: 'such democracy is not a constitution at all', *ou politeía*, and again, *ouk ésti politeía* (*Politics*, 1292a 33–4). With a final gesture, both consistent and fearful, he then excludes it from the realm of democracies, if these are indeed constitutional forms. The words are clear: *oudè demokratías kúrios* – it is not even really democracy (1292a 38).

What is the proper way to talk about this non-constitution, this non-democracy? What name can we give to this ruin of the *arché* perpetrated by the multitude of the *dêmos*? Aristotle lets slip the word 'anarchy' only in two passages. In the first he indicts the misgovernment (the reference is to Thebes, Megara, and Syracuse) that leads democracy into ruin, causing anarchy and disorder, *anarchía kaí ataxía* (1303b 25–32). The expression is repeated twice. In the other he considers the need for democracy to be flexible – that is, to contain a certain amount of disorder – by expanding the body of citizens and admitting into citizenship not only legitimate but also 'illegitimate' children, bastards, the *nóthoi*, descendants from one side only, from either the father or the mother, not from both as would be necessary (1319b 8–10). Openness and inclusiveness befit such a democracy, Aristotle comments, without doing too much to hide his disapproval. In this regard, he recalls the measures adopted by Cleisthenes in Athens and the revolutionary experience in Cyrene. It is, without doubt, a good thing to broaden and unite the body of citizens. But the risk is that the licence (*anarchía*) extended to slaves, women, and children, as well as 'liv[ing] as one likes', could pass for means of democratic government, and thereby gain acceptance (1319b 10–32).

Although Aristotle was a foreigner, he did not look kindly on excesses which – far from meeting his ideal of moderation – border on chaos, disorder, and intemperance. While he took a different and less severe perspective than did Plato, he viewed with similar alarm the drift inherent in democracy, its irresistible anarchic tendency. This becomes clear in a famous passage in which, recapitulating the findings of his analyses and classifications, he points out the two characteristic traits of democracy. Here he is reporting the thoughts of others – the defenders of democracy – not his own, and the tone is somewhat derisive (cf. 1317a 40–b 17).

Freedom, *eleuthería*, is – or is meant to be – the foundation, the principle, the *hupóthesis*, of democracy. Or so it is commonly said. It is as if only in this (non-)constitution could one truly partake, *metecheîn*, in freedom, because – so they say – that is what every democracy aspires to. The interjections mark Aristotle's distance from these claims. But what does this freedom consist of? First of all: 'to govern and be governed in turns', *tò en mérei árchesthai kaí árchein* (1327b 3–4). However, since the *díkaion demotikón*, justice as understood by the people, reduces equality to an arithmetic criterion rather than one of merit, it follows that the multitude is sovereign, *to plêthos … kúrion*. Aristotle repeats the same words he used earlier to denounce that democracy which degenerates into anarchy. Thus, 'in democracies the poor are more powerful than the rich, because there are more of them and whatever is decided by the majority is sovereign'. The second mark of freedom is 'for a man to live as he likes', *tò zên hos boúletai* (1317b 12). If this were not the case, men would live as slaves. From this freedom, which Aristotle considers utterly misconceived, derives 'the claim not to be governed, preferably not by anybody, or failing that, to govern and be governed in turns', *tò mè árchesthai* (1317b 14–16). The one trait is traced back to the other. This is what *eleutheria*, democratic freedom, ultimately amounts to: the rejection of *árchein*, there being no *arché*. Aristotle could not have put it more clearly, even as he avoided calling the spectre by its name: *anarchía*. The foundation of democracy, its principle, is an-archic.

Before describing how such a democracy should function, Aristotle remarks, not without a certain irony, 'these principles having been laid down and this being the nature of democratic government [*arché*]' (1317b 17–18), as if to say: here is a government built on empty ground, without foundations, without substance – unlike what happens in his stable and well-established *politeía*. Given that in a democracy command is non-command, everything else follows from this and its workings should be consistent. All offices are elected by everyone, as a means of exorcizing power, as if ultimately no one were in command. The rotation is, therefore, already a concession. On the other hand, rotation is also present elsewhere, even in oligarchies. What democracy adds is the drawing of lots. Nothing could be further from the criteria of merit and competence, which even Aristotle – like Plato before him – does not reject if the most virtuous, the *mésoi*,[32] are to rule.

The absence of *arché*, of principle and command, makes democracy, in its radical version, a non-constitution that exceeds any archic scheme, any enumeration of titles and modes of command. Understood in the mere negativity of the alpha privative, anarchy cannot rise to the level of a concept. It thus evaporates and dissolves into disorder – a dissolution and a synonymy destined to last for centuries. Hence the images of political chaos, of life without regulation, of a freedom without constraints. Condemned to a dark and indistinct fog, the absence of command defies all imagination and exceeds the possibilities of a thought exercised in the *kósmos* and the *péras*, in order and limit, concentrated on the archic structure of the *pólis*. What escapes the *arché* is excluded from that perimeter. As a pre-politics or an ultra-politics, anarchy is prudently kept outside the gates. Hence the suspicion towards democracy, which seems instead to throw the gates wide open, delivering the city to this devastating spectre.

7. Sortition fell into disrepute, and for centuries thereafter was condemned to oblivion, as if it were a futile – and dangerous – game, a meaningless idea, an anachronistic practice suitable

at best for the democracy of small Greek cities in those foggy beginnings. Surely, it was assumed, such a practice was not well suited for modern democracies, which had in the meantime arrived at other principles and refined other means, such as the election of representatives of the popular sovereignty. But if the drawing of lots was long a repressed memory, it was also linked to others; indeed, it can be considered a further indication or even a proof of them. Sortition has been consigned to the archives of history because the radical meaning of democracy, its anarchic foundation, has been forgotten. The drawing of lots is closely connected to this anarchy.

It is no coincidence that, having recently returned to the limelight, the issue has become so controversial and divisive. It is almost a watershed between different, if not opposing, ways of understanding democracy.[33] The advocates of liberal democracy, while recognizing the split between the masses and the elite and the resulting danger of a pervasive depoliticization, nonetheless defend the established electoral system. Warning against any attempt to give even remote consideration to the Athenian democracy, they emphasize what cannot be repeated, highlighting not only the difference in scale but also the complicated workings of the modern world, whose functioning relies to an even greater extent on competence. This is the increasingly prevalent view that can be called epistemocracy, appealing to the power of experts, or government by technocrats. Here, sortition is abhorred and reviled, seen at best as a populist gimmick, and at worst as posing a mortal threat of incompetence. On the other side are those who call for its restoration, defending a practice which remained in use in other contexts and in later periods, such as in the Italian communes of the Renaissance, and which found support among the most radical currents of democracy from Rousseau to Montesquieu.[34] Whether this means enthusiastically embracing the drawing of lots – as the only impartial criterion and the only real alternative to elections that have become a worn-out ritual – or else looking to it as a remedy for the perpetuation of an unassailable oligarchic elite, the focus is turned towards Athenian democracy. The numbers and measures involved are not important in this context. However, the effort to rescue sortition from the archives and restore it to its original value is not always accompanied by the necessary theoretical clarity. Often, in fact, its proponents end up either generically defending its neutral horizontality or championing a lost cause. Yet, drawing lots is neither a simple tool nor a stepping stone to a government of incompetents. There are other, much deeper reasons why it is inseparable from democracy.

This was how both Plato and Aristotle presented it, well aware that they could not eliminate this requirement, which is the hallmark of democracy itself. It was, in fact, sacrosanct chance that had broken the *arché* of the few – who were not the best but merely the richest – inaugurating an unprecedented relationship with power, which would thus have to change its name. It meant not the assertion of the majority will, but government by those who had no more right to command than to be commanded. The drawing of lots that comes from heaven, the requirement for anarchy – this is democracy.

Long before being applied to the *pólis*, drawing lots was a widespread practice in various fields. It was used in combat, in the division of land, *klerouchía*, including in colonies, in the division of an inheritance, as attested in the *Iliad*, but also in many myths. To draw lots, to throw the *klêros* – which then by extension became the name for sortition in general – was to submit to the divine choice.[35] When it became part of the democratic institutions after Solon, or more likely after Cleisthenes, it had the threefold purpose of avoiding a prolonged concentration of offices in the same hands, mitigating the threats of violence arising from *timé* (the offended dignity of the losers), and preventing manoeuvring by those who ambitiously schemed to remain in government.[36] All citizens who had reached the age of thirty were eligible for office; however, they had to undergo an examination, the *dokimasía*, to assess their general conduct. Submitting to this itself implied a certain desire to put oneself forward. In addition, everyone was always required to give a regular account of their actions. Only a few public posts were elective, namely the military ones of the *stratégoi* and the financial offices. Although combined with elections, drawing lots was considered the emblem of radical democracy: the more it advanced, the more offices, the *archaí*, were drawn by lot. Whenever oligarchs seized power, as they did in Athens in 411 and 404 BCE, they immediately abolished the drawing of lots. Even later, those who – like Isocrates – called for a return to the *pátrios politeía*, i.e. to more moderate forms of government, sought to drastically reduce the use of this practice in favour of elections (*Areopagiticus*, 22).

It is clear that the drawing of lots must have had a symbolic value, one that encapsulated the spirit of Athenian democracy – or perhaps more accurately, its spectre. It is thus hardly surprising that when the possibility of the people coming to power began to be mooted, the lottery was immediately highlighted, as if it were its distinctive feature. Thus we read in Herodotus: 'The rule of the many … is free from all those outrages which a king is wont to commit. There, places are given by lot [*páloi*], the magistrate is answerable for what he does, and measures rest with the commonalty' (III, 80, 6).

The tone is rather different in a famous passage from *The Republic* in which Plato presents democracy. His sarcasm blended with contempt, he ultimately emphasizes the role of chance:

> democracy, I suppose, comes into being when the poor, winning the victory, put to death some of the other party, drive out others, and grant the rest of the citizens an equal share in both citizenship and offices – and for the most part these offices are assigned by lot [*tò polú apò kléron*]. (557a)

For his part, Aristotle, classifying the different forms of government in *Rhetoric*, writes: 'A democracy is a form of government under which the citizens distribute the offices of state among themselves by lot [*klêroi*]' (I, 1635b 30).[37] He repeats this in *Politics*, where he makes it a point of distinction: 'it is thought to be democratic for the offices to be assigned by lot, for them to be elected oligarchic' (1294b 9–10). In his list of points peculiar to democracy he also mentions sortition: 'election by lot either to all magistracies or to all that do not need experience and skill' (1317b 21). Aristotle's harsh judgement is evident when he distinguishes between numerical equality, which is purely quantitative, and proportional equality, or equality based on merit – with democracy leaning towards the former (1301b 30–1). This objection, time and again revived in various forms, would have a long series of consequences throughout history.[38] How can the fate of the city be entrusted to a lottery, and thus risk ending up in the hands of the undeserving, the inexperienced, the incompetent? This roll of the dice is a source of embarrassment for democrats themselves, who mention it only with some difficulty or pass over it in silence. Critics and detractors, on the other hand, are keen to remind us of it.[39]

The two words to consider are *arché* and *klêros*. In its inherent ambiguity, *arché* indicates both power and the position to be covered – understood in a visual sense as a position within the geometry of the city. *Arché* cannot belong to anyone, and if it is not to mutate into a form of domination it must be a power exercised only on a temporary basis, in a position that is always a *service*. Hence the key importance of rotation, alternation, expressed by the formula *en mérei* or, more rarely, *es méros*, which appears as a corrective to the *arché*. Meanwhile, one can both command and be commanded, *árchein kaí árchesthai*, insofar as this happens in turn. Everyone must alternately be able to exercise a position. Democratic freedom does not consist in (self-)obedience, but in obeying and commanding in turn. If it is impossible to avoid the exercise of office, which involves the albeit temporary *árchein* of one over another, rotation nevertheless makes this relationship reversible, neutralizing power.

When we consider Athenian democracy according to the standard models, we think of the people gathered in the assembly. This would be the allegory of direct democracy. But as recent studies have shown, there are other distinctive features, against the backdrop of a much more complex and sophisticated *pólis*.[40] The most accurate image is that of rotation, the orbit of offices, the constant movement in which the geometry of the city takes form. And yet, once power is distributed, the deviations, abuses, and excesses cannot be overlooked. Arrogance and abuse of power arise in the exercise of office – and the threat of *húbris* is always lurking. Rotation is both indispensable and insufficient to prevent power from hardening and becoming concentrated in the hands of a few. It risks ending up in the possession of those who believe they have more right to command than do others. Here and there, even in oligarchies, it is common for control to change hands. What is added to rotation in democracy – changing it, so to speak, from the ground up – is the drawing of lots. Only in this manner is it possible to avoid someone continuously exercising a position in a way that borders on its outright appropriation. The *klêros* is what makes *arché* unappropriable. Rotation becomes random, governed by chance, by sacrosanct fate. The orbital movement risks becoming centripetal and rotating around a possible fulcrum. But it is diverted by the verticality of a fall which, by emptying the space around it, time and again proceeds to disrupt every axis and deactivate every centre of power.

Sortition is the hallmark of democracy, from which it is therefore inseparable. It is not just the means by which public posts are distributed. It is also that seventh title to hold office, which, while disavowing the others and breaking their chain, thereby revokes its own claim to authority. It is the qualification for command of those who have no such qualification.[41] This is the constant shake-up of democracy. The old criteria – the differences in nature, wealth, and knowledge – no longer apply. This does not mean that the incompetent are rewarded. Fate is blind and does not favour some over others. If anything, drawing lots is a remedy for a certain kind of competence, a certain skill for intrigue, the cunning of those who scheme to stay in office. The desire for power should not be indulged. Sortition, on the other hand, can favour those who remain on the sidelines.

Does this mean we end up exposing ourselves to the blind whims of fate, i.e. to the risks of incompetence? This objection is an ancient one and can be found in a parodic version in a passage from *Protagoras*. Here, Socrates wryly comments on the assignment of political offices by lot: no one, he contends, would dare to choose ship's helmsmen, flute players, or city architects in this way.[42] The proper answer to this argument, which would become crucial in modern times, does not lie in pointing to the corrective measures that were already enacted by Athenian democracy. The combination of rotation and sortition aims to put power back into the hands of all citizens, including sailors, the poor, those not born into nobility, the inexperienced, and amateurs, because – as Protagoras explains in response to Socrates – unlike technical skills, which are reserved for the few, political virtue, *aretḗ politikḗ*, has been distributed to all.[43] Anyone, without title or qualification, is worthy of being heard and deserves to participate.

It is here, in fact, where democracy arises from its anarchic roots, that politics comes into being. For the other possible criteria – of paternity, age, wealth, strength, or science – are no longer valid. The democratic break with order, the disappearance of the *arché*, opens up a scenario of unprecedented contingency. Here, no one has the right to govern or be governed, and everyone is called upon to participate.

4

TRAGEDY AND POLITICS

1. The disappearance of the *arché* opens up the new scenario of democracy, and of politics. It is no accident that they arrive in the same moment. This also reveals a further, profound connection between them which, although often overlooked, must be investigated in light of this unprecedented anarchic destitution. The formula 'putting the *arché* at the centre' or 'putting the *arché* in common' seems to encapsulate the gesture that gives rise to democracy. The archic order has always been centred on an *arché*, fixed to a foundation, hardened around a pivot. As it crumbles and collapses, the space of politics opens up. The so-called 'birth of the political' is thus owed to the dethronement of the *arché*. Only because that order has dissolved does it become possible to discuss the ways in which the *pólis* organizes and articulates itself. In this sense, it can be said that the anarchic gesture opens up the space of politics, and at the same time sets democracy in motion.

Contrary to what one might believe, however, from the outset this gesture does not transcend into an archic act, a taking of command, a capture of power. The *arché* is not seized, grasped, or conquered, but deposed. The sequence of command is not repeated, but interrupted. The anarchic gesture of democratic insurgency is in fact an interruption. Precisely for this reason, the *arché* that is laid down and shared is no longer the same – it is no longer *arché*. The anarchic gesture does not leave it unscathed. In the transition to democracy, which cannot be overlooked, the name changes to *krátos*. We should clearly distinguish the two terms. What is now put at the centre is *krátos*, a new form of power which, on the one hand, reveals all the efforts of those who have finally prevailed, and, on the other, already hints at the contrasts, misunderstandings, and dramas of sharing. The *krátos* in the middle, in the *koinón*, the common centre, can never be concentrated in one set of hands if it is to belong to the community of the *dêmos*.

Here, the deposing of the *arché* raises all the many questions of democracy. How should we understand the *méson*, the middle, the median point, in which the *krátos* resides? It is certainly not fixed, rigid, and petrified (like the seat of a palace or the office of an archive). It does not rise up vertically, nor does it tower above – otherwise it would once again be *arché*. The temptation to occupy the *méson*, to appropriate it, to restore it to its hard, archic fullness, will always remain one of the great risks to which the *dêmos* is exposed.

What, then, does it mean to share *krátos*? This is the decisive question for the existence of the *dêmos*, that multitude united by an inappropriable *krátos* around a mobile and hollow *méson*. In the new anarchic political space that takes shape, a space of *eleutheria*, no one commands and no one is commanded: neither *árchein* nor *árchesthai*. This expression – reiterated wherever even the most surreptitious mention of democracy is made – rises up as the motto of the democratic revolution.

2. It may seem that we have stumbled here upon an anarchic strand of Greek thought which, in supporting and proclaiming a radical freedom, remains distrustful of the ruling power. It may thus appear as an unrealistic and extreme approach, seeking to exorcize power, considered in its evil and demonic form, forever keeping it at a safe distance. This sounds like an individual, libertarian choice made by a few fanatics. In reality – many will respond – *everyone* knows that power is indispensable for keeping order in the city; at most, this power can be constrained and mitigated. In short, we hear, it is necessary to show a measure of realism and adapt to the forms of power, preventing excesses and abuses, but without denying or rejecting power and falling into inane wishful thinking.

On closer inspection, however, that is not how things really are. The tragic vision of power is not the whim of some anarchist fringe, but the result of an epoch-making event, the collapse of the *arché*, which the *pólis* itself had to acknowledge. What comes to light here is the tragic nature of democracy, which is also the tragic nature of all political action. Much has been written on both topics; indeed, there is a long tradition in this regard. And yet, few have reflected closely on the connection between tragedy and democracy and investigated their relations with each other. What was the political dimension of tragedy? And in what sense is democracy an ontologically tragic political form?

3. These questions must be raised against the backdrop of an unparalleled juncture, a fundamental convergence between the advent of the *pólis* and the new image of the world that emerged at the beginning of the sixth century BCE. As the political space of the city, which gravitates around the *agorá*, is reorganized, physical space is reconfigured in new cosmological conceptions. It would be a mistake to look for any causal relationship here. It is, rather, a game of mirrors that, beyond the astonishing similarity between the geometry of the universe and the architecture of the *pólis*, points to a radical revolution in thought.

The topic has caught the attention of interpreters from Gregory Vlastos to Marcel Detienne.[1] Following in their footsteps, Jean-Pierre Vernant wrote two crucial essays on this theme, one dedicated to spherical astronomy, the other to the connection between political concepts and the structures of the cosmos. Both feature Anaximander of Miletus.[2] To understand this revolution, we must first look at the way in which the architecture of politics took shape, as it assumed a circular form culminating in the *agorá*. It is possible that this innovation first established itself in the colonies and then later 'at home'; it cannot be found among other peoples, however open to trade they were and however much they were drawn towards the sea. A central space in the urban fabric was not alone sufficient. 'The existence of an agora', observes Vernant, 'depends upon a system of social life that implies public debate on all communal affairs.'[3] The etymology of the word refers to the verb *agheíro*, which means to gather, to convene – implying an assembly. We should note the properly spatial dimension of the movement with which a circle is outlined, as the place of public debate. Here, people take the floor and discuss. The *agorá* always combines the sense of gathering with that of discourse. Hence *isegoría*, composed of *ísos* and *agoreúo*, to speak as equals, that 'equality of speech' which will remain the hallmark of democratic freedom. Those who speak step forward into the centre of the circular space, *en mesôi*, and, after speaking freely, they give way to another; this succession of equals constitutes the assembly of equals. The military gathering of warriors, depicted in the scenes of Homeric epic, is replaced by the assembly of the *dêmos* which marks the advent of the *pólis*. In the political space, where people discuss and argue freely, this advance to the centre, which also means making something public, remains decisive.

As Vernant clearly explains, *en koinôi*, to set in common, is synonymous with *en mesôi*, to place in the middle. The *méson* thus indicates the sphere of what is public, common, the *xunón*, which is distinct from the private, the particular. This middle should not, therefore, be read as a fixed central point, but rather as a dynamic medium. Only through their common participation in this centre can citizens form a *koinonía* or a *xunoníe*, a political community. It should not be forgotten that the *méson* represents both what is common and what is shared. Insofar as citizens have access to this circular space, they belong to the *pólis*. But as the semantics of *agorá* suggests, this implies not only the existence of a political sphere, but also the development of political discourse. In short: not only are the citizens bound by a new, unprecedented link to the *pólis*, but they themselves reflect on this link, discuss their participation, and together decide on the *pólis* and its destiny. This is the ultimate meaning of *koiná*: common things, public issues, must be the subject of free debate, of open discussion, in the full light of the *agorá*.

The space of the *pólis* is not organized hierarchically, as in the monarchy dominated by the king. There, his subjects are subjugated, divided into different castes and classes, deprived of ever more privileges and rights the further they are down the pyramid. In democracy, on the contrary, the equidistance of every position from the *méson* means that all citizens are always *ísoi* or even *hómoioi*, whatever their differences and whatever the contrasts between them. To complete the picture, it should be added that this equality is not static and fixed, but achieved through reversibility: one citizen replaces another, in a continuous succession. The political space of the *pólis* unfolds in a geometry of reversible relationships, in a symmetry of egalitarian relations. There can be no domination, because no one is subject to anyone else. Vernant writes that in Greek political thought, as in astronomy, 'we find exactly the same terminology, the same fundamental concepts, and the same conceptual nexus of ideas involving "centre" (*méson*), "similarity" (*homoiótes*, *isótes*), and "nondomination" (*ou kratoúmenos*, *autokratés*)'.[4] For those who consider themselves equals, to depose power, to place it at the centre, is to depersonalize it, to neutralize it. It is this which ensures that everyone can participate in it and no one can appropriate it.

This is what Demonax did in Cyrene around 550 BCE. Tasked by the oracle of Delphi with establishing a new constitution, while retaining the priestly functions for Battus, 'he placed in the middle [*es méson*], at the disposal of the people [*tô dêmoi*], everything that the kings had previously possessed' (*Herodotus*, IV, 161).

The same applies to Cadmus of Kos at the beginning of the fifth century BCE: 'He had received from his father a well-established tyranny; of his own free will, without any danger threatening him, but obeying a sense of justice, he returned power to the centre [*es méson katatheîs tên archén*] for the people of Cos' (IV, 164).

In Samos in 522 BCE, upon the death of the tyrant Polycrates, his designated successor Maeandrius aspired to rule justly. After erecting an altar to Zeus Eleutherios and drawing a circle, Maeandrius gathered the entire citizenry in assembly and delivered this speech (III, 142):

> To me, as you know, have come Polycrates' sceptre and all of his power [*sképtron kaí dúnamis pâsa*], and it is in my power now to rule you. But I, so far as it lies in me, shall not do myself what I blame in my neighbour. I always disliked it that Polycrates or any other man should lord it [*despózon*] over men like himself. Polycrates has fulfilled his destiny, and inviting you to share his power in the centre [*es méson tèn archèn titheís*] I proclaim equality [*isonomíen*].[5]

Placing the *arché* at the centre – *es méson*, or *en mesôi* – appears to be the gesture that, while opening up the political space of the *pólis*, also allows the *dêmos* into this no longer hierarchical space. Vernant emphasizes how important this is, but limits himself to noting the transition from the privilege of supremacy to a power fixed at the centre – which for citizens would mean asserting themselves as free from all domination.[6] When the two terms *arché* and *krátos* are not duly distinguished, and instead used almost as synonyms, some important questions raised by this gesture are left unanswered.

4. The revolution in the space of the *pólis* is reflected in the new spherical conception of the world. Vernant argues that clear traces of this influence can even be found in the political vocabulary. But the revolution brought about by Anaximander is certainly no less radical than that initiated by Maeandrius. The movement is analogous: the deposition of the *arché* at the centre. What effects does this have on cosmology? With reference to Anaximander, it would be no exaggeration to speak of an an-archic cosmology (and ontology).

The image of the world appears profoundly different from that of Homer and Hesiod, where the Earth is a flat disc surrounded by Ocean, a circular river that flows back into itself without origin or end. If the sky is a bronze dome, symbolizing the immutability of the gods, beneath the Earth lies the abyss of chaos. This is the source of different cosmogonies, where, however, the Earth, solid and secure, sinks its roots, guaranteeing its stability. Like a monarchy, the cosmos is organized into three planes. In the first, Zeus reigns with his retinue of immortal gods; the second is inhabited by human beings; and the third is the realm of death and the gods of the underworld. Anaximander's revolution is not so much a matter of freeing himself from an exegesis that resorts to mythical schemes and invokes the gods. He does not limit himself to a desacralization, as some believe, but proceeds to de-hierarchize the cosmos. This is also very clear from the doxographic texts collected and discussed by Charles H. Kahn in his masterful work.[7]

The Earth does not need a base, or foundation, or roots. It does not even need a founding discourse, because all that needs recognizing is that the Earth stands firm like a truncated column at the centre of the cosmos. The hierarchical space of myth is replaced by a spherical one, geometrically determined by relationships of distance and position. The Earth does not move because it is located at the centre, equidistant from all the points that mark the extreme ends of the universe. It is thanks to this equidistance that it remains still. No support is necessary – neither another base, nor air or water to hold it up, nor any other, higher force to command it from outside. Centrality, equality, and absence of domination are also correlated here, as in the *pólis*; they open up a symmetrical space where high and low, right and left are always reversible. There is no high in itself, no low in itself; the directions of space are not absolute. What is high for us will be low for the inhabitants of the 'antipodes', and vice versa.[8] This geometric-mathematical space explains the position of the Earth, which remains in equilibrium in the *méson*, in the centre, not at the mercy of other forces. Hippocrates uses a telling expression to summarize Anaximander's thesis: the Earth is *hupò medenòs kratouménen*, 'not dominated by anything', or – and it is the same thing – 'not supported by anything'.[9]

It is not difficult to detect, in such lines, the traces of a new political lexicon. The centrality of the Earth implies its autonomy, always in equilibrium between opposing tensions, between contrary forces. This is suggested by the verb *krateîn*, which excludes an absolute and archic domination.[10] Like the other Milesian philosophers, Anaximander believed that the order of the world could not have arisen by decree of a god or by sovereign imposition. Instead of referring to water, air, or some natural element, Anaximander spoke of the *ápeiron*, the unlimited, the un-dominated. As such, it has no *arché*, which would limit it.[11] It could in turn be *arché* (a term that Anaximander introduces for the first time in philosophy), except that it not only imposes no archic domination in the cosmos but, acting as a mediator in the *méson*, guarantees an egalitarian cosmos in which opposing forces balance out and none can prevail. This is not a hierarchical order or a monarchical government. In its mediating function, the *ápeiron* exercises *krátos* at the centre as a common law which, by promoting commonality, *koinón*, prevents all abuse, avoids all usurpation, and maintains the *díke* of *isonomía*, the justice of equality. The revolution initiated by the *ápeiron* evokes the revolution which is taking place in the *pólis*.

5. An anarchic ontology, analogous to the one underlying Anaximander's image of the cosmos, also takes shape in the political arena. This provides a starting point to investigate the tragic nature of democracy. Without an *arché* on which to base itself, and without a *télos* to refer to, democracy stands out in a precarious balance, constantly on the edge of the abyss.

Perhaps no one understood this radical and irreparable rupture as well as Cornelius Castoriadis. The Greek experience is above all an experience of chaos – of magma, of disorder – in relation to which the cosmos, as the human order of the world, has a secondary and derivative character. 'What makes Greece is not measure or harmony, nor the evidence of truth as "revelation". What makes Greece is the question of *non-sense*, or *non-being*.'[12] From the chaotic abyss, which always remains to undermine it, there emerges the human world, which is constructed in that void, without supports and without certainties, relying upon its own creation alone. Herein lies that instituent capacity, which is the ability to compensate for the absence of order. The Greek experience condenses one of the most important points in Castoriadis' reflection: self-institution. To his eyes, the Greeks were those who appeared on the stage of history as authors of themselves, of their own world, of their own laws – of their own *pólis*. One can get a sense, in this interpretation, of how ontology and politics are thought in combination. If self-creation rests on chaos, and if there are no pivots or cornerstones to rely on, then this gives legitimacy to an unlimited questioning – to the question about the question, which is to say philosophy. It is no coincidence that politics, philosophy, and tragedy arise together at the same juncture.

> Just as in Greek political activity the existing institution of society is called into question and altered for the first time, similarly Greece is the first society where we find the explicit questioning of the instituted collective representation of the world – that is, where we find philosophy.[13]

If the Greek experience is ontologically tragic, in the radical freedom of its self-positioning, the heart of the tragedy lies in the political dimension. Democracy is the culmination of this experience, the apex of the creation of a world based on nothingness and perennially exposed to the threat of nothingness. This is why Castoriadis writes that democracy is a 'tragic regime'.[14] Unlike other regimes that do not know danger because they are all certain of servitude, democracy risks its own existence – and is no guarantee against itself. This is also how Castoriadis reinterprets the theme of 'public space', taken up by Arendt, whom he repeatedly credits with having theorized this question. While in other regimes a greater or lesser degree of freedom is granted on the basis of a 'secret of power', only in democracy does a public space exist – *tà koiná, res publica*. However, Castoriadis warns that we must be careful not to understand this space statically, as something that is given once and for all. Rather, we must identify here the 'indeterminacy' of democracy, its openness.[15] Years later, Derrida would speak of 'the democracy to come'.

But if democracy is constantly self-instituting, without external safeguards or restraints, then the real catastrophe, the reversal that threatens and undermines it, has only one name: *húbris*. Because of this self-institution, democracy is always at the same time also self-limiting. It is called upon in each instant to set its own limits, beyond which it is not possible to go. Since there is nothing and no one who can establish these limits once and for all, they will be perennially in question. This is ultimately the crucial question concerning the unprecedented power of the *dêmos*. On closer inspection, while the people can do anything, it must know that it cannot do everything. This is the dilemma of democracy, its gamble.

It is precisely this new, unusual *húbris* that represents the transition from politics to tragedy. But how should this word, which could easily be misunderstood, be interpreted? Its broad semantic range requires the introduction of different terms: arrogance, haughtiness, recklessness, restlessness, a tendency to dominate and bully, but also acts of contempt, offence and mockery. *Húbris* alludes to excess and immoderation. At a certain point, in a given moment, the limits have been exceeded. But what limits? Established by whom? *Húbris* stems almost from the outcome of an action, recognized in its facticity. It results from an excessive and exorbitant gesture, whose effects are plain for all to see, without, however, it being possible to point to the law that has been violated, the rule that has been broken. In this sense, *húbris* is not a transgression. This word becomes a symbol of the new democratic space in which, alongside an unknown freedom, we also discover a fundamental uncertainty, the absence of fixed rules, the lack of precepts and dictates for action. That radiant and promising sky is then clouded by dark shadows: for freedom could slip into arbitrariness, and arbitrariness into abuse. The thrill of creative power gives a glimpse of the monstrous effects of destructiveness. Who can ever press the brakes? Who can prevent a horrendous abyss of wickedness and injustice from opening up within the fate of the individual or the community? If there is no longer an *arché*, if there are no archic principles and commandments and the space of *krátos* has now been flung open, then everything relies on the individual's capacity for self-control, on the *dêmos*'s ability to moderate itself and dampen any conflict.[16] One responsibility is not detached from another, and the limitation of *húbris* has both ethical and political value. Only this measure holds and contains the community, preventing some from dominating others. As in the cosmos outlined by Anaximander, *díke* watches over everything, preventing usurpation and promoting equality. It becomes clear here that the space for democratic questioning is also the space for questioning justice. If there is no norm for the norm, no measure for the measure, then it is necessary not only to give oneself a law, but also to decide what is just and what is unjust. This is what the political community is called upon to do.

6. Many examples could be given of *húbris* portrayed on the theatre stage. But perhaps *Antigone* is the tragedy of politics. In the famous *stásimon*, the song sung by the chorus to celebrate human abilities, the underlying dilemma is expressed: enthusiasm incessantly alternates with a dismayed retreat (332–75). This unfolds in the presence of a being for whom tragedy has no other word than *deinós*. Terrible, extraordinary, formidable, admirable, dangerous, terrifying, fatal. Heidegger translates it as *unheimlich*, disturbing, seeing therein the specifically Greek determination of the human.[17] Who is this lucid and blind being, both innocent and guilty, both acting and acted upon, capable of dominating all nature and incapable of governing himself?

'There are many strange and wonderful things, but nothing more strangely wonderful than man' (332). He moves across the seas foaming white, he wears down the earth with ever-turning ploughs, he captures serene birds, traps sea creatures in nets, and defeats the beasts of the forest with deceit. He has learned speech, the wind of thought, and the passions that establish the city. He knows how to avoid the assaults of the open skies, the downpours of storms, the inhospitable frost – he never waits helplessly for the future, only Hades will never know escape, even if he devises new remedies for untamed evils. His wisdom and art exceed all expectations – but his ambivalence drives him towards good and evil.

Sophocles does not refer to human beings in general, outside of history and political context. The expression *astunómous orgás* (354–5) clearly indicates as much. The reference is to that being who, in addition to being able to speak and think, knows the passions

– *orghé* is impulse, grievance, rage – that give *nómos*, law, to the *astú*, the city. The dilemma raised by the chorus concerns those who already know – or should know – how to live together, because they have already instituted democracy. This means having given oneself a *nómos*.

The chorus continues with verses that seem to clarify and specify the alternative between good and evil, which could be misunderstood and reduced to a moral choice. There are two terms in the dilemma: *hupsípolis* and *ápolis* (370). Those who stand up – *húpsi*, upwards – in the political community incline towards good, while those who withdraw from it incline towards evil. Respect for the laws and for justice sworn in the name of the gods is opposed by reckless audacity, *tólmas chárin*, insolence, arrogance, another way of saying *húbris*. The dilemma is between being sublime, elevated, great in the city, and being inhabited by excess, by the immoderation of haughtiness, and thus detached from the community. The chorus distances itself in the last verses: whoever acts in this way should be *paréstios*, far from my hearth, and should not have *íson phronôn*, equal wisdom, as that shared by other citizens.[18]

Are the tyrant Creon and the rebel Antigone both *ápolis*? It would certainly be more reassuring to take sides. In these two characters, Sophocles presents two unilateral positions which, both permeated with *húbris*, may not be incompatible, if only they were able to 'weave together' human laws and divine justice, instead of blindly defending their own principles. Thus, two irreconcilable absolutes confront each other, two archic attitudes, as abysmally distant as they are dangerously close in their 'polemical intimacy'.[19] Their tragic clash marks a culmination of tension, but also a moment of lethal weakness for the city. That inability to *phroneîn íson*, to share thoughts, to allow the other to be right or wrong – that claim to the last word – places them outside the *pólis* and outside the *lógos*. This is Antigone's 'absolute alienness'.[20] Dionysus and Eros, those nocturnal, mysterious, and elusive deities, close to women and foreigners, to whom the chorus turns, should be favourable to her. Yet, after condemning Creon, they cannot help but condemn the self-destructive madness of Antigone. Closed off in her family *philía*, she ends up devoting herself to Hades, without opening herself to others and to life, in her union with an outsider.

Even a position that, at first glance, would appear anarchic, reveals itself to be profoundly archic. This is exactly what makes it incompatible with the city. And yet: who determines who is inside and who is outside? According to what criteria, what limits and restrictions? Who decides the roles, in the theatre and in the city?

7. Much has been written already on the almost classic theme of tragedy and politics.[21] But we should start by warning against any possible misunderstanding. When we talk about politics, we do not mean examining the political positions taken by the tragedians themselves. Indeed, they were inclined not to take sides, by avoiding explicit reference to the conflicts that were shaking the *pólis*.[22] Nor can the political dimension of tragedy be seen only in the experiences, questions, and perspectives that the new scenario had opened up.

That theatre played a crucial role has been known since at least Burckhardt, according to whom 'the drama was not created merely for pastime or pleasure, which would have kept it a minor diversion, but as a part of a highly important cult of the polis'.[23] The plays were staged during great celebrations in honour of the gods, which, like other festivals, marked the necessary break from the usual cycle of life.[24] The *agorá* was the place where the tragedy contests took place in front of spectators and a jury of ten members chosen by lot. It has been suggested that the theatre of Dionysus was no less important than the *ekklesía*, and not only because of the number of citizens involved.[25] In this sense, tragedy may legitimately be deemed an 'institution' on a par with popular courts and assemblies.[26]

Tragedy arose at the end of the sixth century BCE, when, to quote a famous phrase by Wilhelm Nestle, myth took on a new strangeness in the eyes of the citizen.[27] The confrontation between the archaic *múthos* and the new *lógos* of the city thus agitates the whole of tragedy and always leaves a deep discrepancy, a fracture that is difficult to repair. That legendary past, however inexorably distant it may be, remains inscribed in the tradition of the city which, projected towards new political and ethical forms, nevertheless feels its absence. The prevalence of the *lógos* of the *pólis* – that is, of ideals detached from the mythical background – is thus a source of anguish rather than contented serenity. This laceration runs through every drama where, as Vernant observed, an anonymous and collective chorus, whose role is to express the fears, uncertainties, and hopes of the community, is counterbalanced by the protagonist, whose actions are the plot of the drama, a sort of heroine or hero from another time, whose story and condition are estranged from the citizens' own.[28] Hence the duality of language, but with a reversal of roles: lyrical metre for the chorus – which, continuing the poetic tradition, celebrates the qualities of the protagonist – and an almost prosaic iambic metre for the hero, who is meant to be brought closer to the audience. Ambiguities and tensions emerge even in the semantics of words that end up having opposite meanings. When they speak of *nómos*, Creon and Antigone mean the opposite.

But many other words could be cited that, on stage, give rise to a unilateral interpretation, closed in on itself, incapable of opening up to other meanings. The language of tragedy, in its back and forth of different, if not contradictory, meanings, allows the spectator to move within the semantic uncertainty and conflict between the two worlds. While every attempt to overcome this conflict appears futile, the ever-present tension ensures that the question posed by the tragedy remains unanswered.

However, it would be reductive to see this as merely a clash between the archaic past and the democratic present. Through myth, tragedy tears the city apart, calling it into question. Vernant and Vidal-Naquet, in a couple of quick references, speak significantly of a 'border zone' or 'intermediary zones'.[29] Perhaps, however, what is at stake along that boundary is not only the demarcation between divine order and human order. The stigma of *ápolis*, which emerges in Antigone's dilemma, should offer some guidance in this sense. In a famous passage from his *Politics*, Aristotle takes up this theme to repeat that the *ápolis* – sometimes beast, sometimes god, and sometimes both together – remains outside of the community (cf. 1253a 3). Perhaps tragedy has something to do with the boundaries of the city? In what way?

In attempting to answer this question, we cannot ignore the fact that there is a long and established tradition weighing on tragedy, no less than on democracy. Aristotle himself introduced a first, brilliant misunderstanding because – thinking on tragedy without any reference to the city, and therefore not seeing the citizen in the spectator – he considers cathartic emotion to be the only tragic effect aroused in the individual (cf. *Poetics*, 1453a 7). With this seemingly modern interpretation, undergirded by his own imposing authority, Aristotle ended up long hindering any other access to the tragic. How can we retrieve the viewpoint of the city?

Nor can we forget Plato's condemnation in Book X of *The Republic* (607b 5–6), which has over time come to constitute almost a crime scene to which philosophy must necessarily return. However, the accusing finger pointed simultaneously at both the theatre and democracy suggests an important link between them. Such is the explosive connection that Plato feared, and which led him to denounce the danger that tragedy represented for the *pólis* (cf. *Laws*, 371a 1–7).

If democracy is ontologically and politically tragic, then what role does tragedy play in democracy? An explicit anti-Platonist like Nietzsche, whose theory on the birth of tragedy made history and sparked a long trail of debates and controversies, may open a way into this question. The classic image of Greece, dominated by the idea of harmony, measure, and beauty, has contributed to repressing its most vital moments. Behind the calm and balance of the Olympian gods – the highest figures of classical antiquity – there transpire all those aspects of the Greek world that remained in the shadows. Concealed beyond the Apollonian is the Dionysian, but the one cannot be understood without the other. The harmonious images, which offer reassuring stability, originate from the painful chaos of life. It is thus impossible to separate the Apollonian from the Dionysian without falling into misleading abstractions. Although other phases are marked by vicissitudes and alternating dissonances, the incessant interplay of the two impulses finds its perfect synthesis in Attic tragedy. Nietzsche writes: 'the drama is the Apollonian embodiment of Dionysian perceptions and influences'.[30] The recovery of these two impulses finds expression in the thesis that tragedy originated from the Dionysian chorus. Hence the obligation to 'look into the heart of this tragic chorus as being the real proto-drama'.[31] Thus, the veil covering that half-hidden backstage, the chaotic fluctuation of the 'Dionysian mass', is torn away. But on the same page on which he formulates this thesis, Nietzsche adds polemical and scathing phrases aimed at immediately dispelling any possible doubt: one should not believe that the people are involved here, perhaps in opposition to sovereignty, as if 'the immutable moral law [*Sittengesetz*] was embodied by the democratic Athenians in the popular chorus [*Volkschor*]'.[32] He specifies that this did not affect the 'purely religious beginnings' of tragedy, which were free from any political influence.

While Nietzsche opens up a possible interpretative horizon here, he then seems to immediately close it again. The question concerns democracy, caught up in the accusation of decadence levelled at the Greek world that had devoted itself to the Apollonian. Attic tragedy committed suicide at the hands of Euripides, who wanted to please Socrates and, pandering to the demands of that one spectator, bent tragedy to a consolatory optimism, where nothing bad can happen to the righteous either in this life or the next. The regret for the tragic seems to extend to regret for the lost aristocratic order. This should not lead us to believe that Nietzsche is an irreconcilable enemy of democracy; after that first phase, his conception becomes much more complex and differentiated.[33] What cannot be accepted, however, is the gap that he introduces between tragedy and democracy. It is precisely the opening created by the Dionysian that provides cues to reflection.

Tragedy is situated in a border zone because it separates the city from itself, questioning its limits and putting on stage the boundary between inside and outside. It should thus be understood as a transgression whose political meaning should not be overlooked. Rather less convincing is the hypothesis of 'anti-politics' advanced, albeit in different forms, both by Euben, who sees it as a call to think that 'the city cannot be all', and by Loraux, who sees it as a call to accept the 'bond of division', of conflict.[34] Concealed behind and beyond what is defined as anti-politics is something further, which requires clarification.

The tragic frontier is opened by the chorus, composed mainly of marginalized people: women, slaves, foreigners, the elderly, the young – all those who do not fit into the political order. They are responsible for honouring Dionysus, the god most alien to the city. In the tragic corpus, foreigners enjoy a prominent status.[35] Nor should we forget that many tragedies take place in border areas or at the confines of the known world, not least the one that divides the living from the dead. Furthermore, there are often moments of transition, violation and cross-fertilization, for example between family ties and citizenship: those who were considered foreigners discover that they are citizens, and vice versa.

However, we should not believe that this marks the transition from the order of political domination to disorder and chaos. If it is true that tragedy is not simply a mirror of the city, it is equally true that it is not a broken mirror either. What prevents a deeper understanding is precisely the idea of chaos, which many interpreters – including Castoriadis – cling on to. The risk is to see only a potential threat to the city and its institutions, its looming loss of structure and destruction. The fragments convey this image well. It is as if the political meaning of tragedy were either the creation of a 'civic consciousness' or a return to the underlying disorder, albeit with the intent of revealing what lies beneath.

The transgressive passage is a gateway to the source of order, to the source of the *arché*. The theatre finally allows us to glimpse the backstage of the city. Here, what begins to emerge is the question of the distribution of roles – which could have gone differently (not in the theatre, but in the city). In fact, we can see in this background those who have been excluded, ousted, and distanced. Here are the women, the goddesses, the slaves. In his own way, even the craftsman acquires visibility – this humblest of workers, who according to Plato should have remained in the shadows of his workshop, relegated to that space, without concerning himself with the common affairs, for which he has no time.[36] Did this worker not help to fashion the backdrop which – standing as an artefact, beyond the drama – reflects his own production? Tragedy opens the doors of the *oîkos*, the private sphere, which thus passes into the public sphere of the *pólis*.

It is understandable why Plato sees in the tragic scene not only the prestige of illusion, but also the danger of the democratic syndrome. There, in fact, not only are copies of copies displayed, but fearsome ghosts are exhibited, anarchic spectres ready to unmask the supposed *arché*. All one has to do is open the doors leading to the backstage of the city, where the *arché* has been established, where the parts have been divided and the belonging, the boundary of the *ápolis*, decided. But who arranged all this? And who is in command, in the city? These are the questions that the chorus helps to raise, even in its own apparent political impotence. In this sense, tragedy is an anarchic transgression. It questions the boundary between inside and outside, opens the curtain on the backstage of power, allowing the invisible to emerge into the light of politics.

8. The distinction between *oîkos* and *pólis*, between the private space of the home and the public space of the city, is a longstanding topic of investigation. We need only mention, for example, Henri Francotte's work *La pólis grecque*.[37] However, it takes on new contours and raises new questions in light of the most recent research in anthropology, psychology, and history that has helped to dispel some of the shadows over the 'pre-political' Greek world, and in the heated debate currently underway in contemporary philosophy. The boundary – which is anything but clear-cut, being laden with symbolic significance and traversed by a latent tension – is already a problem for the Greek imagination, as Sophocles' *Antigone* exemplifies. Perhaps, beyond the rigid antithesis between *oîkos* and *pólis*, what is instead at stake is the blurred and conflictual threshold between inside and outside, within and without.

It is worth noting first of all the lack of information and documents concerning the private sphere. Monumental history begins with the Greeks, so what prevails in the self-representation of the city is the public and agonal side. This is evident in epigraphic and artistic evidence as well as in historiographical sources.

> We meet the Greeks, as it were, in their Sunday best; we do not catch them unawares but see them as they choose to represent themselves. These representations, further, are with few exceptions representations of public life. History, once it had reached its canonical mode with Thucydides, concerned itself almost exclusively with politics and war.[38]

It is the marginal observations, the scattered notes, the minor documents that reveal what lies hidden within. The Greek word *oîkos* has three closely related meanings: the house as a dwelling, as a family, as property. It is in this space that the life of the master and his wife, their sons and daughters, and their slaves both male and female unfolds. Relationships are hierarchical and roles clearly defined. All the other inhabitants revolve around the *kúrios*, the head of the family as husband and father, who is also the *despótes*, the master as slaveowner. They are all subject to his authority: the women, who are not fully free; the underage sons (legitimate and illegitimate), who are not yet free; and the slaves, who are completely deprived of freedom.[39] Already in Homeric verse, the *oîkos* is described as a protected shelter, a destination yearned for by the heroes, warriors, and sailors returning from wars, adventures, and travels.[40] Much more than the space enclosed by domestic walls and marked by boundary stones indicating ownership of the soil, the *oîkos* can be understood as a way of life, the ultimate horizon of its members. They are bound together not only by strict rules and solid traditions, but also by a deep connection with their ancestral past, the cult of which keeps the hearth burning, as a source of nourishment for their descendants. The care of the fire is thus tinged with the sacred, as a gift that guarantees the continuation of the lineage and the constancy of the house over time. An extinguished fire means the extinction of the family, the abandonment of the *klêros*, the plot of land that is their property. In this respect, the *oîkos* is conceived as a 'living organism'.[41] Its perpetuation ensures that the land itself remains the property of the same unaltered *ghénos*, the progeny that has its home there.

A community of life, but also of survival, the *oîkos* produces what it consumes. From the *thálamos* – the dwelling that houses the treasure, the valuable objects – the space extends to the fields, the flocks, the vineyards. The set of the activities that take place there constitutes the sphere of the *oiko-nomía*, the administration of the whole house.[42] This etymological meaning could not be further from the current sense of 'economy', which, having lost all reference to the house, has encroached upon politics. It is now the state that oversees and administers production. Thus, the expression 'political economy', which sounds self-evident in the modern context, would have been an oxymoron for the Greeks. For *oikonomía* refers to the administration of the home – of possessions and living beings – detached from political relations.

However, it should be noted that Aristotle's image of a pre-political, apolitical community constituted according to nature is misleading. In his words, 'Hesiod was right when he wrote "First and foremost a house and a wife and an ox for the ploughing"' (*Politics* 1252b 10–11). Rather, we should think of a historical process in which, as the *oîkos* gradually breaks away from the fabric of phratry (*phratría*) and tribe (*phulé*) in which it is embedded, it is projected externally towards the *pólis*.[43]

But the *oîkos* also has an interior and an exterior. It thus appears divided between the realm of Hestia and that of Hermes, the two divinities who, in addition to living on Earth among human beings, preside over their dwellings.[44] Permanence, stability, and fidelity distinguish Hestia – the name of the goddess and the noun for the hearth – who dominates the centre of the house, *mésoi oíkoi*.[45] The interior space is oriented and organized around this point. In contrast, Hermes is the wandering god, the master of the roads, the traveller, the mediator. Ubiquitous and elusive, he appears suddenly and disappears just as abruptly. He is *ánghelos*, the unpredictable messenger, who abolishes distances with his winged sandals. He represents movement, passage, change and exchange, transition, translation. Hermes passes through walls. He protects the house from thieves, because he himself is like a thief who 'passed edgeways through the key-hole of the hall like the autumn breeze, even as mist'.[46] He moves transversally, climbing over fences and crossing borders. He is thus present at the city gates, at territorial borders, at crossroads and meeting points, but also on tombs, where the route into the underworld opens up. Hermes leads from wakefulness to sleep, from life to death.

Hestia and Hermes are each the reverse of the other. The reassuring shadow of the house, the warm intimacy of the hearth, the quiet intensity of *chiaroscuro*, correspond to everything that is projected outside, exposed to the harsh light of day and the impenetrable darkness of night. 'To Hestia belongs the world of the interior, the enclosed, the stable, the retreat of the human group within itself; to Hermes, the outside world, opportunity, movement, interchange with others.'[47] Between Hestia and Hermes there is not so much opposition as complementarity. They cannot therefore be taken in isolation, because they represent the two poles – centripetal and centrifugal – between which space is organized. In the tension between the two poles, the threshold is always unstable.

The most hidden point, where the round hearth burns, is the *omphalós*, the navel that represents the heart of the private space, the immediate connection with the earth, the umbilical cord that binds generations, the intertwining of past and future lives, the encounter between infernal, chthonic, and celestial powers. What allows the house to be solid and well established is the *omphalós*, the root of the womb, the principle of the offspring's rootedness in the paternal home, of the lineage in the land where it is established. The political resonances of this intimacy soon become apparent.[48] Artemidorus writes in his *The Interpretation of Dreams* (I, 43):

> The navel itself signifies parents to those whose parents are still alive; but to those who no longer have parents, their native country, from which, as from one's navel, one's nature and existence derive. Therefore, if anything happens to the navel, this signifies that a man will lose his parents or leave his native country, and, in the case of anyone who is abroad [*epì xénes*], that he will never again return home.[49]

Goddess of the hearth, Hestia thus reveals her two faces, which may otherwise not clearly come to light: that of the virgin, capable of guaranteeing purity, and that of the mother, capable of procreation. Thanks to this female figure, virgin and mother (in an alternation of roles), the *oîkos* can not only remain stable but also endure over time, unaltered and identical to itself. This outlines the tendency to close oneself off and separate, in the chimera of an introversion that would culminate in strict family endogamy and complete economic self-sufficiency. The outside world is confronted in order to bring goods inside, preserve them, and accumulate them, in a proprietary economy – an economy of one's own and of appropriation – based on the plot of land, the basis of sustenance.

The centre symbolized by Hestia, a hearth dedicated to remaining pure, furthermore presupposes other, similar centres, which are equally closed off and separate. Yet, even amidst fear and caution, it is also necessary to pursue trade and exchange, if not actual alliances, with these others. The verb *hestiáo* means to welcome into the domestic hearth, to receive at a banquet, to host. At the tables laid out in the sanctuaries, where Hestia reigns supreme, the justice of Zeus Xenios is observed.[50] But the guest who enters the house, a potential enemy, must undergo a kind of purification in order to be accepted and included in the domestic circle. This is the purpose of the feast, the meal, the food. Thus, the stranger who has wandered in a foreign land, the supplicant who begs for asylum, is received in the hearth, the symbolic threshold of welcome and integration.[51] Another family and a new life await him.

At this point, however, a new and decisive split emerges, confirming the importance of the polarity between internal and external. This time, it is the woman herself who splits in two. This comes to light in the institution of marriage. If Hestia, pure and faithful virgin, maternal protector of the home, must necessarily remain by the hearth, there will be another female figure who moves, travels, and enters into relations with the outside world, passing through the marital union and ensuring the bond between different families. This is the bride who breaks away from her father's *oîkos*, who is, in fact, painfully torn away from it. The heart-rending separation is echoed in Sappho's verse (104a):

> Hesperus, bringing everything that shining Dawn scattered, you bring the sheep, you bring the goat; you bring back the child to its mother.[52]

The foreigner, the bride, moves from one family unit to another in a sort of migration, before she is integrated into her new home, where she always remains an outsider. It is no coincidence that the verb *sunoikeîn* is used; it indicates a woman cohabiting with her husband. It is she who joins from outside and must thus adapt, becoming similar, while her husband welcomes her into his *oîkos*. Here is sealed the symbiosis of lineage and soil, the sacred flow of generations and the ancestral bond with stable and unalterable paternal possessions; here takes root the powerful myth of autochthony.

Yet, while the duality ascribed to women – both the most intimate and the most alien – emerges in marriage, Vernant aptly explains that it would be a mistake not to see its broader, primarily political, repercussions. The world of the patrilineal *oîkos* corresponds well to the dream of purely paternal inheritance that occupied the Greek imaginary with regard to both politics and the family. Women, relegated to passivity and considered a repository of life, imitate the earth, welcoming the seed, but in such insignificance that they can be supplanted. Greek men preferred to believe that they were born from the earth, that they were autochthonous. On the margins, then, lurks the woman who is a stranger to the *oîkos*, a foreigner to the *pólis*, unassimilable or not yet assimilated, a migrant waiting for refuge, perhaps a supplicant.

9. The question of the emergence of politics in Greece requires a perspective that, rather than focusing on the form of the *pólis*, looks instead at its formation or staging. This is what Claude Lefort suggested.[53] Hence the theoretical interest of the perspective – one which would obviously be genealogical – taken up by the German historian and Hellenist, Christian Meier. In his 1980 collection of essays entitled *Die Entstehung des Politischen bei den Griechen*, the question of the emergence of democracy, which had already been touched upon elsewhere, gives way to the related, and in some ways prior, question of the emergence and manifestation of the political. In Meier's words, 'The first democracies in world history could only emerge when the political coexistence of citizens became the centre of their lives.'[54] Only in a broader context can we attempt to understand Greek democracy.

It is almost superfluous to note that such an investigation finds linguistic justification in the adjective *politikós*, derived from *pólis*, an adjective whose substantivation as a neuter noun is already attested in Greek, in what Bruno Snell calls finding the general by itemizing the specific.[55] Unlike the 'beautiful' or the 'just', however, the 'political', *tò politikón*, floats away from rigid conceptualization and ends up presenting a broad semantic spectrum that varies according to the context.

But what did *politikós* mean? The answer is emblematic. Since it referred to the community of the *pólis*, to the whole structure of citizenship to which the Greeks felt they belonged, *politikós* was the antithesis of *ídios*, that which is private, selfish, and self-interested. It was thus synonymous with *koinós* or *xunós*, that which is common and unites. It was so characteristic of the bond uniting free and equal men that it ended up standing opposed to *despotikós*, i.e. to any form of command, or the exercise of power by the few over the many. To soften the despotic character of an oligarchy amounted to making it more political. It is worth emphasizing once again that, while *politikós* referred to action within the *pólis*, it was not suited to describing the relationship between different *póleis*.[56]

Perhaps this observation also prompted Meier to formulate the hypothesis that the emergence of the 'political' among the Greeks was influenced more by the community than by war. This may seem surprising considering the decisive role played in his work by the thought of Carl Schmitt, to whom an essay in the collection is dedicated.[57] Without forgetting the controversies that always accompany this name, it is worth asking whether it is appropriate to project a modern concept onto Greek antiquity. Meier, however, offers an original interpretation that can in many aspects be accepted. Schmitt's eminently theoretical concept of the political indicates, in contrast with the state and institutional sphere of politics, the sphere of mutual relations and tensions, where people act and decide together, starting from the order of coexistence, and where conflict therefore arises. This is what Schmitt calls the terrain of antagonisms.[58] Meier transfers this to the Greek world, using the incisive expression '*politischer Dispositionsraum*', a space for political initiative which, in democratic *póleis*, opens up at the centre of power, or rather at the centre of sovereignty.[59] *Das Politische* and *tò politikón* are therefore comparable and one sheds light on the other. Meier is keen to point out that, for Schmitt, the 'political' does not indicate a concrete field, but rather the 'degree of intensity of an association or dissociation'.[60] It would thus be wrong to see this as a definition of the essence of the political, rather than a simple formulation of a criterion. He adds that only 'by opposition (or enmity?) to Carl Schmitt' has the concept of the political been bent out of shape and reduced to the friend-enemy opposition.[61] In short, it is not necessarily true that extreme conflict is required in order for political unity to exist. However, Meier acknowledges the further step that led Schmitt to an ill-advised conclusion: the closer to the extreme, the more opposed to an enemy, the more political the sphere of relations. Here, 'political' ends up becoming equivalent to 'existential' or 'intensive'.[62] It is at this point that, according to Meier, the paths diverge. This does not, however, prevent him from resorting to the concept of *Handlungsfeld*, 'field of action', to understand the space that opened up in the *pólis* and which marks the emergence of politics.[63]

It can thus be said that Meier looks less to the outside than to the inside, less to the many wars among the Greeks than to the formation of a political community. Of interest to him is the unprecedented political bond that united citizens, tearing them away from their ancient family ties; this fuelled a deep sense of belonging to the city, which was combined with widespread participation.

> The Greek political … is the specific form that this field of action took on in the classical period and especially in democratic Athens. While increasingly large and ultimately vast strata of citizens struggled to gain effective and stable participation in politics, that field changed and expanded until it reached the opposite pole of what in previous cultures had simply been 'political' (in the general sense of the category).[64]

What seemed immovable, rigid, and almost excluded from any change, was returned to conflictual contingency, to action and to the participation of citizens, who discovered themselves sovereign because the very order of the *pólis* was in their hands. It was then possible to raise the question: who rules the city? Those who had previously been dominated questioned domination, speaking for themselves and sensing a previously unknown power to act. As they learned to raise their eyes and look at alternatives, their relationship with time and events also changed: having overcome all submission to fate, they decided the destiny of their own community. Their confidence in their own abilities grew, although they must have been aware that this was an unprecedented risk: 'The great scope for action was matched by the experience of the full difficulty of decision-making; the freedom of being left to their own devices was matched by a full awareness of human suffering.'[65] This was to be the source of the drama of *deinón*.

Meier says no more about this turning point, which he occasionally alludes to as a horizontality that interrupts the vertical order of high and low. Nor can we fail to point out its still metaphysical imposition, which leads him, despite everything, to reduce *Entstehung* to a *Begründung*, to consider the emergence of the political as an archic act of foundation, almost an act of will on the part of citizens, who could sovereignly arrange an order and 'establish a constitution'.[66] In any case, what really interests him is the process of politicization, which he – with good reason – repeatedly emphasizes.[67] For this must have been a remarkable phenomenon even for contemporaries, deeply affecting their existence.

Moreover, it cannot be a coincidence that in his famous epitaph, considered a proud claim to democracy, Thucydides has Pericles say that Athens considers 'him who takes no part in these duties not as unambitious but as useless' (II, 40, 2).[68] This theme has been highlighted in particular by Veyne, who goes so far as to compare the figure of the citizen of that time to that of today's political activist or militant. Those who governed – i.e. those who took office, always temporarily – were no more than citizens who were more active than others at that particular moment. But all were, so to speak, politicians by vocation, animated by militant zeal. This was what citizenship consisted of. And this was why, according to Veyne, Athenian democracy could be nothing other than direct democracy – not because of its scale or the workings of its rules, but because historically it 'was an attempt to remove from the notables the political part of their general influence, by transforming citizens into activists'.[69] From this point of view, the modern-day asymmetry between rulers and ruled would have been suspect to the ancient Athenians' eyes, and considered comparable to the condition of the unfree. If the representatives of the people cannot today consider themselves masters of government, it is only because of elections which, rather than expressing a choice, remind those who govern that they are not summoned by divine right.

In his investigation into the 'emergence of the category of the political', Meier scrutinizes with a historian's eye the remote and largely impenetrable horizon of what he calls *Vorgeschichte*, the 'prehistory' of democracy. He seeks out its various preconditions and multiple causes, without, of course, being able to answer the question: how did the Greeks arrive at democracy? Was it through the first assemblies, the Delphic cult, the unjust division of land, debt slavery, the phalanx of hoplites, emigration, colonization, the unshakeable faith in justice, or the 'tendency towards isonomy'? These hypotheses intertwine: they are all valid, but do not exhaust the matter.

There remains a suggestive hypothesis that Meier, once again revealing his Schmittian influence, seems to hint at, albeit without developing it further. It is basically an absence: during the late ninth and eighth centuries BCE, the Greeks underwent an epoch-making transformation of unknown nature, which drove them from the agrarian world of their origins, entrenched in inaccessible mountainous areas, to that of the Mediterranean coast, as brightly open as it was disturbingly lacking in supports for their existence. There was no ground for a central power, for the possibility of a monarchy that could unite the small scattered communities. The worrying vacuum at the centre corresponded – in the Aegean area – to an extraordinary dissemination of the sites of power.[70] We get the sense that, as Meier outlined this something that was missing (a defect that later turned into an advantage), he was thinking of Schmitt's reflections on land and sea, though he does not mention them.[71] His investigation stops there.

The archipelago must have played a significant role in the an-archic opening up of democracy. With the *nómos* of the land abandoned, the bonds of the *oîkos* loosened, and all fixed points of reference surrendered, the promise of a new freedom unfolds:

> The space of the Archipelago is by its nature intolerant of subordination and hierarchical succession; no island constitutes its fixed axis, capable of structuring the whole in the form of a State. In the mobile and changing space of coordination and cohabitation – which is also the meaning of *pólemos*! – the singularities of the Archipelago belong to each other because none of them has its own Centre, because the centre is in truth nothing more than that impetus that compels each of them to 'transcend itself' by sailing towards the other and all of them towards the absent homeland.[72]

The sea surrounded by land, jagged coasts, beckoning promontories, inlets and straits, a blossoming of islands: this is the landscape of the democratic epic. A space that unites and separates, forces the sharing of risks, spurs the overcoming of limits, prompts cunning, opens up to endless questioning, and exposes to shipwreck. The *pólis* itself set sail. It sailed like a ship.[73] It faced stormy seas, glided lightly on the surface of the water, challenging the depths and ingratiating itself with the skies, always in balance, without an *arché*. Was it guided by some helmsman? Some would have wished so, starting with Plato and Aristotle. But on closer inspection, it was the sailors who rowed it, who steered and governed it. It was a ship without the passengers or tourists that representative democracies have. Everyone was part of the crew.

10. It is hard for us to imagine what an epoch-making change, what an outright revolution, was brought about by the emergence of a bond which, breaking into tribes and crossing families, uprooted the pernicious roots of lineage, broke the chains of atavistic submission, and projected the people thus constituted into a space and time that had become political. This people would be the new protagonist of the democratic city that aimed at *isonomía*, the constant reversibility of power.

The exegesis of the bond underlying the *pólis* can be ascribed to the great insights of Hannah Arendt, formulated in decisive pages in her *The Human Condition*, where she sets out her vision of politics for the first time. She takes her point of departure from two traumatic personal experiences: the tragedy of refugees, deprived even of the right to have rights and condemned not so much to statelessness as to the loss of a community; and the rise of totalitarianism understood as *totale Herrschaft*, total domination. This is the perspective from which her often misunderstood, if not outright overlooked, pages on the Greek *pólis* should be read. It is neither an irrelevant idealization nor a theory of escape from government, but a way of rethinking politics, of retrieving its dignity. As Lefort wrote in this regard:

> Arendt's reading of totalitarianism, in both its Nazi and Stalinist variants, governs the subsequent elaboration of her theory of politics. She conceptualizes politics by inverting the image of totalitarianism, and this leads her to look, not for a model of politics – the use of the term 'model' would be a betrayal of her intentions – but for a reference to politics in certain privileged moments when its features are most clearly discernible: the moment of the Greek City in Antiquity and, in modern times, the moments of the American and French Revolutions. The moment of the workers' councils in Russia in 1917, and that of the Hungarian workers' councils of 1956, might also be added to the list.[74]

It is thus by looking at these periods of council rule, so eccentric in the history of Western democracies, and considering the forms in which the revolutionary spirit manifested itself, that Arendt investigates the Greek *pólis*. In an article commemorating her, Dolf Sternberger talks about a 'resuscitation' – a calling of the *pólis* back to life which, regardless of the niceties of philology and historical subtlety, is peerless in terms of its philosophical force.[75] We can fully embrace this viewpoint, though it is to be regretted that philologists and historians have shown such a lack of interest in these pages, confirming a lack of dialogue between different fields. A friend and fellow student from her Heidelberg days, Sternberger remained in contact with Arendt for decades, as illustrated by their correspondence. He was himself animated by a passion for politics.[76] In his article, he recalled certain telling scenes. For example, during a seminar in Chicago on Herodotus, Arendt's face lit up upon hearing the words of the Greek Otanes: 'I have neither a mind to rule nor to be ruled.'[77] Her love for this passage did not owe to mere nostalgia. Arendt moved in the ancient *pólis*, Sternberger observes, 'like a *Sonntagskind* in the alleys of a vanished city'.[78] At ease, confident and content, as if in the most lucid dream, she opened her eyes and recognized the *agorá*, the assembly, the market; she felt as if she could hear those words, see those scenes again. Above all, she was breathing that air of freedom.

The *Sonntagskind*, the Sunday child, the one born under a lucky star, is a figure from legend and folklore. According to Walter Benjamin, in German fairy tales, 'Sunday children see magical gardens where other people see nothing; they come across treasures that others carelessly pass by.'[79] They thus differ from ordinary mortals. But if they have the power to see beyond, these visionaries also have to deal with ghosts. Thus, the praise given by Sternberger, for whom Arendt's name represents a radical renewal of politics (or rather, of the political), seems to turn into a drastic rebuke. For with the disappearance of the ghost town, abandoned and extinct, politics may also have vanished forever.

This critique, which was already doing the rounds at the time, had its spokesman in Jürgen Habermas, who criticized Arendt not so much for her idealization of the *pólis* as for her lack of strategic action, of a normative and teleological (or teleocratic?) approach. This brought the risk of an escape from government – an an-archic flaw.[80] Sooner or later, some decision would have to be made, as Sternberger reiterated.[81] And yet, Arendt was well aware of the need to make decisions in politics. It was just that she intended to question that normative-institutional view of politics that reduces it to the preservation of order.

It might be hypothesized, here, that Arendt recognized in the Greek *pólis* one of those 'great strokes of luck in history', and that she turned around it like a pearl diver, searching for hidden treasures that could restore dignity to politics. She, after all, had survived the effects of a politics caught up in a teleological vortex, bent to an extreme decisionism, subjected to sovereign subjectivity, degraded to absolute domination. In this sense, *totale Herrschaft*, totalitarian power, is the opposite of the Greek *pólis*. Since that German expression for totalitarianism translates no more nor less than *arché*, Arendt moves within the *pólis* to seek the an-archic space of politics. More than that: where there is *arché*, there can be no politics. *Arché* as domination is 'impolitical', *unpolitisch* – that is, it does not belong to the *pólis*.[82] It thus constitutes its outer limit. When the *arché* asserts itself – when *totale Herrschaft* appears – it is politics itself that is eliminated. If totalitarianism represented the apogee of Western metaphysical politics, with its craving for a sovereign foundation and its archic perversion, the post-totalitarian age must start again from the freedom of the *pólis*.

We can say, then, that politics exists where *arché* is banished. To understand this thesis, we should reread the pages in which Arendt, examining the political bond that connects the city, gets to grips with interpreting the distinction between *oîkos* and *pólis*. To this end, she draws in particular on Aristotle's *Politics* and just two secondary works, namely Fustel de Coulanges' *The Ancient City* and Werner Jaeger's *Paideia*. The emergence of the *pólis* – a simple historical fact and not a philosophical theory – was preceded by the 'destruction of all organized units resting on kinship, such as the *phratria* and the *phylē*'.[83] This made possible a phenomenon that we can only imagine today with 'extraordinary difficulty', namely a clear demarcation between the private and public spheres, between the individual and the common, the familiar and the political. Arendt cites an incisive phrase from Jaeger to explain how the *pólis* meant each man receiving 'besides his private life a sort of second life, his bios politikos. Now every citizen belongs to two orders of existence; and there is a sharp distinction in his life between what is his own (*idion*) and what is communal (*koinon*).'[84] Her view differs from that of Coulanges – criticized for this in a footnote – who argues, in line with Aristotle's reading, that the Greek city, no less than the Roman, was based on the model of the *genos* and emerged from a union among tribes. Nothing could be further from Arendt's thesis, which instead emphasizes the gap between the two spheres. It is worth quoting the passage in full:

> The polis was distinguished from the household in that it knew only 'equals,' whereas the household was the center of the strictest inequality. To be free meant both not to be subject to the necessity of life or to the command of another and not to be in command oneself. It meant neither to rule nor to be ruled. Thus within the realm of the household, freedom did not exist, for the household head, its ruler, was considered to be free only in so far as he had the power to leave the household and enter the political realm, where all were equals. To be sure, this equality of the political realm has very little in common with

> our concept of equality: it meant to live among and to have to deal only with one's peers, and it presupposed the existence of 'unequals' who, as a matter of fact, were always the majority of the population in a city-state. Equality, therefore, far from being connected with justice, as in modern times, was the very essence of freedom: to be free meant to be free from the inequality present in rulership and to move in a sphere where neither rule nor being ruled existed.[85]

The line of discrimination, then, lay directly in *arché* itself. To command and be commanded was characteristic of the *private* sphere, where natural inequalities and hierarchical relationships could exist, starting with the *despótes*, the head of the family. The private sphere was considered sacred because – thanks to the work done by slaves and women – it ensured survival. Yet, this remained subordinate to the public sphere, that second chance that allowed freedom, i.e. the condition of not being subordinate, not being subject to any *arché*, any command. This is why an existence relegated to the private sphere of the *ídion*, of one's own, was literally 'idiotic' in the Greeks' outlook, because it was a *deprived* condition like that of stateless persons and refugees. It meant a life exposed to coercion and violence, one 'outside the world of the common'.[86] Obscurity – the 'curse of slavery' and of those condemned to pass away without leaving a trace – contrasts with the public sphere of seeing and being seen, of listening and being listened to, the space of reciprocity where the other is not a subordinate but an equal.[87]

Politics can only exist where there is freedom from *arché*, where relationships are no longer debased by subordination – that is, where *isonomía*, equality, prevails. Arendt takes the intertwining of these three concepts directly from the Greek context. Her vision of freedom is thus far from the liberal tradition, which conceives of it in a purely negative sense with the clear aim of reducing, if not eliminating, all public coercion over the private, individual sphere. For Arendt, in contrast, it is the public sphere that can open up the space of freedom. This takes real form in *isonomía* – the term for equality, taken up as the banner of the Greek democrats. If Arendt only occasionally referred to 'democracy' (preferring 'politics' or 'republic'), and thereby risked counting herself out of the radical theorists of democracy, this was, she tells us, out of a concern to avoid the word 'originally coined by those who were opposed to isonomy'.[88] Equal freedom, which after the Athenian *pólis* would re-emerge in the early stages of modern and contemporary revolutions, is for Arendt the epiphenomenon of politics.

> Isonomy guaranteed *isótes*, equality, but not because all men were born or created equal, but, on the contrary, because men were by nature (*phúsei*) not equal and needed an artificial institution, the *pólis*, which by virtue of its *nómos* would make them equal. Equality existed only in this specifically political realm, where men met one another as citizens and not as private persons. The difference between this ancient concept of equality and our notion that men are born or created equal and become unequal by virtue of social and political, that is man-made, institutions can hardly be over-emphasized. The equality of the Greek *pólis*, its isonomy, was an attribute of the *pólis* and not of men, who received their equality by virtue of citizenship, not by virtue of birth.[89]

Arendt often returned to her favourite passage – Herodotus on 'neither ruling nor being ruled' – to highlight that the equation between freedom and non-*arché* also has repercussions for those who do rule.[90] A leader surrounded by men who are not his equals would not be free, either. To dominate others is to deprive oneself of those peers with whom alone freedom is possible. Where there is command and obedience, where power becomes violence, the true public space is destroyed. In this respect, the rule of the worst despot cannot be as perfect and unchallenged as that of the head of a household.

The energy with which Arendt distinguishes between private and public ought to be understood in the context of her goal of rehabilitating politics in the aftermath of the totalitarian experience. Concerned to discern the phenomena that attested, despite everything, to a continuity, Arendt denounced the disturbing expansion of the *oîkos*, which transformed national organizations into gargantuan versions of the administration of the home. This implies the primacy of the economic and the consequent disappearance of politics. It is reduced, at best, to a mere instrument for protecting a sort of collective hyper-family called society, directed towards production and subsistence. In this regression to a pre-political condition, the dominant bond comes through labour. Arendt points an accusing finger at Marx, said to have encouraged this alienation, and above all at the Marxism that has contributed to making politics a mere superstructure. This has its devastating effects in the form of privatism – a retreat into the private sphere, which becomes the only space for life – and the loss of the 'world of the common', meaning depoliticization.

The spread of *oiko-nomía*, as Arendt understands it, also implies the affirmation of the familiar – and familistic – model, which leads to the formation of closed natural communities based on birth, descent, lineage, and ties of blood.[91] 'Families are founded as shelters and mighty fortresses in an inhospitable, alien world into which we want to introduce kinship.'[92] The embrace of the family principle by the body politic allows the exclusion of those who do not belong and the erasure of all diversity, in an obsessive search for boundaries and barriers. The unity of the herd is achieved, along with the perversion of politics. However, the ideal of the nation-family, both hostile to internal differences and fuelled by a general hostility towards the outside world, had already been realized by Nazism. Insofar as politics means the coexistence of diverse subjects, it is divested of its functions wherever the unity of the *arché* triumphs.

But without the freedom of public space, action itself disappears. Arendt looks to revolutions to trace their phenomenology and to understand their beginnings. Ultimately, acting and beginning are synonymous. Unpredictable, unexpected, free from any chain of causality, a beginning is like a birth. This leads Arendt to a further step, in which she takes natality as a central category of politics.[93] Precisely because everyone comes into the world through birth, they are already a beginning, and can in turn give birth and initiate something new. This is not a *principium* coming from nothing, a sovereign principle, such as that which gave rise to the world. Rather, it is an *initium*, an action that is always a re-action in the plural intertwining of human actions. In the political sphere, the possibility of beginning is the hallmark of freedom of action. *Totale Herrschaft* is what happens once nothing new is allowed, when everything is predictable and calculable. The aim of totalitarianism is to erase once and for all the human capacity to begin and start again. In other words, total domination attempts to close and bar every beginning.

The total *arché* puts an end to every beginning, to every *arché*. Arendt draws a clear distinction between the two meanings – beginning and command – contained both within the noun *arché* and in the verb *árchein*, which means to begin but also to guide.[94] Only insofar as the one is in fact separable from the other, only insofar as the beginning can be freed from command, is politics possible. Anything else would affirm the right to command of those who come first, and the power to begin of those who exercise command. Arendt clearly sees the need to break this circle.[95] This makes it unthinkable, among other things, that she should be excluded from a panorama of the new anarchism in philosophy.

In her last years, as she increasingly questioned the unresolved nexus between thought and action, Arendt focused on judgement, which she considered the political faculty par excellence. She was unable to develop her thinking before her death; however, she did write important pages on this theme. What especially stands out is the figure of the *theatés*, the spectator who sits in the stands watching a drama, with enough distance to get an overview.[96] This *theatés* is distinguished by her liminal condition, neither completely outside nor inside. She is neither absent like someone who is elsewhere, nor involved like the actors on stage. The stands are the site of public space. The spectator is under no illusion that she can grasp a truth beyond what appears before her, but she can compare her point of view with other people's, gain new perspectives, and formulate common judgements. In her lectures on Kant, Arendt emphasizes this common dimension, in which the public practice of thought is articulated.[97] But this should not be understood as an expanded empathy, i.e. the opposite of conformism. Rather, it is a broadening of the horizon, as when one travels and – thanks also to the imagination – visits other people's points of view. This means moving away from the immediacy of one's own world, leaving behind what is familiar, resisting the temptation to feel at home, and instead *becoming estranged.* The spectators are citizens who know how to become foreigners, passing from inside to outside and vice versa. The second life beyond the *oîkos*, that is, the *bíos politikós*, then presents itself as *bíos xenikós*, life as a stranger, a life that estranges itself.[98] Only in this transition can politics exist. Arendt stopped here, leaving to others the task of developing this theme further.

With Arendt, beyond Arendt, we can thus say that the democratic *pólis* takes form in a scenario that is no longer archic. Here, the link between beginning and command has been severed. The *arché*, the solid foundation, the pillar that held together the walls of the fortification, has disappeared. It gives way to a city that can no longer provide security; it is no longer sheltered within the rigid boundaries of family belonging, of the community based on birth, of the principle of lineage that claims to rule. This is the an-archic opening of the *dêmos*, united by its political bonds. Just as it has called the *arché* into question, this *dêmos* cannot help but continually question its own, ever-indeterminate boundaries.

5

REFUGEE WOMEN, AND THE VICTORY OF THE PEOPLE

1. Perhaps the time has come to finally discuss a judgement that has become too clear, too widely accepted, almost a postulate: the exclusion of women from the city. Such a task seems all the more thankless given that the documentation is scant and the texts handed down to us were written by men. The same applies to epigraphic and iconographic sources. It is thus impossible to talk about women without passing through a narrative, philosophical, and figurative filter that does not allow them a voice or an image in the public sphere. Everything seems to converge towards the orthodoxy representing the *pólis* as a club for men. This only further confirms the idea of a uniform and ahistorical Greece, the absolute beginning and – entirely masculine – foundation of the West.

A widely repeated quote on this count comes from Vidal-Naquet: 'The Greek city, in its classical model, defined itself through a double rejection: the rejection of women, making the Greek city a "club for men", and the rejection of slaves, making it a "club for citizens".'[1] Given that we are attempting here to bring out the repressed anarchic element at the source of the archic *pólis*, it seems appropriate to question whether women really did not belong to the city. If slaves are starkly non-citizens, the position of the *ghunaîkes*, the 'Athenian brides', appears elusive and uncertain. Not strictly excluded, they are part of the city in an indirect way – through a father, a husband or another family member, a *kúrios*, a leader and guardian. However, it is through this link that they are part of the community, enjoying the full protection of the law guaranteed to every citizen.[2] So, in or out? Indecision already undermines the secure boundary and takes on sinister and gloomy overtones. Neither included in the sphere of citizens nor registered in the group of non-citizens – because this composite group is in any case thought of as male – women risk becoming a threat to the androcentric order of the city.

In a famous passage from *Politics*, where he refers in particular to Sparta, Aristotle does not include women among the categories of non-citizens, but adds that they are 'half the city' (1269b 12–19). Divided 'so to speak' into 'two separate groups, that of men and that of women', the *pólis* presents a split, a sort of original cut, which cannot be overlooked. Aristotle goes on to explain that it is important to take care of the half made up of women. To do otherwise would repeat the error of the Spartan legislator, who, in aiming for a strong city, neglected women, leaving them to 'live without restraint'. Hence the parallel between *ánesis*, the loosening of constraints, the excessive freedom granted to slaves, and that granted to women. In both cases, there is a political danger: indulgence towards slaves stirs revolt and demands for equality; excessive tolerance towards women, on the other hand, has a different outcome, which Aristotle wryly sums up in the question: *kaítoi tí diaphérei ghunaîkas árchein è toús árchontas hupò tôn ghunaikôn árchesthai?* 'What difference does it make if women rule or if women rule over those who rule?' (1269b 34–5). This question is harder and more intricate than it may at first appear. There is no direct, open confrontation with women, as there is with slaves; rather, there is a splitting of power, which opens up a flaw, a crack, a dispersion. For if command can be commanded, then it is no longer the original, sovereign *arché* that it passes for. It can spring up here and there, and even end up in the hands of women who put it into question, whether just for fun (there is no lack of irony in Aristotle's question) or with their usual twists and turns. Power is scattered to the winds. Is the feared and derided gynocracy not already an anarchic fissure in the *arché*?

So, we should not underestimate the diffuse phenomenon whereby the androcentric Greek city is conceived by way of its opposite, projecting an inverted *pólis* onto the outside world. Echoes of this reversal can be found in myths that hint at the memory of a legendary female power, such as the Amazons, a tribe of female warriors who did not allow men into their community except as slaves; or the cruel Lemnia, who, because of the rejection they suffered, slaughtered all the males and formed an exclusive community of women on their island. Myth intertwines with historiography, and even philosophy, to recount the origins of the Greek cities of Italy, colonized by slaves and women, or women and slaves – or women alone. A famous, much-debated example is Locri Epizefiri, possibly founded by Spartan women joining forces with slaves.[3] Beyond the artefacts, discoveries, and evidence that point beyond the myth to the historical event, we must question the meaning of a fabulous and extravagant, paradoxical and absurd – ultimately, unfounded – 'foundation'. What could be more inconceivable to a Greek than the power of slaves and women? The projections of the world turned upside down would thus seem to reinforce and strengthen the image of the androcentric city.

Further, decisive confirmation comes from the comedies. *Lysistrata* and *The Ecclesiazusae* are Aristophanes' two emblematic works. In the former, women occupy the Acropolis headed – so to speak – by Lysistrata, whose name means 'she who dissolves armies'. Together with representatives of the main cities at war (the year is 411 BCE and there is rising anger and unrest after the catastrophic defeat in Sicily), they decide to stop having sex with their husbands until the fighting is over. The men give in to the women's blackmail and sign a peace agreement. In *The Ecclesiazusae*, the Athenian women, tired of male rule, decide to take power. Disguised with beards and cloaks, they arrive at the assembly where they pass a law that excludes men from the command of the city.[4] A new political project is launched, a communism presented as the full realization of democracy: land, money, and all types of property are to be shared; the family will be abolished; a decree will provide for old and ugly women to be spared unjust treatment; while children, not knowing their parents, will respect all their elders.

It is almost superfluous to point out Aristophanes' mocking sarcasm, blended with a sad lament for a past version of his homeland of Athens, now replaced by a city that has fallen into the hands of democratic and even communist women. Once again: what could be more humiliating and grotesque? One can at least laugh about it. The upside-down world is a source of hilarity and indignation, curiosity and fear. Hence we cannot overlook the obvious intention, not only in comedy but also elsewhere, starting with matriarchal myths, to exorcize the very idea of female power.[5] However, Aristophanes' utopia seems to allude to a horizon that goes beyond that negative reflected image.

'Women and children' and 'women and slaves' are surely recurrent phrases, but they should not lead us astray. Women are not entirely passive like children, and they also appear distinct from slaves, who are completely excluded from the *pólis* – an exclusion that itself raises no doubts or problems.[6] On the contrary, women are still 'half the city', according to Aristotle's telling expression. Even when they are taken hostage, led away and enslaved, women do not remain inert, however resigned they may be to their conditions. The same ambivalence emerges where, in association with slaves, they become an emblem of fearsome disorder in the city, the *taraché*, the turmoil, the agitation or, even worse, the *thóribos*, the tumult. But even in this case, disorder indicates more than mere confusion: an interference between inside and outside, a disturbing overlap.

Women press at the boundaries of the *pólis*. They threaten the politics of the *ándres*, putting pressure on them from the side of the political. The infrequent incursions by this unthinkable collective, which can be glimpsed in the dense fabric of narrative (and even in historians' narratives), attest to the two great threats that are feared. There is the threat of secession, and the threat of conflict and revolt. The resistance to war (what could be more archic than war?) seems to correspond to a necessary connection with *stásis*.[7]

Separation from the outside or division from within – these are the two mirror images of the one same disorder that undermines the *pólis* within the equilibrium of its borders. It is not a question of a definition through opposition to other cities, but of a distinction from what is most intimate, namely a feminine element which is only partially relegated to the *oîkos*. The alien intimacy, the intimate alienness of women, creates the danger. However much men want to keep them at bay, setting limits and trying to exclude them, they cannot separate themselves from them, starting with the sexual union. The more women are excluded, the more they are repressed, the more they reappear. They bring with them noise, agitation, confusion, contamination, and turmoil – on closer inspection, the spectre of a fundamental *an-arché*.

This helps us better understand the upside-down world of matriarchy. It is by no means a form of female power, but rather, according to its etymology, an *arché* granted to the mother, who remains at home, within the *oîkos*, to protect a matrilineal marriage and the right of succession, while in the *pólis* it is the *ándres* who rule. This concession is, however, dubious and uncertain, given that even the mother is ousted, uprooted from the earth in the great political myth of birth. Mother Earth is the true *arché*.

Left out are those strangers who migrate from one *oîkos* to another, the daughter, the bride, the sister, the virgin, who has not yet entered into a union, or has already broken it. Such a woman is as fragile and vulnerable as she is resistant and incorruptible, as apparently weak as she is powerful and intense in her ability to bring redemption, reverse the course of events, and suggest new beginnings. It is tragedy that brings her onto the scene, confirming her transgressive role, capable of revealing the repressed background of the city.

2. Women's *stásis* brings democracy into existence. This is not surprising if we remember Plato's mocking warning that democracy

is a paradise for women. But the context has dramatic notes. The women who burst onto the scene are foreigners fleeing domestic violence, refugees seeking political protection. The appeals made by these women, who have just arrived after a long journey, put democracy to the test – and attest to democracy. Before, no one had known that it existed, no one even knew its name. It is remarkable that this emblematic coincidence has not been grasped in all its significance and its manifold implications.

Democracy is born on a threshold, by the sea. It is born between the sacred space where the migrant women stand still and the city assembly where the people is summoned to vote on welcoming them – or not. It springs from an an-archic pressure, a sudden arrival that turns out to be a return, an exchange between the outside and the inside, a suspension of boundaries. And not without threats on the horizon. The drama of migration and the drama of democracy are one and the same.

There is, therefore, no founding act, no constitution, no date of origin, no initiator – nor even a proper name to define it. The birth certificate of democracy is a poetic verse, a question laden with anxiety, a circumspect and allusive periphrasis, a rhythmic impulse that risks succumbing to a dramatic catastrophe. It is a memorable snapshot: hands raised together to vote, that mobile and shared sovereignty of the people, passing by lightly and stirring in the air. *Demokratía* is the word that can be glimpsed unwritten between the lines, perhaps because it cannot be established or defined. It is ever-poised in the unstable balance of the relationship between *dêmos* and *krátos*.

At the height of the Athenian revolution, when even the last *archaí* fell, Aeschylus' creative genius staged that political event in the tragedy of *The Suppliants*, dating from around 463–461 BCE.[8] The intricacies of the myth beautifully weave together the story of the unprecedented events that led to the people's victory. Aeschylus projects onto a mythical Argos of times past the Athens of his own time. By now, the *dêmos* has finally appeared on the stage of history, amid enthusiasm to accelerate things and fears that they will dramatically come to a halt. Even in its contingency and precariousness, this revolutionary event is already worthy of immortalization in a tragic narrative.

3. Aeschylus draws on ancient myths and memories of the archaic era, bound up in the knots of a tragedy suspended between relentless violence and the anxious search for refuge, between a revolt permeated with hope and an impotent uncertainty in the face of a recurring nightmare. It is like a black, threatening sail

that stands out on the horizon, between the clear sky and the foaming sea.[9]

In the background is the legend of Io, a priestess at the sanctuary of Argos, who sets Zeus's heart ablaze. This prompts the relentless vengeance of Hera, Zeus's lawful wife, who, out of jealousy, transforms Io into a heifer maddened by the stinging bites of a gadfly into wandering endlessly. Like an incestuous daughter punished by her mother's wrath, Io is forced to flee without rest, condemned to a perpetual meandering, as if – being her mother's rival – no land could ever adopt her. In her frenzy, she runs across Europe, wades through the stormy strait between the two opposite shores, the Bosporus, *boós póros*, and passes through the river-rich regions of Asia, before finally reaching the coasts of Africa.

Io's journey is very different from that of Ulysses. For he, despite many detours and changes of route, charts a sure return to himself and his homeland. Her delirium is also far removed from the drama of Oedipus, the son who, despite being tormented by passionate love for his mother and homicidal rage towards his father, is driven by a desire to know, even if it costs him his eyes. Io – a daughter who defies the maternal authority of Hera, the priestess of marriage rights – remains at the mercy of her obsession, prey to an unstoppable psychosis.[10] Her descendants, too, will be left with the mark of her distress.

In Egypt, at the end of her wanderings, Zeus wafts across her with his divine breath, 'touches' her on the forehead and restores her female appearance, thus allowing her to give birth to a son. He will be called Epaphus, the progenitor of the kings of Egypt, begotten by the 'touch' of Zeus (from *ephápto*, to touch). Only in a foreign land does Io seem to return to herself, to her true self. It is as if her mother had severed all ties with her origins. And Hera's curse hangs over the subsequent generations. A conflict breaks out between the brothers Aegyptus and Danaus, the great-grandchildren of Epaphus, when the fifty sons of one demand to forcibly marry the fifty daughters of the other in order to acquire royal rights over the land.

This is the story of the Danaïdes, who rebel against their cousins' brutality and escape the attempt to seize their dowries through recourse to the custom of endogamy. In their exile, it is not difficult to detect the memory of their ancestor Io. This translates into a symmetrical yet opposite gesture, outside the land, law, and marriage – that is, outside the spectre of incest that haunts them. They thus allow themselves to be led by their father Danaus to Argolis, the region where Io's wanderings began, the region of their first provenance. The rest of the legend has more than one version.[11] The Danaïdes finally agree to marry their cousins, who have caught up with them, but on their wedding night – perhaps on their own initiative, or perhaps at their father's instigation – they kill them. Only two sisters refuse to take part in the crime and declare themselves exceptions, thus highlighting the ambivalence of these female figures. The first is Amymone who, united with Poseidon, god of the deep waters, not only became a water-bearer but also presided over marriage rites under the complicit gaze of Hera. The other is Hypermnestra who, having spared her husband Lynceus and saved the marriage, is put on trial by her own family but ultimately acquitted. From her descend the kings of Argos and the marvellous offspring Heracles, the Doric hero. What became of the others? The next myth condemns them to Tartarus, punished by having to fill a bottomless barrel with water, as if to emphasize their excess that reached such criminal heights. In other versions they are condemned to a mediocre fate or, as in Pindar, to sterility.

But what does Aeschylus think of the Danaïdes? How does he interpret their actions, and how does he judge their behaviour? Was their escape justified? Was this all done to avoid incest, out of an innate hatred of men, or out of respect for the legendary era of matriarchy? Before philosophy and before laws, tragedy prompts us to reflect on the role of these women who, violating the boundaries between inside and outside, burst into the city to demand recognition of a bond other than the immemorial ties of consanguinity.

4. Aeschylus' text opens with an invocation to *Zeus aphíktor*, protector of suppliants. The chorus of the Danaïdes, having just landed in Argos, rises to appeal to the ancient right of hospitality. Having set sail from fine sands, fleeing on the waves of the sea, they drift without any sure destination. This is not because 'the decree of a city' condemns them to exile after a crime – that is, the shedding of blood (7). Rather, they point to a *stásis*, a revolt, an internal sedition (12). They seek escape from sacrilegious marriages. Holding in their hands twigs wrapped in wool, the emblem of suppliants, they ask for protection against the swarm of violent men who pursue them, and they call for justice.

But are the Danaïdes foreigners or not? As they arrive from abroad, they claim to descend from within. They have come from the hazy land of Egypt, but they declare that they belong to the region of Argolis. Outside or inside?

With cheeks tanned by the Nile sun, colourful clothes and a foreign accent, they are 'more similar to the women of Libya' (69–70; 279).[12] The signs in the text follow one after another. They belong to a 'dark sunburnt race' (154–5), are 'clothed in foreign attire and luxuriating in closely woven and barbaric robes', and their 'apparel is not that of the women of Argos, nor yet of any part of Hellas' (236–7). Not to mention the inflection: 'O land, you understand my barbarous speech' (117–18; 129); 'All the world is ready to cast reproach on those who speak a foreign tongue' (972–4). They beg 'as is fitting for aliens' (198). Their Greekness is doubtful: 'this band we address' is not Greek (235). But the Danaïdes themselves are ready to offer the inhabitants of that land 'reliable proofs' of their origins, and 'other evidence, though unexpected, will yet appear' (51–2). They insist on their Argive origins: 'Argives we claim to be by birth ... the truth of this I shall confirm in full' (274); 'it is from this, our homeland, that we went forth' (536–7). Therefore, they cannot fail to arouse suspicion and surprise: 'Foreign maidens, your tale is beyond my belief – how your race can be from Argos' (279). The Danaïdes are thus 'strange foreign women'.[13]

Strange foreign women, threatening to break into the *pólis* from outside, after causing a rift within the family, a wound in the kinship. They say that they fear their blood relatives – 'kindred, yet foes' (225). This group of fugitives remains temporarily not far from the sea, near the city, in a sacred space where altars and statues of gods are set up. This raises the question of asylum.[14] But are the suppliant women entitled to it? Or are they asking for protection as fellow countrywomen?

In the distance, a cloud of dust rises, signalling an army on the march. Danaus sees a crowd armed with shields. They are the *archégetai*, the 'princes of the land', the lords (184). The foreign women, who have dared to venture there without heralds, guides or escorts, are addressed by one who could perhaps be the 'ruler of the realm', the *póleos agós* (248). He is the first they encounter. His name is Pelasgus – a name derived from the root of words indicating pre-eminence. His entire manner is a continuous assertion of dominance. 'I am Pelasgus, offspring of Palaechthon, whom the earth brought forth, and lord of this land; ... I am the lord ... [I] rule' (251–5). The son of *palaiós chthón*, 'ancient soil', was born from the womb of that land, with which he has been one for generations, and thus claims possession of it. Precisely because he is indigenous, he is *archégetes*, 'lord'. First in order, Pelasgus is the sovereign citizen, emblem of the archic vision of the *pólis*.

The contrast could not be more striking, or the opposition more clear-cut (cf. 347–52; 423–7). On the one hand, the son of ancient soil, the native, the first, the leader, the supreme ruler, 'who hold[s] sovereign power over the land', *ô pân krátos échon chthonós* (425). On the other, the fugitive, *phúgada*, the refugee driven into exile, cast out, banished – the suppliant (349, 420). What could the latter possibly have against the sovereignty of the former? The comparison is unbalanced.

The imploring, more or less persuasive entreaties may turn out, despite everything, to be in vain. In fact, the Danaïdes' extreme and desperate ultimatum – threatening that they will turn to Hades by hanging themselves from the altars where they sought refuge – is useless. This would result in a *míasma*, the defacement of a sacred place (473). However, the stain spreads and the danger grows, like a contagion that spreads without remedy. For the alternative to divine wrath against the inhospitable city would be war against the children of Egypt: meaning, 'men's blood to stain the ground for women's sake' (475–7). All the more so because they would be fighting against those who are *homaímoi*, relatives, blood 'kinsmen' of the supplicants. The spectre of *stásis*, of civil war, looms large. Are these exiles, these migrants, the bearers of division and disorder? Pelasgus is aware of the reproach that could be levelled at him: 'You honored aliens and brought ruin upon your own land' (401).

It seems impossible to help without suffering harm. Between uncertainty and fear, *amechanía* and *phóbos*, the question is: to act or not?, *drâsai te mè drâsai?* (377–80). The dilemma contained in this phrase is at the heart of every tragedy. Any decision will lead to catastrophe. As disasters pile up on the horizon, every way out of the problem seems to be denied. Suddenly, however, the parts in the drama change and everything seems to shift in a sort of political upheaval. The *arché* is not the *arché*, the sovereign is not sovereign, the foreign women are not foreigners.

To finally be accepted, the suppliants turn to the first citizen, the native ruler, urging him to make a choice. But the issue is not private, nor can it be reduced to a moral gesture of charity. Pelasgus knows how to distinguish between his own home and the city. Therefore he replies to the Danaïdes: 'It is not my own house at whose hearth you sit' (365). If the *míasma*, the stain, the contagion, affects the entire *pólis*, it is up to the people as a whole, in common, *tò koinón*, to find remedies (cf. 366). This is why Pelasgus cannot make promises before consulting the *astoí*, those who have lived in the city for a long time. The surprise of the Danaïdes is then fully expressed as they call the *póleos agós*, the head of the city, to his archic role. They project onto him the idea of an absolute sovereignty analogous to that of the divine (370–5).

> You are the state, you are the people. Being subject to no judge, you rule the altar, your country's hearth by your will's sole ordinance; and, enthroned in sole sovereignty, you determine every issue.

Sovereign power is one with the *pólis*, one with the *dèmios* – it encompasses the city and the people. All that remains is to exercise the *krátos* in its various forms: *kratúneis*, 'you rule'; *pân epikraíneis*, 'you determine every issue'. The dominion is that of a *prútanis ákritos*, a leader, an advisor in office, who is sovereign insofar as he is not accountable to the judgement of others. *Mónos* is repeated to emphasize the uniqueness of a power that requires only a single irremovable vote, a single gesture that decrees, a single sceptre – the monarch.

But Pelasgus will not make any decisions, nor will he be a judge; even though he is powerful, *krâton*, he can do nothing without the consent of the people, *dêmos* (398). The foreign women have perhaps misunderstood the connection between the two words, because they are unaware of the great political upheaval that has taken place in the Greek city. Having in mind an archic view of power, such as has been maintained in Egypt, they believe that *krátos* over the *dêmos*, dominion over the people, is also being exercised in Argos. The terms are correct, but the connection must be reversed: it is the *dêmos* that exercises the *krátos*.

While the chorus of the Danaïdes continues to speak of Pelasgus as the one who has all power over this territory (425), he appears increasingly in the stylized role of the *proxenos*, the citizen, protector, and friend who speaks in defence of the guest (cf. 419, 491). It is his task to mediate, seeking the right balance between the needs of the citizens and respect for the refugees. His intention to persuade the *pólis* to welcome them is clear, as he sets off towards it accompanied by Danaus; but in reality he can do no more than promise protection. The decision is for the people to make.

Left alone, at the mercy of their anguish, the suppliants address a prayer to Zeus, an emphatic hymn to his infinite power, an invocation that he may welcome the recollection of their mythical ancestor into his vast memory and come to the aid of her descendants. The opening verses are echoed in the closing ones (524–7; 590–9). They celebrate the power of Zeus, *ánax anákton*, 'sovereign of sovereigns', with perfect *krátos*, father and lord, the great generator who planted their stock with his own hand – *autócheir ánax* (592). Word and deed coincide in the realm of Zeus, who sits on his throne, subject to no other power. To carry out his divine will, he needs only to raise his hand. Thus the suppliants imagine the monarchical power that Zeus exercises over the cosmos, and thus they imagine the same principle of a single sovereign power on earth.

The plot twist comes immediately, with 'tidings most welcome': a radical political change. The people has pronounced the decisive decree, Danaus reports. The daughters, full of anguish, pose their question more sharply: *dḗmou kratoûsa cheír hópe plethúnetai?*, 'to what end has the decision been carried', or more literally, 'How has the powerful hand of the people decided?' (604).

Here we see the connection between the two terms: it is the *dêmos* that exercises the *krátos*. And this *krátos* is concentrated in the hand that rises supreme. This mirrors the image of monarchical power. The reversal could not be rendered more vividly: the *autócheir*, the right hand of the absolute sovereign, who had claimed to legislate standing alone, reveals his impotence and his impolitical nature. For he is swept aside by the sovereign hand of the people. This is the dawn of the democratic revolution.

Aeschylus offers a poetic-political game: the hand of the people, *dḗmou cheír*, dominates, *kratoûsa,* in a present participle, an unfinished verbal form, in the active voice, declined in the feminine. The revolutionary compound, the explosive mixture, referred to continuously throughout the second half of the tragedy, is broken down, dismantled and reconstructed in many different ways. Its parts are inserted into turbulent contexts and alternating emotional atmospheres. In this way, the semantic value of the segments is etymologically recovered, while the ever-new agreements between *dêmos* and *krátos* open up equally many political horizons.[15]

However, it would be a mistake to believe that there is only one hand – there are many. They rise together. At that moment, *krátos* passes from hand to hand, no longer concentrated in the gesture of the sovereign, but passing and running between the raised right hands of the *dêmos*. The power of the people excites and enthuses. Aeschylus depicts it in the air teeming with hands, *éphrixen aithér*, where *phríssein* is the verb used for fields rippling with ears of corn, for ranks waving spears, for skin furrowed by convulsions. It is the thrill of democracy. That emotion must have gripped the *dêmos* itself as it gathered in assembly.

This is how Danaus tells his daughters about the vote he has witnessed in the city, a verdict of salvation for the suppliants, as their request for asylum was accepted. The Argives decided without hesitation: 'the air bristled with right hands held aloft' (607). The hands that crowd the air, rising unanimously, confirm that the migrant women are to be welcomed. They have ruled that

> we are settlers in this land [*metoikeîn*] and are free, subject to no seizure, and secure from robbery of man; that no one, native or alien, lead us captive; but, if they turn to violence, any landholder who refuses to rescue us, should both forfeit his rights and suffer public banishment. (609–14)

There is no democracy without hospitality, and there is no hospitality without democracy. The hand is raised to save and welcome. The *krátos* of the *dêmos*, the sovereignty of the people, is at one with the asylum-seekers' victory. It is no coincidence that a few verses later Zeus is mentioned as *hikésios*, defender of suppliants (616). The Danaïdes, who have just acquired this new status, remember him as *xénios*, the guardian of guests (627). But it is the people of Argos whom the Danaïdes celebrate, by singing a real hymn to the *dêmos*. Those 'hands that crowd the air' for benevolent decrees are answered by propitious vows, asking for protection for this hospitable city (621–9). The wish is clear: 'May the people who control the state guard its privileges', *tò dámion tò ptólin kratúnei* (699). And with other poetic expressions, in which the scratchy and disruptive *kr-* of *krátos* resounds, the sovereignty that runs unstoppably towards the *dêmos* is sealed by that epochal passage sanctioned by *demópraktos* (942), the unanimous decree of the people which, like a nail driven through and through, cannot waver.

'Never, under compulsion, to surrender this association of women' (943–4). This is the substance of the decree. The city is called upon to push back against violence, brute force, arrogance, and outrages. From the outset, the role of women in the public sphere of the *pólis* is at stake – where they burst in to demand justice, even before they demand hospitality. They arrive from outside, fleeing unwanted marriages, refusing to be bound by matrimony, opposing such unions between blood relatives.[16] In this way, they denounce the 'foundational' violence that invades the marital sphere.[17] They dissolve intimacy in order to make binding demands on the stranger. They go in search of another bond, which is never solely intimate, but always already marked by estrangement, separation, and non-belonging. This seems possible only in the democratic city, which renders justice by making private troubles a public matter. The breaking of the bond of kinship gives rise to the political bond.

Foreign to their community of origin, the Egypt of their exile, separated from the marriage bond to which they were destined, the suppliants present themselves – openly asserting their foreignness – on the threshold of the *pólis*. But they also appear unmistakably foreign in the eyes of the citizens. They are thus rather 'strange foreign women', given that these women do boast a connection with the community they have arrived in, a relationship of descent, a commitment to memory. More than just 'strange foreign women', they reveal themselves to be external and internal all at once. Aeschylus renders their condition paradoxical using an oxymoron:

astoxénoi, composed of *astós* and *xénos* – the supplicants are 'citizens and foreigners' (356; translation edited).

In this lies these women's fundamental ambivalence: in the external brought into the internal, and in an internal which is deeply marked by the external. Their journey itself is a sort of backward path, a departure that turns out to be a return. Outside and inside are reversed and thus appear already to have cross-fertilized each other. Here, we sense the subversive power of these figures who, from the *an-arché* of the threshold, urge the people to vote and prompt the decision – the raised hands with which democracy is awakened and asserted. Both inside and outside, internal and external, the suppliants are welcomed by the hospitable city, which rises as one to protect their lives. They are welcomed with the verb *metoikeîn* – to reside as foreigners. They are not simply changing their abode. Rather, this is a form of residence that marks a return into the realm of foreignness. The suppliants are foreign residents who, knocking on the door of the *pólis*, stir up democracy from within it.[18]

The fear of a *pandemía* runs through the entire text. Having fled from *míasma*, the migrant women could bring *míasma* with them. Once again, the threat comes from two sides, external and internal, *xenikòn astikón*; that is, a 'twofold defilement – from strangers and from natives at once' (618–19). On the one hand, *pólemos*, war; on the other, *stásis*, conflict within the city. But are they the ones defiling a pure and intact community? Or is it that the boundary between inside and outside was anything but clear, and these kindred strangers are merely proving it? The *míasma* they represent is a salvific contamination, that self-immunization that alone can protect the city outside and inside. This seems to be the challenge of democracy, an open community that is always threatened by the dangers of external war and internal discord.

5. 'And may Zeus award power to the women' – *kaí krátos némoi ghunaixín* – the chorus of refugees pleads in unison (1068, translation edited). A victory for women, then. And victory for the *dêmos*. A multiplied and contagious *krátos*. On the other hand, Aeschylus had taken sides very early on. Not hiding his own enthusiasm for the new revolutionary era, already in 472 BCE, in *The Persians*, he had contrasted the irresponsibility of a monarch with the democratic urge for accountability before the *pólis*.[19] Elsewhere, scattered references to the *isonomía* and freedom of Athens prelude the passionate eulogy contained in *The Suppliants*. It is possible that the formula *édochsen tôi démoi*, 'the people have decided', echoes in that culminating scene, reporting the vote of the people gathered in assembly. This almost ritual formula, attested in a document on

residence at the end of the sixth century BCE, is both a symptom of the awareness assumed by the *dêmos* and a seal of the new power.[20] In a decree from a few years later, the complete formula comes to light: *édochsen têi boulêi kaí tôi dêmoi*, 'the council and the people have decided'.[21] Perhaps Aeschylus' verse, which projected the new word into the future on the wings of a periphrasis, preserved the memory of that formula, and this also bore the image of the gathered assembled.[22]

But what happened next? What happens when the poetic periphrasis in the feminine form, referring to the victory of the people, is contracted and stiffened – giving rise to the noun *demokratía*? Although it might seem to have established itself, this noun turns out to be elusive, evasive, almost evanescent. Attestations to it are sporadic and rare throughout the fifth century BCE. In the body of literary and historiographical texts handed down to us – from Herodotus to Thucydides, via many poets and playwrights – the word *demokratía* appears about fifteen times. Furthermore, among these occurrences, the term refers to the Periclean and post-Periclean *pólis* in twelve cases, all relatively late, dating to the last decade of the fifth century BCE. Further confirmation comes from onomastic traces – plaques, dedicatory inscriptions – which document a proud and assertive use of proper names such as Demókrates, 'Power of the people', or Demóchares, 'Grace of the people'. These are militant-spirited names given to children by those who, in the heat of strong political passions, applauded the democratic upheaval.[23] The chronological framework for these newly minted names is the decade from 470 to 460 BCE. Everything seems to be concentrated in that handful of years.

The rare references to 'democracy', the uncertainty over its use, the tendency to replace it with other words such as *isonomía*, the clear reticence over even mentioning it, and the silence surrounding it – all this should raise many questions. What are we talking about when we say that we are talking about 'democracy'?

This problem is especially stark given that no similar difficulties are apparent either for monarchy or for oligarchy – by opposition to which the new power of the people clearly shows all its fragility. As if that were not enough, in the few instances in which 'democracy' is referenced – apart from Herodotus – the word always has a pejorative meaning, i.e. it has a critical connotation, a polemical stamp. The term sounds provocative, irritating even, and was used and abused by its detractors. Democracy: a subversive word, a reference to the popular revolution at which an accusing finger is pointed. 'These democrats' sounds a bit like 'these anarchists'. If the term became something like a stigma, the democrats also distanced themselves from it. In the fifth century BCE they preferred to pass over it in silence, not to reference it too much, not to make too excessive a challenge. *Nomen est omen*: in all this we should recognize the difficulty of accepting not just the name, but also the thing itself. The linguistic problem barely conceals a major political issue. *Demokratía* suffers a paradoxical fate, for under the blows of a virulent reactionary propaganda it is gradually tamed and emptied of its explosive potential. It is reduced to an irenic and reassuring version, to the point of becoming synonymous with *politeía*, or rather being supplanted by it.

Perhaps this unease towards words is indicative of a discord which, beyond ruptures and rejections, continues to trouble Western tradition, manifesting itself in a recurring tendency to water down democracy, neutralize it and regiment it, to the point of it becoming the generic name for that well-tempered regime that is desired everywhere in the world. We should therefore reflect on that initial prohibition of speech that was supposed to make the thing acceptable. However, this is precisely one of the Greek aspects of modern democracy that has been overlooked and forgotten, with the focus instead on the modern aspects of Greek democracy.

It is generally understood that *demokratía* means 'government of the people' or (supposedly the same thing) 'rule of the people'. In this compound noun, the real problem would seem to be the term *dêmos*, on which most attention has always focused. The second element, *krátos*, would seemingly create no grounds for uncertainty.[24] From this, depending on whether *dêmos* is understood to refer to a part or to the whole, the alarming question arises: is this the rule of the majority or the entire city? Is democracy factious partisanship, or totalitarianism? This is seen as the dilemma inherent in democracy. On closer inspection, such an interpretation, which fails to express all the potential meanings of *krátos*, is not at all favourable to Greek democracy but rather casts a shadow over it – and, ultimately, over democracy *tout court*. Democracy may nevertheless be taken seriously, accepted and approved, insofar as it is framed and ordered within the modern framework. This applies to those (i.e. most interpreters) who uphold the majority version of democracy as liberal and moderate, respectful of minorities, and filtered by representation. It applies even more to those who have shown some inclination towards the whole, understood as the anticipation of a modern dictatorship of the proletariat. There again arises the problem, already discussed, of the hermeneutics of texts, and of a desirable exercise in anachronism; that is, starting from current questions and then returning to them also weighed down by ancient problems. This back-and-forth, which is in many ways unsettling and disorienting, is, however, a game with narrow margins, which any single interpretation would put an end to.

Here, it is worth referring to Nicole Loraux's important insights. She cites, as a successful example, the book *Les Oligarques*, written by the French Jewish historian Jules Isaac in 1942, at the height of Philippe Pétain's collaborationist regime. While recounting the events that marked the last years of the fifth century BCE in Athens, the book describes the French disaster, almost predicting the Vichy regime.[25] But allusive history has its limits, and Loraux warns against any attempt to modernize Athenian democracy in a one-sided manner. The polemic involves a certain recourse to texts by detractors, justified in part by the scarcity of documentation, and is directed in particular against the use of an anonymous pamphlet attributed to an old oligarch who was said to have understood democracy better than anyone else, seeing in it a sort of dictatorship of the proletariat *ante litteram*. In addition to the weight of an overly burdensome present, Loraux sees the risk of reading Athenian democracy in terms of a detested and unacceptable regime, a forced interpretation that is relatively late, dating back at most to the period 429–424 BCE. Since it is difficult to contextualize this criticism, the danger would be to reduce democracy to an unacceptable, distorted, and caricatured portrait, similar to what people today ultimately mean by radical democracy. Loraux concludes: 'Athenian democracy was not and could not have been a dictatorship of the proletariat.'[26]

It should be emphasized, however, that critical or even disparaging texts can often open up interesting perspectives – provided, of course, that they are taken as a heuristic device, and as a supplement to the few accounts of democracy written from a 'democratic' perspective. If interpreting things from today's perspective is unavoidable, we must surely guard against both facile projections and equally hasty and misleading translations across space and time. The use of terms such as 'constitution', 'regime', 'state', and 'civil society' (the list of examples could go on), and the abuse of modern vocabulary to talk about *demokratía* and *pólis*, are part of a questionable appropriation of the past. Words are not indifferent, and rigid translations, held up as established terms, play a prominent role at the beginning of traditions and monumental histories.

We would do better to mount a careful deconstruction of these layers, a cautious archaeology that looks at the complex etymology and ambivalent semantics of Greek words. To that end, we should attempt to outline a grammar of the use of *demokratía* by comparing texts. However, this turns out to be a rather arduous task, due to the remarkably scant available evidence. Most of the accounts left to us are undemocratic or even openly anti-democratic in character. We may even legitimately ask whether there is a democratic way of talking about democracy. Is it possible that there is no text that gives voice to the *dêmos* as the protagonist of a new era, rather than being written by some oligarch keen to paint it in the grimmest colours? Perhaps the democrats did not have time to write during those years of struggle. But unfortunately, writing is what remains, and has the last word. So, it is necessary to confront more directly the problem of the lack of a democratic theory of democracy. In short, it seems that the democrats decided against formulating their own theory and articulating their own language. We cannot rule out the possibility that this choice had a political significance of its own.

6. If the thought of Protagoras, a sophist and foreigner to the city, is perhaps the closest thing to a reflection on democracy, another foreigner – Herodotus of Halicarnassus, a citizen of Turii – offers the most passionate eulogy to democracy.[27] His enthusiasm is comparable to that which runs through Aeschylus' verse. In the fragmented and scattered democratic constellation, the historian and the tragic poet thus provide decisive testimony on democracy through their 'literary works'. This should come as no surprise, considering how democracy proceeds through the political becoming a common affair. This explains why in fifth-century BCE Athens no speech in the public sphere was not political speech. In this sense, the modern conception of a literary work, which could also be simply an expression of the author's life and character, seems entirely inadequate for these genres – historiography and tragedy – so marked by the *pólis*.

There is no more radical and fierce advocate of democracy than Herodotus. His words are profound and clear, and his testimony is of particular importance. It cannot be inserted, as is often the case, into an indifferent sequence, a homogeneous succession. Arendt, who loved to quote Herodotus and to take him as a point of reference, was correct in this sense. But, precisely for this reason, it seems necessary to draw a distinction between the different accounts. There is a link connecting Herodotus to Aeschylus: their fervour for the revolutionary events taking place before their eyes with the thrust towards popular sovereignty; their applause for its decrees, for the votes, the popular scrutiny; their admiration for sortition and transparency; their unconditional defence of freedom against all forms of slavery, of political equality against all hierarchy, and of open citizenship against all forms of national closure. It matters little that Aeschylus limits himself to an evocation, to the use of a periphrasis, and that Herodotus prefers the term *isonomía*.

For both took sides and offered an image of democracy permeated with enthusiasm and pride.

The tone is quite different in Euripides and Thucydides. In many respects, these authors can be considered a kind of counterpart to the other two. For Thucydides, deigning to use the word *demokratía* – a concession which barely conceals a critical detachment from the term, an embarrassed aversion to it – becomes an opportunity to exalt Athens, the homeland of valour and merit, obedience to authority, and a sense of honour. In short, he presents an oligarchic city that has erased almost everything that democracy stands for. The same can be said of Euripides, whose *Suppliants* shares little with Aeschylus' tragedy other than the name. In both cases, a king expresses his willingness to submit to the popular judgement the difficult question posed by the arrival of a crowd of refugees. But while Aeschylus' Pelasgus acts as a protector, Euripides' Theseus proves incapable of finding a 'fair pretext' (247) for persuading his citizens to accept them. Some time passed between the two tragedies. By now, democracy seemed to be on the defensive, riddled with mistrust, unsettled by scruples, suspicions, and perplexities.

There is surely no abyss between the two, and there remained a backdrop of continuity – and yet the discrepancy is clear. We must thus assume that, closest to its point of origin, democracy had an explosive force, an exhilarating momentum, which dissipated once this system seemed to have secured itself on solid foundations. This is what the funeral orations demonstrate. Thus, at its first appearance, democracy has an image of itself that is destined to fade. Herodotus referred to the turning point marked by Cleisthenes, who helped to strengthen the political bond of the egalitarian city by eradicating family ties. For his part, Aeschylus alludes to Ephialtes' move to abolish certain posts. In both cases, democracy surges forth – a beginning, and a new beginning.

7. While Aeschylus uses a periphrasis, the term *demokratía* appears for the first time in the sixth book of Herodotus' *Histories*. There are four significant mentions of it. Two instances involve the verb *demokratéomai*, which means to place oneself under the power of the people, to be governed democratically. In both cases, it is used in an anti-tyrannical and liberating sense.[28] There are also two instances of *demokratía*. In one passage, it is recounted that Mardonius, son-in-law of Darius, upon arriving in the Greek colonies of Ionia, 'put down all the despots' and 'in lieu of them established democracies [*demokratías*]'. In the other, the explicit reference is to Cleisthenes, who 'made the tribes at Athens, and set up the popular government [*tèn demokratíen*]'.[29]

However, we should look elsewhere, to Book III, for Herodotus' passionate praise of democracy. Using a literary device, he tells of a debate staged at the Persian court, involving three dignitaries who had opposed the failed plot against the king (III, 80–2). Their concern is to establish which is the best form of government. The protagonists are Otanes, the supporter of democracy, opposed by Megabyzus, who favours an oligarchy, and finally Darius, the king, who is – obviously – responsible for defending the principle of monarchy. The scene here narrated is set in the past, back in 520 BCE, but the content of the debate was a highly topical question, which Herodotus – exiled in Athens in 445–444 BCE, in the years of Periclean democracy – must have been accustomed to addressing in the successful public readings of his work. He thus addresses the broad audience of his own day, aware of their intense participation and the sharp contrasts among their number.[30]

The first to speak is Otanes, who immediately proposes to place the questions of government 'in the midst' of the Persians. Here again emerges the formula *es méson* + *títhemi*, i.e. to dismiss, to de-pose (sometimes accompanied by the prefix *katá*), to put down, with a movement that is both vertical, from top to bottom, and horizontal, towards the centre. This symbolizes the democratic destitution of power. All of Otanes' arguments are directed against monarchy, where the *arché* is concentrated in one person, *mónos*, who is allowed to do as he pleases without having to answer to anyone; even the best man, invested with such authority, would be led astray from the common good. *Húbris*, combined with this immense power, could lead him into the worst atrocities. It is at this point that Otanes opposes monarchy with *isonomía*. It is worth noting the subtle play on words here, which accentuates the antithesis: the *mónos*, the single ruler in whom the *arché* is concentrated, ends up exceeding, violating, and annulling the *nómos*, the law; on the other hand, in *isonomía*, the *arché* is subject to the *nómos* in accordance with the meaning of the verb *némein*, i.e. to divide, to share, to have an equal share.

> The rule of the many on the other hand, has, in the first place, the fairest of names, to wit, isonomy; and further, it is free from all those outrages which a king is wont to commit. There, places are given by lot, the magistrate is answerable for what he does, and measures rest with the commonalty. I vote, therefore, that we do away with monarchy, and raise the people to power. For the people are all in all. (III, 80, 6)

In this famous passage, which has been widely discussed and interpreted in various ways, Otanes defends democracy, conceived as *isonomía*. He forcefully claims, even through his choice of vocabulary, that power should be shared. This translates into the most radical and emblematic of institutions: sortition for the *archaí*; the obligation of transparency, that is, of accounting for the *arché* exercised in the name of the people; and the publicity of decisions taken *ex tò koinón*, in the common assembly.

Both in these lines and elsewhere in the debate, the word *arché* often appears to indicate a power that may well be illegitimate, but which seems to be recognized in reality. This also applies to the verb: hence, when Otanes speaks of *plêthos árchon*, he means nothing other than 'the people who govern'. This is, in short, the mere acknowledgement of a *de facto* power.[31] It may be surprising that he uses *plêthos*, where one might have expected *dêmos*. However, Otanes rightly prefers the term that designates the multitude to indicate the 'government of the greatest number', echoed in the proposal to raise 'the many' to power.[32] The emphasis is on the dimension of the assembly and the community built therein. Thus, *plêthos* can be considered a synonym for *dêmos*, which has a more pronounced political value. In referring to the greatest number, Otanes does not want to exclude anyone, not even the upper classes; when a decision is made, it is inevitable that the majority will prevail. The government of the greatest number implies an equal distribution of power: *isonomía*.

In the years when Herodotus was writing, the terminology was anything but fixed and established. Fluctuating and uncertain meanings marked a nascent political lexicon, for which Herodotus himself can be considered the forerunner. This also explains the absence, throughout the debate narrated here, of the use of the word *demokratía* to indicate a possible political form. It was so recent, so new and unprecedented, that it raised doubts even about its designation. Only after Herodotus introduced it was the word revived and used in new ways, albeit with pejorative connotations. These latter owed not so much to *dêmos* as to *krátos*, and to the idea of domination.[33]

When it was his turn, Megabyzus, who supported oligarchy, immediately seized the opportunity to criticize those who wanted to transfer *krátos* to the multitude. He thus highlighted the precarious condition of an unrecognized power (III, 81, 4). His arguments, which do not hide his aversion to tyranny and the rule of a single man, give vent to all the clichés of anti-popular rhetoric. For Megabyzus, 'there is nothing so void of understanding, nothing so full of wantonness, as the unwieldy rabble' (III, 81, 2). Ignorant, incompetent, unaware – what trust can be placed in the people, which can produce only ruin? Better to choose a small group, the best, the *aristoi*, and confer power on them. For his part, Darius, although he agrees with the criticisms levelled at popular rule, argues that the most effective form of government is monarchy, alluding to the two risks that democracy and oligarchy respectively entail: on the one hand, *stásis*, sedition; on the other, the plot.

This paradigmatic dispute, destined to become the basic text of the *lógos tripolitikós*, clearly illustrates how much easier it is for democracy to present itself as *isonomía*, as opposed to the power of a single man. In this case, the divide could not run any deeper, because ultimately it is the contrast between freedom and slavery. Things are very different when democracy has to distinguish itself from oligarchy, because here the difference is between *olígoi* and *dêmos*, in either case with reference to the city and its citizens.

At the end of the debate, the vote goes in favour of monarchy and Otanes is defeated. He then rises for a final speech in the middle of the assembly, beginning: '*stasiôtai*' – comrades of struggle, comrades of *stásis*.[34] He admits that he has lost; there will be no isonomy and someone will have to be chosen as king. Not him – he prefers to withdraw from the competition. And he explains why: 'I have neither a mind to rule nor to be ruled [*oúte gàr árchein oúte árchesthai*]. … I withdraw, however, on one condition – none of you shall claim to exercise rule over me or my seed for ever' (III, 83, 8). Neither to exercise *arché*, nor to suffer it. This provides a way of reaffirming the meaning of *isonomía*, but also of *eleuthería*, of freedom.[35] It entails not a private withdrawal, but rather a remaining outside, an anarchic exception, which will endure so long as politics must remain the non-politics of a single man's exercise of the *arché*.

8. In the heart of winter, a procession of carts carrying cypress coffins with the remains of the fallen proceeds along Akadimias Street towards the public cemetery, the Kerameikos, in the most beautiful suburb to the northwest of the city. They are followed at a distance by an empty litter covered with drapes to commemorate the missing. Citizens and foreigners attend the ceremony, against a backdrop of wailing and weeping from the relatives.[36] At the end of the funeral, Pericles, a man distinguished by his reputation and appreciated for his intelligence, takes the floor. Rather than issuing words of glory in honour of the dead – who are, in truth, barely remembered – the Funeral Oration addressed to the living is a homily delivered in times of war. It is a statement of patriotism, with stark political and practical implications. The climax is reached when, with a sustained rhythm and engaging talk of what 'we' do, Pericles proudly presents a paradigm of the city. He casts it not as an ideal model, but as an order that has already been achieved:

> Our constitution [*politeía*] does not copy the laws of neighbouring states; we are rather a pattern [*parádeigma*] to others than imitators ourselves. Its administration [*oikeîn*] favours the many [*pleíonas*] instead of the few [*olígous*]; this is why it is called a democracy [*demokratía*]. If we look to the laws, they afford equal justice to all in their private differences; if to social standing, advancement in public life falls to reputation for capacity, class considerations not being allowed to interfere with merit; while as to poverty, if a man is able to serve the state, he is not hindered by the obscurity of his condition. (Thucydides, II, 37)

For a long time, throughout most of the fifth century, the name given to the revolution that took place in the Athenian *pólis* remained vague and uncertain. Only in the Funeral Oration, which Thucydides has Pericles pronounce in 430, the first year of the Peloponnesian War, is *demokratía* openly asserted as such. Some have therefore seen this speech as the manifesto of Greek democracy in its classical form.[37] At the tomb of the fallen, Pericles celebrates the double victory of Athenian democracy: over the Spartans and over the former aristocratic regime. The *dêmos* has taken power. Yet the Athens described is not the Athens that saw Aeschylus' *Suppliants*, but Athens in arms, ready to defend the freedom of the Greeks. From its first lines, the oration seems to offer a democratic version of the patriotic tradition.

The most famous phrase, the one that introduces the name *demokratía*, proves to be the most problematic. The question is formed by the verb *oikeîn*, which means to live, to settle, to reside, but also to be administered, to be governed. As is often the case, the exegesis of a word becomes the starting point for different, if not outright opposed, interpretations of a text. Is it called democracy because it is ruled by the majority? By the many and not by the few? In that case, *oikeîn* becomes almost *árchein*. Or is it because it serves the interests of the many, not the few? Is it oriented towards the majority? The difference lies in whether the *dêmos* is seen as the *subject* or as the *recipient* of government: on the one hand, a positive and edifying view of its role; on the other, a much more limited one. In both Renaissance and modern interpretations, from Lorenzo Valla and Thomas Hobbes to the present day, scholars have long been divided.[38]

While Thucydides' vagueness is apparent to all, the grammatical construction around *oikeîn* seems to leave little doubt. It is clear that the preposition *es* designates the object of administration, not the subject of government. The *dêmos* is not itself sovereign, but a beneficiary of this system.[39] The idea that the multitude can take part in government is not itself considered; indeed, any such prospect is carefully left to one side. Pericles says that the *pólis* is governed for the people, not by the people. This is confirmed by the non-central position attributed to democracy. If Pericles comments 'As for the name [*ónoma*] ... it is called *demokratía*', does this imply an antithesis between name and thing? Is this democracy in name, aristocracy in practice? And who calls it that? Its opponents? In any case, this elision cannot be overlooked.[40]

If the canons of monumental history tell us that this speech represents the highest praise for democracy, on closer inspection it turns out that it empties the word of meaning.[41] A slogan that is good for popular use covers up the reality of power concentrated in the hands of one man. Elsewhere in Thucydides' account – outside of this official setting – his judgement is quite clear: 'what was nominally a democracy became in his hands government by the first citizen' – *demokratía ... toû prótou andròs arché* (II, 65, 9). On the other hand, Thucydides, who certainly does not sympathize with democracy – 'the men of sense among us knew what it was' (VI, 89) – seems to believe that popular government is acceptable only if it is led by figures of high standing such as Pericles.

The rest of the Funeral Oration also follows a pattern of corrections and limitations. An epitaph for democracy? An official eulogy that amounts to its embalming? All the traits highlighted by Herodotus, from sortition to transparency, are here passed over in silence, while aristocratic characteristics are celebrated, from merit to obedience to unwritten laws. Instead of being presented as a break with the past, democracy is traced back to an immemorial origin. Thus the Funeral Oration becomes another narrative of *foundations*: 'I shall begin with our ancestors ... They dwelt in the country [*chôra*] without break in the succession from generation to generation, and handed it down free' (II, 36, 1).

The key word is *arché*, which is here proudly proclaimed. The *arché* of time is added to the *arché* of space, and that of fathers to that of sons, multiplying its power. Hence, Pericles refers to 'our fathers', who 'added to their inheritance the empire [*arché*] which we now possess', yet 'our dominions [*arché*] ... [have also] been augmented by those of us here' (36, 2–3). Empire, dominions – but also principle. Nothing is more relevant in the present than an origin. This means looking to the future by going back to the past. It means celebrating the endless repetition of generations on the same soil in order to exalt the permanence of Athens, its unviolated and stable identity.

The spectre of autochthony peers out from the heart of Athenian democracy at its inception. The archic device arrests the democratic paradigm, aligning it to the foundations, the origin. This also has consequences for the *dêmos*, pushed to recognize itself within the pure boundaries of the *éthnos*. This means banishing metics, foreigners, suppliants, women – in the name of the beautiful homogeneity of the self and the integrity of the inhabitants, all children of their own soil, belonging to the patrilineal progeny, to the homeland and its order. The *arché* is the principle of the homeland. Democracy becomes naturalized, demands citizenship, and takes root in its much-vaunted native origins.

9. To grasp the importance of this archic legitimization which comes to light in Pericles' Funeral Oration, it would suffice to consider other speeches which also express the need for Athenian democracy to assimilate the values and benefits of aristocracy. But it is Plato who exposes the clichés and conventional motifs of patriotic prose in the *Menexenus*, offering a peerless parody of funeral speeches.[42] It is no coincidence that one of the rare occurrences of *demokratía* is found in this same text.

The young Menexenus, eager to enter the world of politics, invites Socrates to repeat the epitaph pronounced the day before by Aspasia, beloved of Pericles. The allusion could not be clearer. These words are also attributed to a woman, indeed a foreign one, which provides a further, paradoxical corroboration. The eulogy of the fallen warriors, emphasizing their nobility of *eughéneia*, their good birth, is one and the same with the eulogy of the Attic land that gave birth to them:

> as regards nobility of birth, their first claim thereto is this – that the forefathers of these men were not of immigrant stock, nor were these their sons declared by their origin to be strangers in the land sprung from immigrants, but natives sprung from the soil living and dwelling in their own true fatherland; and nurtured also by no stepmother, like other folk, but by that mother-country wherein they dwelt, which bare them and reared them and now at their death receives them again to rest in their own abodes. (237b–c)[43]

Plato refers to an immemorial motif of ancient Greek tradition, a rhetorical theme of whose powerful political significance he is well aware. This is the foundational myth of autochthony, a useful means not only for boasting of *ghénos*, noble lineage, but also for asserting exclusive possession of *chthôn*, the territory of the city. This is what *autóchthonos* means, a term composed of *autó* and *chthôn*, self and soil – he who belongs to the soil and to whom the soil belongs.[44]

The political myth of autochthony is linked to the eminently Greek myth of Mother Earth, asserted in origin stories and attested to in the traditions of cities. Plato himself provides a famous formulation of it in his *Statesman*, where he calls *ghegheneîs*, the children of the *ghê*, earth, the first kind of living beings: not the offspring of coupling, but sprung from the earth's life itself (270e–271c).[45] There is almost no gap between that fabled beginning and human time: the Earth, from whose fertile womb men are spontaneously born, remains the Mother, the solitary archetype of all female births. In her shadow, like a stranger, is woman, *ghuné*, this other than herself, this surrogate of Mother Earth, whose role she can only imitate. She joins from outside the *ghénos* of the *ándres*, the men who constitute the body of the city, the only citizens, the natives. No matter how deeply we probe the fabric of myths, there are no native daughters. Women, always in an ambiguous place in humanity, instead appear as acquired relatives.

In *Menexenus* the absolute *arché* of humanity, devoid of maternal shadows, is found in Attica, the land of the Athenians' fathers, their *patría*, from which their patrilineal progeny descends (237e–238b). While other cities boast of having been founded by a prestigious foreigner and do not disdain such contamination, Athens is a shining example of pure autochthony. Children of their own soil, the Athenians have remained 'the same', bound to the identity of their origins, and guaranteed the purity of their birth and lineage. Thucydides has Pericles say similarly at the beginning of his Funeral Oration: Attica 'never changed its inhabitants'. But in the *Menexenus*, the celebration of autochthony reaches its height. The purity of birth is not enough; loyalty to the ancestral soil is also required, which translates into immobility. Remaining in the same place, avoiding change and mixing, strengthens genetic unity. A single lineage – one which remains intact, unperturbed by departures and arrivals, undefiled by foreigners and unshaken by immigrants – is the model of the *pólis*. This suggests that the perfection of the political regime stems from the purity of its origins. Revived by Aristotle, who saw stability in the identity of *ghénos* and *éthnos*, this argument was destined to enjoy great success throughout the modern political tradition (cf. *Politics*, 1295b 21–9).

Plato does not shy away from taking a further step: from autochthony to democracy. A focus on 'good birth' must not lead to a neglect of *politeía*, for the one influences the other. The Athenians, he contends, have always governed themselves with the same principle, since time immemorial: 'One man calls it "democracy" [*demokratía*], another man, according to his fancy, gives it some other name; but it is, in very truth, an "aristocracy" backed by popular [*plêthos*] approbation' (238c–d). Once again, democracy seems to be a matter of name rather than of fact. The mocking tone is unmistakable, as reflected in the subsequent lines, which are almost a parody of Pericles' Funeral Oration (see 238d). But the twist comes when Plato reinterprets democracy, reverses the relationship between politics and nature, and deliberately misrepresents the ideal of equality:

> the cause of this our polity lies in our equality of birth. For whereas all other States are composed of a heterogeneous collection of all sorts of people, so that their polities also are heterogeneous, tyrannies as well as oligarchies, some of them regarding one another as slaves, others as masters; we and our people, on the contrary, being all born of one mother, claim to be neither the slaves of one another nor the masters; rather does our natural birth-equality [*isogonía*] drive us to seek lawfully legal equality [*isonomía*], and to yield to one another in no respect save in reputation for virtue and understanding. (238d–239a)

Political equality, an essential ideal and decisive proof of democracy, is thus traced back to – and reduced to – the natural equality of origin. Meanwhile, there can be equality insofar as there is kinship, genetic commonality. There are 'neither slaves nor masters' – as the slogan of the democrats has it – because we are all *adelphoí*, all brothers of Attica, purely autochthonous.[46] Those who are not – those who do not belong by soil and blood – are not equal, and have no right to equality. Democracy becomes a family matter. Good birth would be the *aitía*, the cause, the condition. The low-born are bound to remain outside. Those of foreign origin, those who come from mixed marriages, but also those who have moved away and perhaps wish to return, such as the *astoxénoi*, resident-foreigner women, end up on the margins of the city.

This 'democracy', founded on the *arché* of the fatherland, is rooted in genetic origin, in *homophulía*, racial commonality (see 244a). It functions by exclusion and proceeds by division. It builds up borders and readily dives into hatred:

> So firmly-rooted and so sound is the noble and liberal character of our city, and endowed also with such a hatred of the barbarian, because we are pure-blooded [*eilikrinôs*] Greeks, unadulterated by barbarian stock. For there cohabit [*sunoikoûsin*] with us none of the type of Pelops, or Cadmus, or Aegyptus or Danaus, and numerous others of the kind, who are naturally barbarians though nominally Greeks; but our

> people are pure Greeks and not a barbarian blend; whence it comes that our city is imbued with a whole-hearted hatred of alien races. (245c, 245d)

In *Menexenus*, the self-referential homeland triumphs in emphatic and extreme tones. It is an autochthonous Athens, an authentic Greece, the solid Centre of the world, the City par excellence. Here, where everything is placed under the sign of the self, of the *oikeîon*, of what is intimate and familiar, people live firmly on their native soil, where they were born, and they live with their own kind, reiterating their origins, their identity of birth, lineage, and ethnicity.

We should not underestimate the repercussions that the powerful myth of autochthony has had on ways of understanding – or rather, misunderstanding – democracy. The confusion between *dêmos* and *éthnos* has in fact led to the upheavals that have marked democracy's most recent history.

10. For how long was *demokratía*, the word that announces and proclaims the victory of the people, uttered with pride and satisfaction? For a much shorter period than we might imagine. A realistic estimate would be the timespan of 'a generation'.[47] We should not lose sight of the mark of infamy left on the term by the opponents of democracy. Its supremacy points to the division of the *pólis*. The *dêmos* turns out to be problematic because of its inherent ambiguity: it bends to partisan and biased use, while also being so extensive as to include the people as a whole. But in the city, even *krátos* is a suspect term. The attempts to erase it came immediately, as soon as the compound *demokratía* took shape and the concept became clear. This is evidenced by official discourse, in both historiography and civil eloquence. In the same moment that *demokratía* burst onto the scene, the repression of *krátos* began. This could not fail to have a backlash on the *dêmos*, which ended up taking a backward step.

As the sovereign people seemed to establish itself in the city, the reticence and restrictions also grew. There was a mounting fear that democracy, born of a *de facto* superiority, was not on the right side. To openly assume *krátos*, to raise its banner, could spell its ruin. Hence the veil of silence with which democrats themselves shrouded their words during the fourth century BCE. Even the building of a cult of *demokratía* was but a pretext for stiffening and embalming it, as often happens in political strategies regarding memory. In the compound noun *demokratía*, the unmistakable echo of *krátos* rings out, and the spectre of civil war rears its head. The *dêmos* bears the burden of having brought to light the *stásis* that disturbs the archic image of the city.

An epochal transition then takes place: from *demokratía* to *politeía*.[48] Enough of these divisions, enough of these quarrels and clashes. Harmony and stability are needed. While the subversive potential is neutralized, institutional aims and administrative concerns prevail. This is all the more necessary because the democratic victory is frightening in its radicalism: it is not just a rough-and-ready policy cobbled together by a miserable, incompetent, insolent people, but a policy that responds to the interests of the people. Harnessed and tamed, democracy is brought back into the fold of the *pátrios politeía* – the slogan used to claim an *ancient* constitution in order to surreptitiously justify *change*.[49] For its part, the *dêmos* is driven to identify with the rediscovered unity of the *pólis*. This was supposed to mean, first of all, *politeía*, that is, the totality of citizens; only later would it refer to the political order, the constitution.[50] In this passage, the *dêmos* is overcome, removed, in the totality of the *politeía*, and it is ultimately the *pólis* that governs.[51] Power thus flows from the people and towards a stable, perennial, capital-C City whose one and indivisible essence has survived countless misfortunes and upheavals. The revolutionary word *demokratía* is banished in favour of a long-enduring reference to the *pólis* alone. This term would be used to praise Athens, the *pólis* par excellence. Only in the Hellenistic era, once all subversive echoes had faded away, would *demokratía* reappear as the generic name for any moderate regime.

This legacy has been preserved throughout Western tradition, through many ruptures and changes. And yet there remains an unease towards this word, and a more or less pronounced tendency to water down its meaning. As the power of *demokratía* is defused, the power of the people is also hollowed out. What has been inherited, therefore, is not only the term and the concept of democracy, but also the Greek *problem* of democracy.

6

STÁSIS: TWISTS AND TURNS IN THE HISTORY OF THE *PÓLIS*

1. The monumental representation of democracy's history traces a gentle arc from beginning to end, from *arché* to *télos* and vice versa. In this account, democracy appears as a constitutional form, established almost with a stroke of the pen and instituted by one or various brilliant and prudent leaders. Already traceable to ancient historiography and the Aristotelian perspective, this image inspires the search for the *prôtos heuretés*, the first discoverer. Thus a few names stand out – those of the main characters, the drivers of change, the distinguished precursors. Whether they acted out of personal interest or for altruistic purposes, out of foresight or a thirst for power, they are imagined as the only true protagonists. Every change, every twist and turn, is ultimately interpreted in terms of a conflict between elites.

This elitist and institutionalist view of democracy, perpetuated over the centuries, still has considerable influence both on the way we investigate its ancient form and on the way we consider present-day democracy. From this stem many preconceptions and misunderstandings. One is the idea that one *arché* is replaced by another *arché*, with the difference that more people are in command. This explains the tendency to cast democracy as a constitution – an approach sharply critiqued by Sheldon S. Wolin, one of the most original voices in US radical thought. Wolin advances the idea of a 'fugitive democracy', i.e. a transitory, fleeting, disruptive democracy which cannot be contained within the bounds of a fixed constitution, except at the price of becoming rigid and empty. Here, he indicts a certain way of reconstructing the history of Athenian democracy that is reflected in political philosophy. Thanks to Aristotle's considerable influence, it has long been believed, and still is, that democracy is one form of constitution among others, distinguished only by its peculiar guarantee of equal rights.[1] This sort of passive democratization not only overshadows and conceals the novelty of that change but also prevents recognition of the *dêmos*'s decisive role. The effect of such accounts is that 'a "true" political actor [is] portrayed as an individual'.[2] Neither philosophy nor history does justice to the struggle of the people to occupy the stage previously reserved for heroes, kings, and nobles. That hard-fought struggle, capable of overcoming or destroying centuries-old barriers, clashes too much with the prevalent dramaturgical model. This is unsurprising, considering that democracy's enemies played a crucial role in handing down this concept, both domesticating it and hollowing out its meaning. It thus becomes almost self-evident that it should be read within the framework of a constitution, in an attempt to tame it. Hence the widespread image, today, that identifies democracy with its constitutional form. Against this image, it seems more appropriate to 'accept … the familiar charges that democracy is inherently unstable, inclined toward anarchy, and identified with revolution'.[3] These traits should, in fact, be the basis for another conception, an *a*constitutional idea of democracy. If we look at the roots of disorder, we see the revolutionary transgression that distinguishes democracy, starting with Athenian democracy. Marx was well aware of this, and saw it as the basis of every constitution. Wolin concludes: 'Revolutionary transgression is the means by which the demos makes itself political. It is by stasis not physis that the demos acquires a civic nature.'[4] In this sense, the history of Athenian democracy should be considered a 'succession of popular uprisings'.[5]

It is precisely the close link between *demokratía* and *stásis* – the spectre of anarchic sedition, the ghost of internal division – that has led to the construction of the archic paradigm, conforming to the linear narrative. Starting from its reassuringly elitist origins, the history of democracy is conceived as a constant arc of progress. If there are moments of acceleration or slowing of its advance, these have no bearing on its overall evolution. It is as if, from the moment the democratic constitution is first established, there is a gradual democratization, in line with the development of its primordial constitutional principles. There may be divergent judgements, squabbles over the dates or chronology, but the archic paradigm remains at the heart of things.

Democracy is thus only rarely seen as a revolution. Those who search for the *arché*, the founding origin, the guiding command, neglect the event that marks the deeper rupture. History is read as a chain of connected events, forbidding any drastic and sudden changes. Unnoticed, in the blank spaces, lies the impossible to which alone the appearance of the unexpected possibility can be traced. The revolutionary unknown is not taken into account; it is dismissed *a priori*. Since the extraordinary event could not happen, it did not happen – or so goes the line of argument that underpins much of the history of democracy.

The difficulty lies in imagining the disruptive moment when the people climbed onto the stage of history. It was then that the *dêmos* – obscure and nameless, the multitude hidden in the darkness of the margins – broke through and showed its *krátos* to the light of the *pólis*. It was then that it became a protagonist in its own right and in its own name; then that it proved its effective and surprising ability, demonstrating the possibility of opening a new chapter in politics, breaking the traditional lines of authority and deposing the *arché*.

To dig deeper into the archives of democracy, taking an alternative approach rather than the already known paths, is to dwell on the cracks and fragments, heading into the crevices to scrutinize the momentary points of emergence. It means getting a picture of an uprising without chiefs or leaders, of anarchic movements in the spirit of equality, of more or less drastic changes which often took the form of a *stásis* within the city. Democracy bursts forth in a site of conflict, where the empty space around which it is articulated clearly comes into view. The deeper and further-reaching the uprising, the more this constitutive void comes to light. Hence two needs. One, to examine the fabric of history for those slums and margins forgotten or passed over in silence in favour of the march of memorable events. Two, to pay attention to unmasked domination, to the reversal of power relations, to the unheard speech issued as a motto of defiance or repeated as the seal of a victory also triumphant on the terrain of language. To unpick the sequences of rebellion amidst the tangle of stories and accounts demands working through each scenario in turn. This means, in each instance, finding a frame for a philosophical anarchaeology that avoids the pitfalls of the elitist and institutionalist vision inherent in the idea of linear progression.

This does not exclude the possibility of a more decisive uprising, and perhaps a revolutionary interruption, such as that of 508–507 BCE in Athens, where accounts of the past already indicate a watershed moment. It is to Josiah Ober's credit that he not only retold that story, but also showed the possibility of historical inquiry responding to a political vision of democracy that avoids reducing it to a constitutional form. It is no accident that, while Wolin refers to Ober to point to an alternative history of Athenian democracy, Ober in turn explicitly takes both Arendt and Wolin as points of reference in his treatment of the events of 508–507 BCE.[6]

In the specialist field of classical studies – separated from public debate, and traditionally isolated even within the humanities – Ober presents, in the US context, the possibility of a bridge between Greek history and contemporary political reflection. From his earliest internationally acclaimed works, such as *Mass and Elite in Democratic Athens* (1989) and *The Athenian Revolution* (1996), he makes clear his intention to fundamentally re-examine entrenched prejudices and cornerstones of interpretation that are usually taken for granted.[7] Ober distances himself from any archic conception of democracy that reduces it to an institutionalized procedure or decision-making mechanism. At the same time, he also distances himself from the caricature of the tyrannical majority. In the wake of Arendt, he offers an interpretation of *krátos* understood not in the sense of superiority but as a capacity to do things. It was thus that, in its great uprising, the Athenian *dêmos* found its own ability to act and discovered itself to be a political actor.[8] One may disagree with the way in which Ober ends up reducing the scope of the revolt – and it is also essential to criticize his project of *Demopolis*, as a neo-Athenian alternative to liberal democracy, which is nevertheless anchored to liberal principles[9] – but it remains the case that his historical and political research has made valuable contributions.

To argue that democracy arose from an anarchic event is not to claim that this revolutionary charge would alone have sufficed. As Ober has clearly explained, the action of the *dêmos* would have had no effect had it not been channelled into – and articulated in – institutional innovations.[10] Some of these changed the way the Athenians conceived of citizenship and communal living, while others represented an unprecedented attack on the archic power of the city. Without the new laws and democratic practices, the victory of the *dêmos* would not have been possible, although it must always be seen against the backdrop of the tremors that prepared the way for it. In this sense, it can be said that Athenian democracy is also a laboratory for examining the relationship between the anarchic and institutional moments.

2. The meagre ambition of establishing a beginning, at all costs, also appealed to Athenians of the fourth century BCE. Even when the *pólis* was already in crisis, they pointed to Solon as the 'founder' of their democracy.[11] Beyond labels, however, such a judgement on the reforms introduced by Solon in 594–593 BCE has always raised doubts. Even the moderate Aristotle, whose *Athenaion Politeia* – together with the pages of Herodotus and Plutarch – represents one of the most valuable sources, appears perplexed. Outlining the scenario of that time, he writes:

> Afterwards it came about that a party quarrel [*stasiásai*] took place between the notables and the multitude that lasted a long time: for the Athenian constitution was in all respects oligarchical, and in fact the poor themselves and also their wives and children were actually in slavery to the rich; and they were called Clients, and Sixth-part-tenants (for that was the rent they paid for the rich men's land which they farmed, and the whole of the country was in few hands), and if they ever failed to pay their rents, they themselves and their children were liable to arrest; and all borrowing was on the security of the debtors' persons down to the time of Solon: it was he who first became head of the People [*toû dêmou prostátes*]. (*Ath. Pol.*, II, 1)[12]

There is a looming danger of *stásis*: the internal conflict that has threatened to cut through the city ever since its inception. This all has to do with the *méson*, which may either be shared – breathing life into the political community – or split, chasm-like. The different sides clash, almost like two armies. How, then, can this split into armed factions be resolved? In one sense, it is about setting limits. But it is also a matter of removing old boundary stones. This sums up Solon's difficult task, as he was called upon to act in that *méson* of the archaic city which, far from being a place where different ideas met in confrontation, appears more like a war zone. There, under the aegis of Ares, the citizens were pitted against each other, on two hostile fronts.

Some present Solon as a precursor of modern liberalism, but this is an error of historical interpretation, an exaggerated projection onto the past. Interpreters who have taken this approach have been prompted in part by a certain image of the moderate politician, fed also by Aristotle when he cast the struggle between a few rich aristocrats and the dispossessed masses in the most conflictual tones of his century. Solon's endeavours are, however, better seen in the light of the new political space. 'How was he to take into his own hands, the hands of one man, the arche that must remain *en meso*?', asks Vernant, commenting on Solon's arbitration when he acted in the name of the community.[13] But perhaps the failure of that mediation lies in this – partly misleading – question itself.

Power, people, victory – *dêmos, dámos, krátos*. The words circulate, spread, bounce from one city to another, from Sparta to Megara. At the dawn of the fifth century, the Greek cities were swept by winds of revolt, shaken by violent tumult. A handful of men prospered at the expense of the many, and they did so in a haughty and brazen manner. As the power of the *dêmos* strengthened, there was a growing aspiration for equality. Three paths then opened up for the cities: a legislator to outline a new order; a single ruler, mostly in the guise of a tyrant; or, as was more often the case, sedition.[14] The three paths were not clearly distinguishable; they could be combined or overlap.

From an almost mythical past emerges the figure of the *sáphos*, the wise man, skilled in politics, capable of being an arbiter, the *nomothétes*. One telling such name is Zaleucus, a lawgiver in Locri around 662 BCE. It is unclear where he sits between legend and reality. According to Aristotle, he was a *poimén*, a shepherd – leader of flocks and leader of peoples – who lived in seclusion outside the city and who, having been a slave, became a free man when, with his fine laws, he liberated his fellow citizens from the great *taraché*, the political disorder that oppressed them.[15] The legislator can be a liberator no less than the tyrant, the *túrannos*, who does not necessarily have negative connotations; indeed, he is often a tribune of the people. The widely taken path of revolt – as, for instance, in the case of the Megarians – seems to slip more easily into the unprecedented dissoluteness of popular power. The spectre of anarchy loomed large. Referring to that episode, Plutarch, perhaps drawing on Aristotle, used the adjective *akólastos* to describe an 'unrestrained' democracy.[16] Questions remain about the dates, but not about the radical nature of the experience.

This must have been inspired by the uprising in Athens in 594–593 BCE – the one which Solon was called upon to deal with. On the one hand, there was the impoverished and humiliated *dêmos*, oppressed by obligations, enslaved by debts, to the point of being completely excluded: 'they found themselves virtually without a share in anything [*metéchontes*]' (*Ath. Pol.*, II, 3). On the other hand, there were the landowners, the greedy and insatiable aristocrats, avaricious and unjust, who, proud of their blood ties and property, called themselves *eupatrídai*, sons of good fathers. Solon was also a *eupatride*, but he had experienced the crisis among the people who were rising up, in a *stásis* that 'lasted a long time' (*Ath. Pol.*, II, 1).

The poet Solon claims for the *árchon* Solon the role of the intermediary, the mediator. In the middle between two fronts of now belligerent citizens: 'I stood between them like a boundary-stone [*hóros*] in no man's land [*metaichmíoi*].'[17] These are the words of the strategist of yesteryear who, despite the demands of the people, did not set himself up as a tyrant: 'I spared my land/My native land, and unto tyranny and violence implacable/Did not set hand.'[18] If his ideal is finding a middle way, his intention is to find a point of reconciliation, a means of putting things right.[19]

Solon denounces the *dusnomía*, the condition of 'bad order' in which the whole city finds itself and which is about to turn into downright catastrophe. There seems to be an imminent threat of Zeus enacting divine punishment for its abuses and injustices. It is but a short step from debt slavery to civil war – and the division of the *pólis* may prove irreversible. Previously, some had taken that catastrophe almost for a natural curse inflicted by heaven, resorting to oracles and prophecies, or seeking shelter in their own homes, as Hesiod suggested.[20] However, Solon indicates an opposite path. It may seem obvious to attribute adverse fate to the gods. And yet the direct responsibility for the turmoil in the city lies with the citizens alone – and especially, of course, with the nobles in their unbridled iniquity. Solon's appeal marks a decisive shift towards the political dimension, in which sterile individual grievances, like ineffective outbursts of anger, may find some shared response. Some interpreters thus see in this the so-called 'discovery of the political', since the focus is not so much on a return to order as on the manner of the ordering itself.[21] Solon is not a monarch, but a sort of representative of the citizenry who addresses those who believe they can escape the plague that threatens the *pólis* by retreating into their private corner. Engraved in these verses is a powerful image of the 'public evil', the *demósion kakón*, that must be confronted.

> The public evil comes home to each man and the courtyard gates no longer have the will to hold it back, but it leaps over the high barrier and assuredly finds him out, even if he takes refuge in an innermost corner of his room. This is what my heart bids me to teach the Athenians, that *Dysnomia* brings the city countless ills, but *Eunomia* reveals all that is orderly and fitting.[22]

To encapsulate Solon's political message: there is no salvation without community. Here emerges the idea of shared responsibility, the need for everyone to respond to the evils of the city by confronting them. It also refers to the ability to change things, without resigning oneself to powerlessness. But once again, Solon's conciliatory role emerges. While he strengthens the space of the *pólis*, he also consolidates the *oîkos* through his measures on freedom from debt slavery and the restoration of land ownership.[23] The prosperity of the *oîkos*, the private sphere, thus remained essential for the prosperity of the *pólis*.

How far does Solon succeed in keeping the two opposing factions in check? A defensive tone emerges in the verses: 'Had another than myself/Taken the goad, unwise and covetous,/He'd not have held the people.' To convey the difficulty of his task, he resorts to a crude and telling comparison: 'I stood at guard on every side,/A wolf at bay among a pack of hounds.'[24] Aristotle hands down to tradition the image of the peacemaker, the skilful strategist of the *méson*, the champion of moderation. However, the *méson* in which Solon operates is not yet the *agorá*, but rather the *metaíchmion*, the space between two opposing sides in a civil war. Solon's efforts have to do with limits and boundaries. But how so? 'Black Earth would best bear witness, for 'twas I/Removed her many boundary-posts [*hóroi*] implanted:/Ere then she was a slave, but now is free.'[25] This fragment summarizes the *seisáchtheia*, literally 'shaking off burdens', the cancellation of debts and the abolition of loans secured by personal pledges, which made Solon famous. In one fell swoop, the boundary-posts set in the fields to indicate the obligations incumbent upon the people are removed. The land is unbounded and made free, meaning that no one has to work under another man's command. To uproot the many boundary-posts is to eradicate the archic power of the *eupatrídai* in order to open up the *krátos* of the city, the new political space.[26] If the disenfranchised are finally to become citizens, then the *hóroi* of slavery are erased. But just as Solon urges a single, indivisible city, in the centre the fault line of *stásis* splits the citizens, dividing them into two camps. It is a kind of no man's land, the *metaíchmion*, in which Solon seems forced to become a *hóros*, to himself become an archic limit, to interpose himself. That centre must remain empty – a temporary void, which is constantly threatened, yet indispensable. The *árchon*, however, succumbs to the temptation to fill it, to occupy it in order to preserve the possibility of political life. He does not contribute to laying down the *arché* in the *méson*. Yet, as the abyss of anarchy suddenly opens up, he interposes himself, himself becoming the *arché* in order to safeguard the *méson*.

In verse, Salon sings the praises of *eunomía*, good government: lawfulness is restored, things are put back in order, everyone is kept in their proper place. But *isonomía*, equality understood as equal distribution, is not pursued.[27] Hence the ambiguity of his words: on the one hand, 'to the common people I gave so much power [*krátos*] as is sufficient'; on the other, 'Thus would the people with the chiefs [*archôn*] best follow.'[28]

Although aristocratic hegemony based on birth was weakened, and access to the *archaí*, public offices, was expanded, the great power of the *árchons* remained virtually intact. The ancient court for trying murder cases was transformed into the Areopagus, a council made up of former *árchons* called upon to uphold the laws and supervise the *archaí*. Upon the first signal of opening, an archic shelter served as a counterweight.

3. No one could have imagined it, although there had been signs: the clamour around the assembly, the public demonstrations. The people of Athens strongly supported changes that would improve the conditions of every citizen. However, it was quite the opposite when the rest of the Athenians suddenly rose up, pouring into the streets of the city. It was a disparate crowd, made up of carpenters, stonemasons, potters, charcoal burners, farmers – and especially sailors and rowers. Unstoppable due to their large numbers and disruptive force, they were bound by the aspirations and filled with the enthusiasm of those who finally emerge from obscurity into the open. There was no one to lead them – they had no chiefs. From time to time, some of them stopped at a corner to give directions to others. So the rest of the Athenians set off towards the Acropolis, resolved to besiege it. They occupied the space around it and camped there. For two days they besieged it fiercely, even though many of them did not even have weapons. But nothing could stem their determination, their revolutionary energy, their need for recognition. What had previously been nothing more than a despised mob prevailed and won. The victorious people experienced its own power, sensing what it was capable of doing. Perhaps it was then that the *dêmos* perceived its own *krátos*, and revealed itself to itself in its own striking force. Such was the moment when *demokratía* erupted.

There had been similar uprisings before this, in 594 and 561. But the one that occurred in 508 was decisive, because it began a new chapter in Athenian history and energized the development of politics. For this reason, Josiah Ober rightly compares it to the storming of the Bastille in Paris in 1789: that, too, was a surprising and violent mass revolt, a semi-armed and anarchic uprising. Provoked by the attempt to dissolve the Assemblée Nationale, it instead accelerated the course of the French Revolution.[29]

There are only two remaining accounts of what happened in Athens: the one provided by Herodotus, the most complete and oldest, written in the mid-fifth century, when the memory of the events was still alive; the other, written a century later, but largely consistent with the first, is found in Aristotle's *Athenaion Politeia*. These are succinct accounts of just a few lines; they outline the episode in broad terms, and gloss over the details. However, they are sufficient to give an overall idea of the extraordinary nature of the events being narrated. They can be supplemented by a few verses from Aristophanes' *Lysistrata*, which contain traces of the oral tradition about the siege.[30]

To grasp the importance of that revolutionary moment, we should first take a quick look at the historical context that preceded it. The innovations introduced by Solon, who had attempted to resolve an acute economic crisis, were mostly adopted by the tyrants who, starting with Pisistratus, ruled Athens through most of the sixth century BCE. Often at odds with the aristocratic class from which they themselves came, the tyrants had encouraged the cohesion of the *pólis* through cults, festivals, ceremonies, new buildings, and the sharing of common spaces. All this had undermined the archic foundation of authority and fostered the emergence of a strong egalitarian tendency. The common Athenian no longer felt like the client of a large family, and nor did he want to be subject to domination by others. He began to see himself as a citizen, part of the political community of Athens.

The situation seemed to accelerate when, after the expulsion of the tyrants in 510, the city became the scene of clashes between aristocratic rivals who had no qualms about seeking outside intervention. When Isagoras obtained the office of *árchon*, he tightened the bonds of citizenship and transferred power to a pro-Spartan elite. His opponent was Cleisthenes, a member of the Alcmaeonidae family, who were considered heretics and cursed for having conspired against the tyrants. Various reasons led Cleisthenes to ally himself with the much-despised *dêmos*, welcoming it into his *hetaireía* (the fold of his supporters), as Herodotus recounts. But he must have sensed that the wind had changed and that the masses, who wanted more voice and more rights, had had enough of the elitist government. So, this *avant la lettre* populist dared to make a surprise move, rallying the people to his side and forming a mass party.[31] He thus put forward multiple proposals in the assembly that would favour the *dêmos* and earn him increasing influence. It is not known whether the reforms were initiated first and lit the touchpaper for the uprising, or whether they were merely its consequence. What is for sure is that Isagoras called on the Spartan king Cleomenes for help, and the latter quickly entered Athens with a military force. This was followed by the great purge of Cleisthenes and his supporters, numbering 700 families in all. Convinced that he had the city in his grasp, Cleomenes attempted to abolish the council, the *boulé*, in order to hand political authority to a body made up of Isagoras' supporters. But the *boulé* resisted – *tês de boulês antístases* – and refused to obey.

Aristotle recounts that 'the multitude banded together': the *plêthos* combined to support the resistance of the *boulé* (*Ath. Pol.*, XX, 3). Cleomenes and Isagoras, together with their supporters, took refuge on the Acropolis. They had been taken by surprise and forced into a defensive reaction. It was then – perhaps also because of the enemy army's affront to the sacred Acropolis – that the *dêmos* surrounded them.

To indicate the multitude that rose up, Herodotus speaks of *Athenaîoi de hoi loipoí*, 'the rest of the Athenians' (VI, 72). The term *loipós* means 'what remains', the remnant, the remainder. This remnant, which had been confined to the margins of the *pólis*, discarded and excluded from the centre of power, was the protagonist of the uprising. These 'other Athenians' – not a small part, but the masses – without leaders or guides, having 'the same feelings and judgements', *tà autà phronésantas*, besieged the Acropolis. It is possible that Isagoras and Cleomenes had retreated to the hill, a sort of fortress, to wait for the tumult to subside. But, as the news rapidly spread, yet others joined the revolt, rushing from the countryside to the city. The siege lasted two days. On the third day, surrender was granted.[32] The people emerged victorious.

What at first appeared to be yet another dispute among aristocrats turned out to be an unprecedented *stásis* with radical effects.[33] Athens entered into a new political era. Echoes of that revolutionary event, which must have remained long in the memory, surface in the verses of Aristophanes. He refers to Cleomenes, who was the first to claim the Acropolis but was forced to surrender his weapons and leave. 'That's how I fiercely hemmed him in, our men in ranks of seventeen we even slept before the gates' (*Lysistrata*, 273–82).[34] But who is speaking of this feat in the first person, here? It is the Athenian *dêmos* itself, the protagonist of a new chapter in the history of the *pólis*.

4. Although in different ways, interpreters agree in emphasizing the novelty of this new actor on the scene. Some even speak of a 'political class', arguing that, unlike what had happened in the past, it is the urban class that is changing, acquiring a previously unknown consciousness.[35] Herodotus' text should be understood in this light when we read: 'Cleisthenes was being worsted in the struggle, he made common cause with the people' (V, 66).[36] This is not the usual move made by aristocrats to exert leverage over the people. Rather, Cleisthenes binds them to his side, brings them into his circle of supporters, mediates and promotes their participation. In this way, the *dêmos* takes on political value.

However, this properly reciprocal relationship must be carefully considered if we are to avoid the risk – a trap which some interpreters fall into – of identifying Cleisthenes as an archic figure, the initiator of democracy, its paradoxical *arché*. Indeed, a long institutionalist and leader-centric tradition sees Cleisthenes as the first 'founder' of democracy – or the second, after Solon. The sources already present him in this way, thus giving rise to this image, although the emphasis varies and the terms have their different nuances. Herodotus says quite explicitly that it was Cleisthenes 'who made the tribes at Athens, and set up the popular government' (VI, 131, 1).[37] For his part, Aristotle writes: 'The people having taken control of affairs, Cleisthenes was their leader and was head of the people' (*Ath. Pol.*, XX, 4). But doubts and questions remain.[38]

The people's anarchic revolution was the disruptive event without which the subsequent development could not have taken place. However, it is a naive fantasy, a distorted view, to believe that this alone would have been sufficient. If that event gave rise to democracy and made possible the people's public role, no less decisive was the ability to sense the right moment and channel the revolutionary energy into the complex and sophisticated institutions that allowed Athenian democracy to take historical form. This was precisely the merit of Cleisthenes' innovations. In this sense, it can be said that, while he bound the people to himself, making them a political force, he unquestionably took sides with them.

This is demonstrated by his institutional endeavours.[39] He introduced radical and profound changes affecting various areas such as citizenship, the council, the army, and control over authority. However, to see these as a series of individual reforms would be to lose the sense of their overall meaning. As many scholars of the Greek world have pointed out, Cleisthenes designed the political framework of the city, which was inscribed in a new space and a new time. Lévêque and Vidal-Naquet, who devoted a famous essay to this topic, thus argue that this turning point – this *metabolé*, to use Aristotle's term – was 'of such capital importance that it in some sort of way formed a screen between the Athenians and their far-off past'.[40] Moreover, if we leaf through studies considered to be classics, by historians such as Henri Francotte or Gustave Glotz, the issue already appears in stark terms. With Cleisthenes, the 'compromise between the *gens* principle and the territorial principle' was broken.[41] Thus, the 'solidarity of the family', hitherto the first organized unit of law, was superseded.[42]

But what does a 'territorial principle' mean? This is too ambiguous an expression, often incautiously and blindly repeated. How does it relate to democracy? And what about the birth of politics? What we intend to argue here is that the break with the traditional conception of public space and time introduces a new politics of inhabiting – or rather, of cohabiting. Those who had earlier perceived themselves simply as members of a family now become citizens and fellow citizens. In their community, resident foreigners are welcomed as new citizens.[43] This is the culmination, the real hallmark, of the project designed by Cleisthenes.

The reorganization of the *pólis* is marked by mixing, unification, and equality. To this end, family ties are broken and traditional affiliations split up. The need to erase the old way of organizing the *pólis*, which had given rise to internal feuds and factions in constant conflict, is accompanied by the need to redesign the city space itself. The criterion of *ghénos* – origin, descent, lineage – is replaced by that of *dêmos*, i.e. district, which becomes the basic unit. The *demes* were grouped into thirty *trittyes*, ten in the city area, ten on the coast, and ten in the hinterland. Each of the new tribes consisted of three *trittyes*: the urban, coastal, and mountain. The whole of Attica was divided into a network of *demes* and *trittyes*, with the city at its centre. In this subdivision, blood ties and links with the territory no longer applied. The *ghéne* and *phratries* survived, but they were excluded from political organization. This was a way of undermining entrenched gentilic power.[44] However, it was not so much a question of erasing the old foundations of life as of proposing new ways of living based on mixing. People who not only came from different families and social classes, but were also accustomed to different lifestyles in the city or the hinterland, were henceforth encouraged to live together. This provided a way of undermining not only the rule of the *eupatrídai*, but also the particularism of the local lords. Mixing above all meant overcoming the division between urban, inland, and coastal areas. This was to be done within a political framework whose vanishing point was projected towards the centre of the *pólis*. It brought together all the buildings linked to the community – everything that was public.

The articulation of space, achieved with refined geometric flair and punctuated by the numbers three, five, and ten, corresponds to an equally complex and earth-shaking redivision of time.[45] Although the lunar calendar continued to guide religious life, the Prytaneic calendar regulated the political life of the city. The year was divided into ten periods of thirty-six or thirty-seven days, corresponding to the ten tribes that would take turns in the administration of the city. Within the exact span of a year, each tribe took turns exercising the *prytany*, i.e. the right to take a seat in the common hearth, delegating fifty of its members each time. The *boulé* was expanded: Solon's Council of Four Hundred became the Council of Five Hundred. This served to broaden participation and allow each tribe in turn to form the permanent commission of the Council during the ten periods of the year.

Space and time were coordinated. We might say that they proceeded in unison, in the name of equivalence. No period was qualitatively different to another, and no festivals interrupted the cycle, as in the religious calendar. The subdivisions of political time were interchangeable equivalents. That was how far the ideal of *isonomía*, permeating the Cleisthenic revolution, had reached. Numerical correspondences, spatial relationships, and political coordinates provided the symmetry and reciprocity that made citizens equals. Literally devoid of hierarchy, the *pólis* appears as a homogeneous space without a summit, where no one can seize the *arché*. The rotation at the centre, in the *méson*, following a regular cycle, ensured that *krátos* passed from one group to another in a continuous succession. Rather than constituting two absolute and opposite poles, commanding and being commanded became two sides of the same coin, the two terms of a reversible relationship. It is precisely this reversibility that prevents and impedes any archic impulses.

When we look at the heart of the *pólis* we find confirmation of this vision of democratic change. Not only is the *arché* laid down in the *mesón* according to a finely articulated geometry, but the remodelled *agorá* forms a new public space. Placed under the protection of Hestia and Hermes, surrounded by boundary stones, the *agorá* houses the *bouleutérion*, the seat of the Council of the Five Hundred, where representatives take turns presiding over the *ekklesía*, the assembly, taking their places at the common hearth. This is a decisive aspect but one that seems to be underestimated. Far from their homes and their territories, the delegates inhabit this space together, in a solidarity that is no longer familial but political. As they share that common space and time, drawing up a shared agenda, they give life to the community of the *pólis*. And they make clear the ideal of *sunoikeîn*, of cohabitation.

In the transition from *oîkos* to *pólis*, the memory of the hearth is preserved. No longer confined to private homes, but projected into the public space of the *agorá*, it becomes the *Hestía koiné*, the common hearth.[46] The ancient bonds of kinship give way to new ties held together by the political *lógos*, without renouncing the centre, which is no longer private but public. As a political symbol, Hestia represents hearths in general, without identifying with any one in particular. She is therefore inappropriable. But if domestic hearths, due to a sort of incompatibility, tend not to mix, maintaining their endogenous purity as much as possible, the common hearth is, instead, the living symbol of mixing and cohabitation. Outside the *oîkos*, in the outside world that seemed foreign and inhospitable, there opens up the common sphere, *tà koiná*, where another way of living is possible and necessary. It is not Hermes who prevails over Hestia; rather, the one inflects the other, in a sharing of the internal and a welcoming of the external. The common hearth is the threshold between *oîkos* and *pólis*, a threshold that can vary and shift towards one pole or the other.

The Cleisthenic revolution is a rupture in the conception of space and time. It gives rise to a new political model surprisingly consistent with the cosmological one outlined by Anaximander. Thanks to *isonomía*, the *pólis* forms a circular *kósmos*, revolving around a *méson*, where every citizen travels the entire circuit, assuming and relinquishing all the symmetrical positions that make up the political space. It is possible that this was influenced by previous experiences of reform in the laboratories that were the colonial cities of the sixth century BCE.

5. However, we must also consider a further aspect of the Cleisthenic revolution, which marked not only a rupture in the conception of space and time, but also a new vision of citizenship. It is no coincidence that, according to Aristotle, it was Cleisthenes who 'offered to hand over the government to the multitude', because by replacing the old tribes he wanted to ensure that the Athenians could take 'control of affairs' (*Ath. Pol.*, XX, 1, 4). This term should not be understood in the more restrictive sense of a constitution, which it would later acquire, but rather in the broad sense of active citizenship.[47]

Cohabitation here becomes a properly political issue. Neglected or ignored by more recent commentators, this issue was highlighted by traditional historiography, which refers to it as 'synoecism', but ultimately sees it as a means of achieving a mixture that transcends gentilic tribes.[48] However, the need for *sunoikeîn*, or cohabitation, is much more than a simple means to an end. It is, rather, the seal of the democratic revolution. It is not enough to break the bonds of blood and soil, to undermine birthrights and descent; it is also necessary to outline an open citizenship. This is precisely how Cleisthenes proceeded, according to Aristotle's account, which is found partly in the *Athenaion Politeia* and partly in a controversial passage of the *Politics*.

When Aristotle offers a detailed description of the division into districts and *demes* – where the motto is *mè phulokrineîn*, 'not to discriminate' – he emphasizes the new figure of the *demótai*. Precisely because the previous differences, marked by the tribes, have been overcome, the citizens living in each *deme* are defined as *demoti* – 'fellow-demesmen of one another' (*Ath. Pol.*, XXI, 4). This is not a question of countering the 'gentilic principle' by establishing a 'territorial principle', as many have argued.[49] The intention, which is much more radical, is to make the people a new political protagonist, not only by severing ties of tribe and family, but also by cutting ties with the land. This process thus involves deterritorialization. Only in this way can the people be transferred to a new political space and time. This is precisely what it means to make the *deme* the basis of the *politeía*: to divide the *chôra*, the inhabited area, by way of a common residence, which becomes the new bond of solidarity. Although the *deme* exists in space, it is not identified *with* space – an interpretative departure that would have a long train of consequences across history. What matters to the *demoi* is ultimately their shared domicile. But this raises the enormously important question of whether residence is sufficient for participation in citizenship. Who, then, would be a citizen? Is it whoever lives in the territory of the *deme*? Does this include the so-called metics, i.e. those who have come from elsewhere? Aristotle would immediately reject this criterion: 'citizenship is not constituted by domicile [*tôi oikeîn*] in a certain place (for resident aliens and slaves share the domicile [*oíkesis*] of citizens)'.[50] However, in explaining how Cleisthenes protected the ideal of equality through the institution of the *deme*, Aristotle specifies:

> And he made all the inhabitants in each of the demes fellow-demesmen of one another, in order that they might not call attention to the newly enfranchised citizens by addressing people by their fathers' names, but designate people officially by their demes. (*Ath. Pol.*, XXI, 4)

The need for isonomy extends even to names, sweeping away patronymics, symbols of powerful patrilineal descent. Every citizen is, so to speak, adopted by the *deme* and must therefore be called by a demotic name. But the decisive argument introduced to justify this change is that it is intended to prevent the *neopolítas*, the new citizens, from being exposed and becoming targets of blame, discrimination, and denunciation.

The term used by Aristotle raises many questions. Who are the new citizens? What relationship do they have with the *deme*? Why take such precautions? One possible answer can be found in a significant passage from the *Politics* where, during a discussion on the right to citizenship in times of revolution, the *metabolé*, Aristotle refers to a measure taken by Cleisthenes:

> But perhaps a question rather arises about those who were admitted to citizenship when a revolution had taken place, for instance such a creation of citizens as that carried out at Athens by Cleisthenes after the expulsion of the tyrants, when he enrolled in his tribes many resident aliens who had been foreigners or slaves. (*Pol.*, 1275b 34–6)

The controversial part is the last line: *pollоús gar ephuléteuse xénous kaí doúlous metoíkous*. Several philological and linguistic problems have been raised in a long tradition of interpretation. Ultimately, they seem in large part linked to the inconceivability of an unprecedented measure, too new and advanced. The verb *philetеueîn* can have no other meaning than 'to place someone in a *phulé*', to adopt, to enrol in a civic body hitherto bound by ties of kinship and territory. There is no doubt, therefore, that Cleisthenes admitted a certain number of non-citizens into the *phulé*, almost contaminating it, so to speak. But who were they? The range of possible answers is very varied and includes the most extravagant hypotheses, from mercenary soldiers to old supporters of the now-expelled tyrants.

On closer inspection, however, some light is shed on this passage by an old commentary from Michel Clerc.[51] In addition to citizens and slaves, the Athenian population also included a group of individuals who, although free, were excluded from citizenship. These were mainly foreigners residing permanently in Athens, as well as freed slaves, about whom ancient sources say little.[52] However, we know that, while remaining in this distinctive condition, they were subject to the payment of a tax called *metoíkion*. This explains why even in inscriptions freed slaves appear alongside resident foreigners. Both groups, despite their differences, fall into the category of metics – *mét-oikoi*, transients, those who join the inhabitants of the city from outside.[53] In the passage in question, *xénous* and *doúlous* relate to *metoíkous*. This means that Cleisthenes recognized metics as having citizenship rights, and that some of them were freed slaves and some were resident foreigners.

Such recognition should not be underestimated or neglected, as some interpretations do, as if this had been a somehow accidental measure.[54] On the contrary, these new citizens represent the seal of democracy. Tellingly, this happens just as the people becomes aware of its full *krátos*, in an an-archic vein. As the people senses its own power, it recomposes itself, without fear of opening up to 'foreigners'. It is not afraid to embrace those who are – not by chance – simply called 'new citizens'. This would not have been possible without the uprooting of the old dynastic and territorial ties that bound the *dêmos*, and which risked closing it off within *éthnos*. This move overthrows not only the power of descent, but also the claim that citizens have some intimate connection with the Attic land. It expresses the exact opposite of the principle of autochthony. Cleisthenes' efforts should be seen as an attempt to superimpose on the *chôra*, the separate region, a network of equivalent *tópoi*, a subdivision of areas that constitute the political space of the *dêmos*.[55] It is not, therefore, just a matter of 'mixing', as claimed by Aristotle, who was clearly unfavourable towards such a project. Rather, it is a comprehensive rethinking of the *dêmos* and citizenship.

Should foreigners be welcomed? Should they not be welcomed? Should they be banished or integrated? In other Greek cities they might be rejected, but at the dawn of democratic politics, Athens, a destination for mass immigration, welcomed new citizens. It did so without 'naturalizing' them. Rather, it treated them as equals with the old citizens in the spirit of cohabitation.[56] Without the Athenians' consent, such a project could not have been realized. They were not the sons of Attica,[57] but the cohabitants of its districts. The name based on the *deme* and not on the father, the demotic instead of the patronymic, is the emblem of democratic citizenship.

But if Cleisthenes thus placed the *politeía* back in the hands of the multitude, this did not prevent the later emergence of ambiguity, closedness, and retreat. Such troubles began already with the idea that inscription in the *deme* could itself be read as a firm normative criterion, of a type with birth. In a paradox destined to repeat itself across history, the democrats were the true conservatives. Like Pericles, with his law of 451 BCE, which restricted citizenship to those with two Athenian parents, they ended up guarding and controlling the borders of the civic body. Despite the revolutionary leap, the *arché* remained in the background, together with nostalgia for origins and the principle of autochthony.

6. The revolution of citizenship had broken down ancient barriers and atavistic bonds, enabling the *demes* to form the *dêmos*, the people. That centrifugal force, from the *oîkos* to the *pólis*, which had translated into openness, had given rise to a new sense of participation that superseded family belonging. The Athenians could consider themselves citizens – and they did so. But the architecture of the *pólis* maintained an unassailable verticality. To the Athenians' eyes, it took on the traits of the Areopagus, the hill dedicated to Ares which, between the *agorá* and the Acropolis, stood out with its haughty cliffs shrouded in sacred terror. It was almost the materialization of the *arché*.

Could that power ever be broken? Would there be another decisive *stásis*, this time with a different intent, a different aim, a direct attack on the stronghold of the *arché*? However much citizenship had been strengthened, increasing its capacity for resistance, the archic power at the centre of the *pólis* endured as a residue of the old order. It was a lasting impediment to democracy.

In the monumental history, few traces remain of the 'seventh *metabolé*'. This unprecedented upheaval is associated with the name of a nightmare, that of Ephialtes (*Ath. Pol.*, XLI, 2). Plutarch dedicates a few damning lines to this event, speaking of an *ákratos demokratía*.[58] The adjective *ákratos* has a range of meanings that are clarified by the noun it modifies: unmixed or pure for a liquid; simple for an object; unmoderated or rigorous for justice; absolute for freedom; intemperate or violent for a person or behaviour. *Ákratos demokratía* could thus be translated as 'absolute democracy' – one that has dissolved all bonds, removed all foundations, a true democracy without compromise. However, the untrustworthy accusation of violence looms large here. Everything is to be dismissed with a political assassination, a sort of unsolved mystery, with no culprits, over which a thick veil of silence soon descends.

The ghostly figure of Ephialtes haunts the open spaces of democratic memory, which is always ready to repress any anarchic interruption, to cancel out each act of *stásis* and erase all sedition. Only in this way is it possible to tell a harmonious linear story of an unstoppable evolution – from the beginning, a well-rooted autochthonous origin, to the democratic end, the *télos* of good government. At the helm is Pericles, the 'statesman' par excellence, to whom Thucydides had already erected a *monumentum aere perennius*. It is thus only fitting that he remains the only famous protagonist, capable of shaping an entire age, the only celebrated face of the democratic constitution. Thus the other characters have been allowed to pass into the shadows, eventually swallowed up by darkness.

But Ephialtes presents a different case. For despite its blurred and evanescent contours, his figure is inextricably linked to the overthrow of the Areopagus in 462 BCE, which shook the foundations of the highest and most venerable Athenian assembly. By removing the last remaining vestiges of the *arché*, it began a new chapter in democracy. It would be more accurate to speak, here, of radical democracy or an-archic democracy. The anchor that kept the ship moored was now removed.[59] This was the event that overturned the traditional order and brought the word *demokratía* to the fore, for it truly represented the power of the people and the peak of politicization. It must have been a moment of intense emotion but also of deep anguish.

To understand the tensions that pervaded the city, it is worth rereading a passage from the *Politics* where Aristotle speaks of revolutions. Addressing their potential causes, he specifies that they occur when one party gains too much honour and too much authority. As an example, he writes:

> the Council on the Areopagus having risen in reputation during the Persian wars was believed to have made the constitution

> more rigid, and then again the naval multitude, having been the cause of the victory off Salamis and thereby of the leadership of Athens due to her power at sea, made the democracy stronger. (*Pol.*, 1304 a 20–5)

Although the *árchons* were also chosen by lot according to the democratic practice, at the end of their term they became members of the Areopagus, where they held office for life. This was considered an affront in Athens at the time, where no office could be held for more than a year. In short, the people felt cheated and deceived because they had no control over the appointment of these *árchons*. The Areopagus was ultimately a council of elders, entirely aligned with the aristocrats and linked to conservative interests.[60] The sources are scarce, and the information available is cryptic and often contradictory. However, accusations were made that supremacy had been assumed thanks to 'additional functions' beyond the established ones, and a guardianship from above, *phulaké politeías*.[61]

In 462, the multitude rose up, and again there was *stásis*. This time, however, it was not to defend the Acropolis, but to attack the Areopagus and remove it from power. The people stripped the Areopagites of their powers, which were then handed to the assembly and the courts. That is why the few brief accounts that do exist speak of a subversion of order. Ephialtes, at that time *prostátes* of the *dêmos*, a member of the democratic party,[62] stood with that multitude.

It is difficult to tear away the veil of silence that has made his figure indistinct and enigmatic, almost ghostly. On one point, however, there is unanimity: Ephialtes was one of the most influential figures in Athenian history, and his death was a disaster for democracy. He was named after one of the giants who rebelled against the gods and a demon who appeared in nightmares. A well-attested etymology links the noun *ephiáltes*, nightmare, perhaps of ancient Mycenaean origin, with the verb *ephállomai*, 'to jump on someone' – an ominous name for someone who would lead the legendary attack on the Areopagus.[63] His *deme* is unknown, as is his family – only the name of his father, Sophonides, is known. He must have been born around 500 BCE, because he was a *strategos* in 467 – which also means that he was an Athenian citizen and of wealthy standing. Yet some later sources emphasize his poverty. This can be explained by considering his political positions and, above all, the qualities attributed to him.

Pure and incorruptible, of 'bronze' integrity, intransigent in punishing any injustice committed against the poor, an ardent opponent of the rich and the oligarchs – this is how he is portrayed by the ancients. To the eyes of moderns, he looks like a radical Jacobin, a 'Robespierre *avant la lettre*'.[64] Not at all inclined to compromise, he was a revolutionary who – as has been said – poured torrents of undiluted freedom into the hands of his fellow citizens.[65] Thus Plutarch recounts:

> when [Cimon] sailed away again on military service, the populace got completely beyond control. They confounded the established political order of things and the ancestral practices which they had formerly observed, and under the lead of Ephialtes they robbed the Council of the Areopagus of all but a few of the cases in its jurisdiction. They made themselves masters of the courts of justice, and plunged the city into unmitigated democracy [*ákratos demokratía*].[66]

The name of Ephialtes remains linked to *ákratos demokratía*, democracy freed from all constraints, from all anchors – a ship ready for the open sea, no longer weighed down by the cumbersome burden of the Areopagus. It is difficult to determine whether the *stásis* in which he played such a leading role can be considered 'year one of the Athenian democracy'.[67] However, it must be assumed that, despite the oblivion and silence to which his radical politics were condemned, the abolition of the Areopagus had more effective and lasting effects than previous changes, including the Cleisthenic revolution in citizenship. It is no coincidence that tradition recognizes at least his gesture of having 'brought down the nómos', the Solonian tables of laws, from the sacred hill of the Acropolis to the *méson* of the *agorá*. This was no merely symbolic act.

We can summarize the broad outlines of the story. From 470, the leading figure of the democratic party was Ephialtes, supported by Pericles who, initially more in the background, was flexible and inclined to compromise. On the side of the aristocrats was Cimon, who, being in favour of an alliance with Sparta, became unpopular and was ostracized, which is to say banished from the city. In his absence, the attack on the Areopagus was launched.

Despite the frustrating lack of testimony to draw on, it can be said that the assault had been prepared by a series of trials that Ephialtes had already brought against the Areopagites in 467, accusing them of having exercised their offices dishonestly (cf. *Ath. Pol.*, XXV, 1–4). Thus, the trial had been introduced as a political weapon to get rid of opponents. The people had transferred most of the Areopagus' functions to the assembly and the courts, and it now retained jurisdiction only over wilful homicides.

Immediately afterwards, in the same year as the uprising, Ephialtes was killed. The name of the murderer is unknown, but it is said to have been a 'cunning murder', i.e. an ambush.[68] As for the instigators, there are various versions. According to some sources, the conspiracy was hatched by the aristocrats – and this is not difficult to believe. A certain Aristodicus is mentioned, a hired assassin who came from outside to carry out the execution. But according to other sources, everything took place within the democratic faction. It is natural to wonder who benefited from Ephialtes' death. This even makes it possible to reconcile the conflicting versions, because one cannot rule out a political assassination planned with the help of his opponents by the second-in-command of the democrats, who had no qualms about getting rid of a friend who had become as popular as he was inconvenient. When Ephialtes was removed from the scene, this marked the beginning of Pericles' power: he became not only the undisputed leader, but also an increasingly authoritarian head of state. A radical democracy gave way to 'an aristocratic and kingly statesmanship'; what was 'nominally a democracy became in his hands government by the first citizen'.[69] This also explains the veil of silence that soon fell over the murder, which no one had any interest in investigating. Thus, Ephialtes was erased from the memory of the *dêmos* and from the official history of democracy, with the record of *stásis* deleted.[70]

7. Vendetta upon vendetta, in an ancient chain that reaches the son who can avenge his father only by killing his mother. What could be worse? An unspeakable punishment awaits him, unless the chain of crimes is broken by leaving the matricide unpunished. Orestes found refuge at the sanctuary of Delphi, clinging to the statue of the god, his hands still dripping with blood, some time after he murdered his mother Clytemnestra. But beside him sleep the Furies, the black, wingless harpies, sinister creatures hated by humans and the Olympian gods, whose task is to punish those who shed 'equal blood'. They are immediately opposed by Apollo, who promises to protect Orestes, urging him not to give in to *phóbos*, fear, when the Furies seek vengeance. He orders him to go to Athens, the city of Pallas, and submit to a trial that will free him from persecution. The shadow of Clytemnestra, who wanders despised among the dead, with no one left on Earth whom she can task with avenging her, suddenly appears, rousing the congregation of the Furies. These are the atavistic ministers who punish the blood shed in violation of the mother's law; she beseeches them to hunt down the fugitive and wash away the shame. The Furies turn their wrath against Apollo. He is guilty not only of having spirited away the man who murdered

his own mother, but also of having taken jurisdiction away from the most ancient of regimes.[71]

The scene shifts from Delphi to Athens, where Orestes appears, seeking a fair judgement. Who will pass sentence? The contrast between the *Díke* of the Furies, who calls for vengeance, and the *Díke* of Apollo, who instead asks for acquittal, seems almost like a war between mirror images: female–male, pre-Hellenic–Olympic, blood relationship–marriage, dark–light, ancient–new. Frank, courageous, and peaceful within, Athena – the goddess who is her 'father's daughter', having no mother and springing directly from Zeus's head – recognizes the seriousness of the dispute, and prefers to hand it to a court that deals with crimes of blood. Thus, the Areopagus reappears. Aeschylus celebrates it as a bulwark of justice which, by instilling fear, is capable of safeguarding order in the *pólis*. The verdict is equally split; Orestes is acquitted only because Athena adds her vote in favour of the matricide.

But hadn't that court, the Areopagus, been dismantled during the democratic revolution of 462 BCE? The great Ephialtes had convinced the assembly to unseat the ancient Council, a now obsolete aristocratic institution that no longer had any reason to exist. It was an unprecedented turning point, a break in political life. The order had been overturned.

In *The Persians*, staged in 472, Aeschylus has the chorus answer the question of who rules the city: 'of no man are they called the slaves or vassals' (242).[72] And in *The Suppliants* of 463, the allusion to the imminent victory of the *dêmos* expresses pride and enthusiasm. Why, then, did the Areopagus return, restored and ennobled, as early as 458 with the performance of *The Eumenides*? Its reinstatement has political significance and should be interpreted as a warning and a hope. The revolution had been too radical. In the future, the city would need to be more prudent, more pacified. But what kind of democracy would remain? This is the question that emerges in Aeschylus' verses.

The political rupture had run so deep that it seemed like a cosmic shift: the new order had sought to erase the old. Aeschylus portrays this political clash as a theological dispute: on the one hand, the Furies, the primordial deities, the daughters of the night; on the other, the dynasty of Zeus, the most recent gods of Olympus.[73] The principle of punishing blood with blood is opposed by the need for a judgement that halts the unending sequence of crimes. The dispute concerns the law itself, which must be established because it does not yet exist.

Victory smiles on the new order – but through the veneration of the past, and not in opposition to tradition. Humiliated by the sentence, the Furies threaten to unleash their rage-filled curse upon the city. But through the power of persuasion, Athena convinces them to let go of their fury and accept honours and worship, and welcomes them as metics into the city. She follows – indeed, guides – their phantasmagorical procession to their underground sacred dwellings, amid songs of jubilation. Thus she transforms them into the Eumenides, the Benevolent Ones, goddesses who destroy the wicked, guardians of prosperity and peace, protectors of the court that they had bitterly opposed. Appeased in their spirit of vengeance, the Furies are entrusted with the memory of misfortunes and, under the name of *Semnaí*, the Fearsome, they remain to protect the city from internal strife – but also to constantly threaten it, as Athena leads it from war to war.

Aeschylus thus narrates the return of the Furies and the restoration of the Areopagus.[74] He seems to care deeply about the recomposition of the *pólis*, its unity. *The Eumenides*' pleas leave no room for doubt: discord must remain outside the city gates, and the blood of citizens should never be shed in feuds. If the citizens keep pursuing their vendettas by committing fresh crimes against each other, this is sure to wound the entire city. The chorus chants in unison:

> I pray that discord [*stásis*], greedy for evil, may never clamor in this city, and may the dust not drink the black blood of its people and through passion cause ruinous murder for vengeance to the destruction of the state. But may they return joy for joy in a spirit of common love, and may they hate with one mind; for this is the cure of many an evil in the world. (978–88)[75]

It is not difficult to see in this a message for contemporary Athens. It had survived a revolution that was perhaps too drastic in the eyes of Aeschylus, whose enthusiasm must have cooled. He would certainly not have demanded a step backwards, through the abolition of the democracy that had been conquered. But he argued the need for moderation, for balance. Nor can we forget that it is precisely in *The Eumenides* that we hear Athena's solemn warning to the citizens, looking to the political future of the *pólis*: 'neither anarchy nor tyranny', *met'ánarkton bíon mḗte despotoúmenon*, a line which is repeated twice (526, 696). Neither anarchy nor despotism. Neither too free nor too dominated. Had the uprising at the time of Ephialtes convinced Aeschylus to see democracy as the extreme opposite of a despotic regime? The conclusion in *The Eumenides* might be interpreted both as a criticism of Ephialtes and a plea in his defence.[76] It is true that in Aeschylus' verses the Areopagus is no longer the 'guardian of the laws' but retains the limited functions that restrict it to judging crimes of blood – as Ephialtes had wanted. This question must thus be considered in the light of tragic democracy: the city recognizes itself in tragedy, which stages order and disorder and dramatizes every form of exclusion, including that of the ancient powers.

The Eumenides is one of the most enigmatic texts, in which the protagonists are the gods but the issues debated are ethical, legal, and political. Christian Meier saw this tragedy as offering a valuable contribution to Greek political thought and, in this vein, coined the expression 'theological politics'.[77] But why this inversion of the well-known formula 'political theology'? It can be explained by the fact that here it is not theological concepts that are secularized, as in modernity, but rather politics that plays a leading role. Aeschylus focuses on internal conflict and the possibility of ending it. Meier thus wonders whether there is not even a 'philosophy of history' or a 'theology of history' behind the *Oresteia*, whose construction would find its keystone in *The Eumenides*.[78] This raises the possibility of a *pólis* capable of leaving behind family feuds, retaliation, and discords – a question that Meier addresses with a view to Aeschylus and a Schmittian exegesis of *The Eumenides*.

The words of the chorus take on decisive significance: 'may they return joy for joy in a spirit of common love, and may they hate with one mind' (984–6). Meier reads this through a Schmittian lens: 'It cannot be a coincidence that the same categories that were important to Carl Schmitt faced with the threat to modern statehood were important to Aeschylus in his "analysis".'[79] The message is: unanimous friendship within, unanimous enmity without. The *pólis* achieves unity only if the friend-enemy opposition is displaced to the outside. This is allegedly the prerequisite for dispelling the spectre of internal division, the ghost of *stásis*. Here, it would seem, there is an impulse towards politicization, a higher vision of the politician *super partes*, which makes Aeschylus the interpreter of an indispensable shift in democratic politics.

According to Meier, in a political landscape marked by tensions and agitated by conflicts, there takes shape the alternative between a 'democracy freer from constraints' and a 'more controlled democracy', between one more loyal to the people and one with a more aristocratic vocation.[80] Aeschylus' 'theological politics' promotes a moderation capable of preserving the city from dangerous extremes. Meier's pages repeatedly feature the term *méson*, laden with political significance, which stands between two opposites: *arché* and *anarchía*. The city must be neither oppressed by despotic rule nor 'without government'. What transpires from Athena's words is a constant effort to maintain the unity of the *pólis* by curbing an overly extensive and extreme democracy and promoting a new synthesis among oppositions. If the gods have readmitted the ancient order into the new one, the city must follow their example and rediscover a balance. For this reason, the *deinón*, the terrible, must be restored and re-legitimized thanks to the Areopagus. Meier thus ends up casting Aeschylus as the promoter of a middle way. The seal impressed by the Schmittian historian on the paradigm of the *méson* – an understanding destined to enormous future historical influence – emerges where it is identified as the form of 'political government/power/rule'.[81] Which, if we return to the Greek, is nothing other than the *arché*. Meier explicitly draws a straight line from Aeschylus to Aristotle:

> Aeschylus also believes that the proper order of the *polis* is divinely determined: Zeus always grants victory (*kratos*) to the middle (*meson*). He refers to the *middle ground* between anarchy (*anarchta*) and despotic rule, i.e. what Aristotle later called 'political government' (or: political form of rule), *politiké arché*.[82]

In this view, Aeschylus is considered the forerunner of Aristotle for having sensed that there was no other way to achieve internal agreement within the city except through *méson*, that form of government which Aristotle would choose as the goal of political action.[83] To avoid possible misunderstandings, a further step is taken: *méson*, the golden mean, which stands out for its superiority, must be recognized as *krátos*, victory. Meier writes: 'it should not be one power, but rather the middle ground, that has *krátos*. It should be added that this is ultimately what it always comes down to.'[84]

And what about the *dêmos*? Suddenly, the *krátos* vanishes, dissipates, as if the *ánarchon* reminiscent of the *demóthrous anarchía*, the anarchic rage mentioned in *Agamemnon* (883), could no longer find a place among the people, and is rejected to the extreme. The link between *dêmos* and *krátos* is broken – the people loses power. Appropriately rehabilitated, passed off as an indispensable bulwark of the city, recentred in the middle, the *arché* is set in opposition to democracy, which has already shown all its anarchic power. This *krátos*, which has been too often evoked, will no longer need to be remembered, and will instead be condemned to oblivion. It is better to prohibit the power of the people, to the point of erasing it, thanks to the archic device. The postulate of the 'golden mean' would become the most widely relied on normative means of neutralizing democracy – and not only in ancient Greece.

8. In *The Divided City*, Nicole Loraux's most important book, the name of Christian Meier never appears, and yet the author's debt to him is evident throughout.[85] Elsewhere, she mentions Meier only in passing, together with Carl Schmitt, with regard to *The Eumenides*.[86] It would be difficult, however, to imagine Loraux's reflection without the category of the political. But before considering this sadly lacking exchange, which touches on a crucial point, it is worth briefly outlining Loraux's work, since it provides essential insights for those who do not wish to stop at the conventional image of the Greek *pólis*.

A historian and Hellenist who ably moves between different fields – philosophy and psychoanalysis, political theory and anthropology – Loraux soon broke away from the disciplinary logic and conservatism of classical studies. Dominated by curiosity about details and a focus on institutions, this discipline ended up immobilizing politics. According to Loraux, we need to dismantle the portrait that Athens painted of itself and which the historiography has largely reproduced. Being and ought-to-be are confused in a reassuring and idealized representation, which projects 'the idea of a city that is at one, indivisible and at peace with itself, a historically embodied model of democratic Athens, ready to be used by both Athenians and moderns'.[87]

In this regard, Loraux openly speaks of 'ideology' – a key term in Marx's thought, but also one revised in light of the French and Italian thinkers who reworked the concept in the 1970s. Louis Althusser broke the ice by theorizing ideology not as the system of production relations that governs existence, but in terms of individuals' imaginary relation to those relations.[88] But especially significant for Loraux is the work of Claude Lefort, who had broken with 'Marxian positivism' in order to recognize the properly imaginary value of ideology. In Lefort's view, analysing the forms of production is insufficient for understanding a society that is always organized through the making and remaking of symbolic forms.[89] Following in this vein, Loraux unsurprisingly distances herself from an orthodox Marxism aimed at shedding light on the dynamics of exploitation in the ancient city, and turns to Marx more as a master of suspicion, useful for deconstructing the overly idealized democracy of Pericles' century.

Loraux identifies ideological discourse in a genre that has often been neglected because of its ceremonial and repetitive traits, namely the *epitaphios lógos*. Delivered in honour of soldiers who have sacrificed themselves for their country, the funeral oration is the place where the ideal of the democratic *pólis* is elaborated. 'Not content with confusing themselves with Athens, the Athenians invented Athens.'[90] This was possible not only thanks to multiple exclusions – in particular of women and slaves, those outsiders within whom the official gaze overlooks – but also through the erasure of the conflict from which democracy arose. For it is instead presented as an institution rooted in the city since its foundation. This offers a staging of social harmony, of an exemplary cohesion. This was the way in which Athens stylized itself, casting itself as paradigmatic of the City as such. Yet it comes at a high price, for the democratic *pólis* thereby takes on aristocratic values, fixing the present to the origin myth. The immortality promised to citizens who have fallen in battle is nothing more than a reformulation of the beautiful death sung about in the poems of the Archaic period. Loraux, however, focuses her attention on the unanimous way in which the city, still in a phase of democratization, recognizes itself in collective *areté*, in civic excellence.

L'Invention d'Athènes, her first work, published in 1981, was initially titled *Athènes imaginaire*. In those years, to invoke the imaginary, another way of saying ideology, was to revive a key term introduced by Cornelius Castoriadis, who had in 1975 published *The Imaginary Institution of Society*. Castoriadis was, together with Lefort, a prominent figure in the *Socialisme ou Barbarie* group, which brought together the heterodox political left in France. He seems to have had much in common with Loraux, who in fact expresses her appreciation for him. However, there are also differences, which are indeed a source of controversy. The issue first and foremost concerns the use of 'imaginary', which for Castoriadis, far from being a reflection of an ideal, is always an instituting imaginary.[91] The context of modern Marxism, to which Castoriadis remained anchored, separates him from Loraux, whose work moves increasingly closer to Michel Foucault's archaeology and Jacques Derrida's deconstruction. However, the reasons for the disagreement run deeper. For Loraux, the funeral oration is proof of a democracy that falls short of itself, incapable as it is of acquiring its own language. Castoriadis passes the opposite judgement: for him, the speech attributed to Pericles in Thucydides' account is not only permeated with democratic values, but reveals the quintessence of the Athenian city.[92]

There are many threads linking *L'Invention d'Athènes* to *The Divided City*.[93] Loraux returns almost obsessively to certain themes, considering them from different angles. However, only later did the theme of division within the city – *stásis*, internal conflict – arise in her work. The anthropologist Pierre Clastres – a dissident student of Claude Lévi-Strauss whose work is close to the positions of Lefort and Abensour – must have exerted a certain influence here. In his book *La Société contre l'État*, published in 1974, Clastres offers a new interpretation of primitive communities marked by a constant struggle to avoid any form of internal division and thus prevent the imposition of power from outside. This struggle for 'indivisibility' proves to be an eminently political problem.[94] It is in this light that Loraux revisits her reading of the city, seeing in Greek politics an effort to evade indivisibility, to ward off *stásis*.[95] But the anthropologist is also an essential point of reference on another related theme. Loraux is reluctant to see war as the political institution able to ensure the internal stability of the city, and refers to the words of Clastres, for whom war is nothing more than the way primitive societies function.[96]

Loraux's distance from Meier – and from his Schmittian way of understanding the 'category of the political' – could not be clearer. She takes a critical stance on two closely related points. First, she sees in the construction of that category the same intention that animates the Greeks to present the city as a united whole, overlooking the contrasts and divisions, and excluding women, strangers, and slaves. The idea of the city rests on the 'ellipsis of the political'.[97] The tacit reproach levelled at Meier is that he places the Greeks beyond conflict, a state which, in fact, even if they wanted to, they cannot reach. Internal strife remains the spectre of the *pólis*. Thinkers of 'isomorphic politics' risk seeing only the beautiful homogeneity of an egalitarian city at peace with itself.[98]

The second point has less to do with Meier than with Schmitt and the friend-enemy opposition, which Loraux considers a distortion of reality.[99] This is not just a matter of doubting the merits of applying a modern category to democratic Athens. Rather, Loraux questions this opposition itself. It is not clear, in fact, why a community should be able to sustain itself only by confronting some enemy. It is as if it were necessary to conceive of external enmity in order to imagine internal friendship. But the internal-external dualism is fictitious, and the inside-outside dichotomy is misleading. It looks for a clear split where there is a continuum: that of a conflict that takes different and intermediate forms, both inside and outside. Hence Loraux's criticism of those – including, it is implied, Meier – who claim to interpret the conclusion of *The Eumenides* in this way. They are, she contends, introducing a causal relationship that does not exist in the Greek text in order to argue that a unanimous enmity towards the outside world creates a unanimous internal friendship. However, this critique also applies to Vernant, who contrasts the political, 'definable as the city seen from within', with war, identified as 'the same city showing its face to the outside world'.[100] Loraux echoes here the 'very Greek' way of assimilating politics to the city at peace, placing conflict on one side only, where it would even be desirable.[101] This, however, risks not only overlooking the continuity of conflict, but also failing to grasp its capacity to unite, which is well known from Homer to Heraclitus. In a striking expression, Loraux calls this the 'bond of division'.[102]

It is unsurprising that, in a context in which the inevitability of conflict is constantly reiterated, *stásis* becomes central. The theme is not new in historiography: scholars such as Gustave Glotz have seen in *stásis* – generally translated as 'civil war' – the very stuff of Greek history, as a tragically recurring episode that even democratic voting cannot keep at bay.[103] But the original dimension of Loraux's essays lies in the radical way in which she sees *stásis* at the heart of the *pólis*, with all the consequences that follow from this.

A disastrous scourge, an inexplicable disease, a long-brewing plague, a misfortune that has sinisterly fallen from above – every effort is directed towards expelling *stásis* from the city. Once struck by it, the city waits hopefully to be freed from its plight and regain its integrity.[104] However, within the *pólis*, which is supposed to have absorbed and transcended the *oîkos*, there remains concealed the *neîkos*, the conflict ready to reignite within the family. Thus, the most horrific misfortune looms, that of the *oikeîos pólemos*, the internal conflict, which seems exorcized only when projected onto an external war. Perhaps this can be achieved by returning from such a conflict with a *níke*, a 'victory that is not evil', as Athena hopes in the closing lines of *The Eumenides* (903). But the effort to avert *stásis*, to expunge it, does not succeed. Any attempt to repress it is bound to be futile, because 'civil war is congenital to the city'.[105] Thus, according to Loraux, in the One-City the division into two must be recognized, and conflict must be identified as lying at the heart of the political. The Greeks looked into the depths of that abyss and recoiled in terror. Yet, despite themselves, they keenly sensed that *stásis* was inscribed in the *pólis* almost as an institution. As Henri Van Effenterre observed: 'To indicate sedition, revolution in the city, the Greeks use the term stasis, derived from a root that clearly evokes the ideas of firmness, permanence, stability. As if their stasis were an institution!'[106]

Recounted with embarrassment, mentioned with reticence, *stásis* is difficult to fit into the category of *pólemos*. The revulsion for a man who kills his brother, for the spilling of the same blood, emerges in Thucydides' masterful description: 'even blood became a weaker tie than party' (III, 82, 6). But the opposite could also be true: the bond of political faction became more intimate than the bond of kinship.[107]

9. Corcyra, 427 BCE. The people are fleeing through the narrow streets, seeking refuge wherever they can, still in a state of shock and confusion after the cold-blooded attack, carried out with brutal and premeditated violence while the assembly was still in session. No one could have imagined a new oppression after the assassination of Peithias and the massacre of his fellow democrats, numbering sixty or perhaps more. In the hours following that vile plot, many remained inert, almost incapable of reacting to the coup by the oligarchs. But with the attack on the assembly, the limit was reached. Night fell on the bloody clashes. Pressed by well-armed hoplites, the people of Corcyra now seemed beaten. Those who still resisted, aided by the darkness, climbed the streets leading to the heights of the city, reaching the acropolis. They gathered there, while some managed to push their way down to the inlet below. But the area around the *agorá* lay in the hands of their opponents, who also controlled the port and the arsenals. All was not lost, however, and apart from a few skirmishes the next day was spent tensely waiting. Yet then, hundreds of mercenaries arrived from the mainland to help the oligarchs. The clash seemed to be turning for the worse. Was the people's fate already sealed? *Eleutheria*, freedom – with a great commotion, their messengers spread this promise throughout the fields, and the slaves soon joined their side. Compared to the others – the few, the well-armed men in power – the people was now a multitude. Another day passed. Then conflict broke out in the city: swords, spears, and shields against daggers and stones. The people has cunning on its side, dexterity in outmanoeuvring the enemy, and the intuition that binds it to the city. Yet, in that strange internal war which they have to endure, they seem to be going down to defeat. But here come the women – heading out of their houses, clambering onto the roofs, and hurling tiles at the enemies. Not at all on the back foot amidst this tumult, they fight amid the chaos and confused cries. Victory goes to the people. The oligarchs retreat. Their silhouettes disappear into the distance as the sky darkens, and a calm seems to descend. In the darkness, however, a flame looms menacingly – and then another joins it, and another. The houses around the *agorá* are already ablaze, while fire begins to devour the warehouses and depots nearer the port. The city is in danger. Everything risks being consumed by the blaze. The others, the few, the enemy, had no qualms about destroying the entire city. The victorious people of Corcyra would long remember this.

These scenes of urban warfare constitute a chapter in the devastating civil war that shook Corcyra between 427 and 425 BCE. One of the first in the varied Greek landscape, and the most bloody and savage, it would become emblematic of *stásis*. Thucydides portrays it in dense, agitated lines.[108] If the focus is on internal events, the background also sees a constant coming and going of ships, ambassadors, and soldiers, indicating the involvement of other forces and other protagonists – Athenians, Spartans, Corinthians – more or less directly responsible for the drama unfolding in the city. For Thucydides, this provides a way to shift the blame for an internal conflict onto external factors. This is his attempt to reduce the *stásis*, in all its incomprehensibility, to a war between great powers, their games and their alliances. It would otherwise be difficult to explain the appalling fratricidal struggle that took place when the Corcyraeans, in a state of ecstasy, began to fight among themselves, falling prey to internal discord (III, 70, 1). But were they mere victims – or active interpreters of their own history? Thucydides is eager to portray *stásis* as a calamity, and to establish a symmetry between the warring parties. Yet, in the course of the chronicle, the historian's position emerges ever more clearly, if only in his choice of words: on the one hand, there is the *dêmos*, the Corcyraeans, the people of the city; on the other, there are the *olígoi*, the few, the adversaries, the enemies, who are increasingly separate from the *pólis*, both physically and politically. They were those, says Thucydides, who 'held power', *oi échontes tà prágmata*, that is, who managed public affairs (III, 72, 2). Yet they did not hesitate to carry out a coup, a conspiratorial attack. This is a serious charge: they are intent on overthrowing democracy, *tòn dêmon katalúousin* (III, 81, 4). But *katalúo* also means to dissolve, and in this sense to ruin. To overthrow democracy is equivalent to breaking up the *dêmos*, which instead resists and regroups. Having at first remained relatively passive, the *dêmos* now reacts by taking a stand, forming itself into a faction in struggle. For this multitude, the fate of the city is a heartfelt concern. The other side, in contrast, set fire to it, showing no interest in the common good. Here, Loraux believes that we can see a certain resemblance to the history of the Paris Commune, to which is added the people's rejection of civil war.[109]

The story of Corcyra continued in a tragic crescendo. The agreements made were ineffective, and the truces did not last. The ongoing spiral of violence culminates in the final massacre of the oligarchs who, walled up in the temple of Hera, are condemned to death and slaughtered as enemies. But others, writes Thucydides, 'were slain also for private hatred, others by their debtors because of the moneys owed to them' (III, 81, 4). Fathers killed their sons and ties of blood became less strong than political ones. These events caused a sensation because it was the first time that such crimes had been dared. This did not act as a deterrent, however; on the contrary, the *stásis* – so the historian relates in a sombre tone – spread to other cities, causing further misfortune and upheaval.

10. What does *stásis* mean? Movement or standstill, agitation or position? This word, with its strikingly ambiguous meaning, encapsulates the enigma of Greek politics. The first attestation of the word is found in the most famous fragment of Alcaeus, where it is used to describe a ship at the mercy of the winds.

> I cannot make sense of the *stásis* of the winds.
> One wave crashes from this side,
> Another from the other, and we in the middle
> Are borne in our dark ship
> Battered hard by this great storm.[110]

The anchors are loosening, the sails are torn, the water in the hold is rising above the base of the mast – the crew seems adrift on the high seas, *to mésson*. As an allegory for the city, agitated by conflict and jolted by internal strife, the verse could not be more effective. The question remains about the word *stásis*, a dilemma and a concern for many interpreters. Some translate it as 'position', others as 'discord'. The two meanings coexist. The winds blow from different points, in different directions, lifting the motionless front of air, provoking the conflict, the whirlwind, that endangers the city itself.

Since its first appearance in Greek literature, the word *stásis*, pertaining to the language of physics, has also had a political meaning. It is no coincidence that Homeric language, expressing a world still built around a vertical axis, contains no trace of it. Only when the *arché* crumbles can *stásis* emerge.

The etymology reveals all its contradictions. Derived from the verb *hístemi*, whose root in Indo-European languages indicates standing, positioning oneself in space, *stásis* immediately reveals itself to be synonymous with *kínesis*, movement. This owes to its continuous and repeated use in political vocabulary. In Chantraine's etymological dictionary, the contradiction is even rendered with a certain nonchalance: 'the act of positioning oneself, of rising, of lifting oneself up'. Hence – although this is not so obvious – sedition, or rather 'rebellion'.[111] On the other hand, it seems that the Greeks were familiar with the double meaning of the word and easily found their bearings in an agitation so powerful as to bring the city to a standstill. In Plato's *Cratylus*, his dialogue on the justice of names, an attempt is made to use phonetic imagery to interpret this singular word that begins with a spirant, the *sîgma*, and with the *taû*, which designates support (426b–427c). What sounds could best convey the political physics of *stásis*? A movement that stops, that takes a position, an insurgent part that separates itself by rising up.

The problem of translation becomes insurmountable. In this case, more than in others, any attempt to modernize the term risks causing misunderstandings, given that *stásis* is a phenomenon peculiar to the *pólis*. It would almost be more appropriate to leave it in the original Greek – but not without first clarifying its meaning. Two temptations emerge in particular in the exegesis. The first is that of rendering *stásis* as 'civil war', reducing it to a kind of warfare and at the same time reattaching it to the Roman context of *bellum civile*. And yet, as Benveniste points out, *civiles* indicates the reciprocity of relations between fellow citizens, which does not disappear in cases of conflict.[112] The second temptation is to translate it as 'revolution' in the modern sense. Mazzarino rightly wrote: 'To indicate our idea of "revolution" the Greeks and Romans never made use of grand cosmic concepts. They could thus indicate it in Greek, as *stásis*, "uprising", or *taraché* or *kinesis*.'[113] Elsewhere, however, Mazzarino himself succumbs to the impulse to translate it as insurrection.[114]

Stásis has a very broad semantic range: faction, party, seditious grouping, sedition, discord, insurrection, revolt, revolution, civil war. As Finley pointed out, in each instance the meaning is determined only in its proper context.[115] This is also due to the development of the word, which spans the entire period of Greek Antiquity and has given rise to a conspicuous series of derivatives, an outright political lexicon revolving around this one word.[116] But what seems to characterize *stásis* as its distinctive feature is the difference between inside and outside. As the accounts passed down to us show, *stásis* cannot take place outside the *pólis*. In the *Republic*, Plato argues that *pólemos* and *stásis* cannot be confused, because they correspond to two types of hostility, the one directed against what is *allótrios*, and the other against what is *oikeîos*. Hence, *pólemos* is directed externally, against enemies, and *stásis* internally, against those who ought to be friends (470b–d).

This is why some speak of *stásis émphulos*, of internal struggle, division. Here, the closest neighbour can suddenly turn out to be the enemy – the one standing in front of us, who is now to be confronted.[117] What evil could be worse than a real plague breaking out in the city? If we disregard derivatives such as *stasiótes* (companion, partisan, seditious), where subjective activity is implied, it is also telling that the noun *stásis* points to a self-producing phenomenon, without any actor being named. It is an event that occurs, that happens.

Stásis is a movement, from a verb denoting a state. It stands up, takes increasingly hard positions, and culminates in internal strife. *Stásis* is the rift that opens up in the city, leading to violent conflict and armed confrontation. Once again, spatial metaphors provide the framework for visualizing political relationships. However, the perspective of *stásis* is particularly obscure and intricate due to its constitutive paradox, being both a movement and a state. This is spatially reflected in the horizontal and vertical dimensions. Iconically, it is a movement that stops, that takes a position by stiffening, separating itself as it gathers its forces – simultaneously from the bottom to the top, from the centre to the edge. A crack opens up that can deepen, becoming an irreparable gash, a fatal laceration, a real fissure. We should not underestimate the centrifugal force of *stásis* – what Hans-Joachim Gehrke defined as its *Schwungkraft*, its capacity for inertia and persistence.[118] An isolated dissent can spread, a group can take harder form, while nevertheless opening up to other factions. It draws in those who were previously excluded, as they are almost trapped in a process of condensation that may prove irreversible. It is impossible to know if and when the ripples will smooth out, if the conflicts will die down and the sides will become more fluid. The *pólis*'s very existence is at risk.

11. But why is *stásis* so dangerous? What makes this such an unparalleled curse, and such an incurable disease? The answer cannot be derived from the anatomy of the internal conflict alone. Rather, it is necessary to take a broader view and consider the *pólis* – which, in this respect, is missing from Loraux as from other authors who have dealt with this subject.

The modernizing view – one that has long prevailed, despite the critiques and doubts that have been raised – has provided a warped perspective on Greek politics. For it has forced it into an anachronistic mould, reducing it to the linguistic-conceptual web that emerged from the Europe of the seventeenth and eighteenth centuries. As is often the case, the distortions are already inherent in translations, which – as in the case of *stásis* – for want of acceptable equivalents end up collapsing the differences between the Greek terms. While seemingly making these categories more accessible, in practice it obscures them by adding a modern filter.

The most striking case, and perhaps the most serious, is *pólis*. This term is often rendered as 'state' or, almost as a concession, 'city-state'. But the Greek *pólis* was not a state. It never had the strict bonds of Hobbes's Leviathan, nor did it possess any institution that monopolized and exercised the legitimate use of force, as per Max Weber's famous definition.[119] On the contrary, the Greek *pólis* was a non-state community, held together only by political ties, in the absence of a coercive apparatus. On the other hand, nor was it a tribal community, underpinned solely by obligations based on kinship. The path of politics had, in fact, attempted to break those ties in the transition from the *oîkos* to the *pólis*. This is why here we cannot rightly think of the tribal societies studied by anthropologists.[120] In short, the *pólis* was a non-state decentralized community, which was not based on family ties and did not revolve around an *arché*, a recognized sovereign authority. Rather, this community relied on political ties alone. This is what makes the Greek experience unique and what makes the *pólis* today a laboratory for a post-state community.

To understand *stásis* as an event in the *pólis*, and in turn the *pólis*'s reaction to *stásis*, we should thus cast off the lens of state politics, which prevents us from seeing this phenomenon in its dramatic depth. The nervous excitement that must have permeated everything, everywhere, together with the demand for active participation, can be explained in light of the continuous risk that the *pólis* ran: namely, the risk of its own dissolution. Nothing, in fact, could have prevented this. There was no central authority – an authority *super partes*, so to speak – capable of resorting to coercion to prevent conflict. The absence of a standing army, not to mention a sovereign police force, and the inevitable distribution of power across different sides, meant that violence could spread throughout the city.[121] The great fear of *stásis* was also owed to the awareness that there were few means to contain it. What could be the dam holding it back, the ultimate limit? In the tribal community, the last line of defence was still represented by lineage, which allowed a certain stability even despite disputes; the dilemma was between the rule of the cousin and that of the king. But in an an-archic community, where the *arché* had fallen, there was no barrier except that between citizen and citizen; lines of family had now been surpassed. The violence of the *pólis* entered into the private space of the *oîkos*.

Nothing was more feared and nothing was more necessary. This is the dilemma inherent in *stásis*, which must be considered one of the arcana of politics. But this can only be understood from the perspective of the *pólis* community. The bond that held citizens together was political, and it was thus essential to participate and to take a position, though this could also itself be a prelude to sedition. Politics thus contained its own negation. It is easy to understand why even voting in the assembly – the *diaphorá*, or vote, partition, dissent – was considered a potential risk, the first dangerous step towards *stásis*.[122] Moreover, it was precisely the most active citizens, those most inclined to take a clear stance, who were exposed to centrifugal forces. The paradox could not be more obvious: was *stásis* itself a kind of civic duty? In a sense, yes, as demonstrated by the law of Solon:

> And as he saw that the *pólis* was often in a condition of party strife, while some of the citizens through slackness were content to let things slide, he laid down a special law to deal with them, enacting that whoever when civil strife [*stásis*] prevailed did not join forces with either party was to be disfranchised and not to be a member of *pólis* life.[123]

This emergency law merely acknowledged the conflict that had always been at the heart of the city. If it is necessary to prevent the outbreak of *stásis* once it has invaded the *pólis* to the point of endangering the community, taking a position is the only way to reunite the two divided halves. Indeed, the hesitant citizen who opts out is excluded from his rights with *atimía*, i.e. declared politically dead. *Stásis* is almost a privilege that can materialize in the possibility of mobilizing as one of the opposed sides. This law against neutrality does not, therefore, imply any disapproval of *stásis*. Fear of its destructive power does not compromise the political judgement on its necessity. To participate is to keep the city alive.

But what does it mean to take part? Unlike rigid familial relationships, political relationships were dynamic, open, horizontally projected, and thus permeated by uncontrollable conflict. It would be misleading to imagine a 'party' in the modern sense. Rather, we should assume that there was a wide and varied range of groupings extending – to borrow the title of an essay by Gehrke – from friendship to programme, from circles centred on *philía* to alignments that identified with a long-term project.[124] The active circles at the centre of internecine wars must have been organized on the model of the *hetairai* – from *hetaîros*, companion – groups within which differences in wealth could exist but which were held together by political ties. However, the phenomenon of *stásis* cannot be understood without considering the fluid morphology of the city, where the radicalization of the conflict led to the formation of wider circles, capable of drawing in those who had previously remained on the outside. The reverse was also true, in that the factions could just as easily break up, not only as a result of persuasion, but also because family ties prevailed on a more or less temporary basis. In general, however, this barrier to conflict broke down, and it was precisely this that characterized *stásis* as *oikeîos pólemos*, civil war.

Stásis is both a fundamental condition of the *pólis*'s existence, and the abyss underlying it.[125] Hence the impossibility of banishing it or of outlawing it, despite its explosive nature. In this sense (and this is worth emphasizing) from the point of view of the democratic *pólis*, *stásis* is not illegal. Far from it: it represents the path that the city *must* follow in order to survive, a path that, depending on the circumstances, may be more or less creative, more or less destabilizing. One oft-sidestepped issue concerns the end (also in the sense of purpose) of the *stásis*, which is not to be found in the state. More generally, the struggle is not directed towards seizing the *arché*. If anything, it is the tyrant who, through his actions, aims to establish sovereign power, a state centre. And we must assume that the bad reputation that did partly surround *stásis* was owed precisely to the possibility of an archic drift. The danger, therefore, lay in the foundation, and not in an impossible usurpation of power.

What, then, was the *raison d'être* of the *stásis*? The story of Corcyra itself formed the backdrop for a heated debate between those who placed particular emphasis on economic factors and those who stressed political motives. The latter include Gehrke. Referring to numerous accounts of the widespread prosperity of the island at that time, he strongly denied that inequalities could have played a role.[126] At the opposite end of the spectrum are those ready to speak of 'class struggle', the real conflict of interests that must be brought to light.[127] Loraux weighed in on this debate in her article comparing Corcyra and the Paris Commune, in a critique of that shortcut that reduces politics to a screen, a veil, behind which the substantive issues will supposedly emerge. Only 'a decision or a reflex, both very classically Marxist and, if necessary, infinitely orthodox', can lead to the understanding that 'socio-economic reality' is the sole legitimate dimension.[128] In this way, the Greek question of *stásis* is left unaddressed, starting with the term itself. In support of this interpretation, a (proto-)'Marxian Aristotle' is called upon as a witness, pointing to poverty as the cause of *stásis*. However, according to Loraux, this image does not stand up to any thorough rereading of the *Politics*: Book V refers to many and varied sources of conflict.[129] The political factors, however, are considered sufficient to trigger *stásis*. Thus, for example, Aristotle writes that this happens 'when some find themselves participating in the politeía not according to the idea they have formed'.[130] At stake in each instance is not only the order of the *pólis* and the distribution of power, but also the recomposition of citizenship and the limits of the political body. *Stásis* in fact jeopardizes the threshold between inside and outside. This is what Agamben observed, taking up Loraux's reflection, which he credited on two fronts: that of having situated the problem in the relationship between the *oîkos* and the *pólis*, and that of having clearly seen that Greek politics does not definitively overcome the *oîkos* in the *pólis*.[131] Precisely because the city integrates the family within itself, it is always threatened by internal discord. Agamben corrects Loraux, however, and wonders why civil war should be considered 'a secret of the family and of blood, yet not a political mystery'.[132] When discord breaks out, the brother kills his brother like an enemy. Civil war no longer allows us to distinguish between the intimate and the alien, kinship and citizenship. In this respect, for Agamben, *stásis* functions as a state of exception, because the family is included in the order of the *pólis* through its exclusion: 'the house is exceeded in the city and the city is depoliticised in the family'.[133] Proof of this can be found in the events of Corcyra 427, as narrated by Thucydides. Suddenly, in the battle within the *pólis*, a breach opens up, from which slaves and women emerge – that is, the people destined to remain in the *oîkos*. At that juncture, they become decisive, as if they were part of the *pólis*. The presence of slaves who are individually promised freedom should be understood in this sense.[134] But it is the women in particular who bring the *thóribos*, the tumult – which is not just noise and confusion, but the disturbing interference between inside and outside. In the uprising of the people, the most seditious move is that of the women who climb onto the roofs to throw down tiles. This is a metaphor for subversion, for the low becoming high and vice versa. It is a revolt within a revolt, because these unexpected comrades-in-arms, who confront the oligarchs with the improvised weapons of non-combatants – these women to whom the fate of democracy is once again linked – threaten the politics of men and press at the borders of the *pólis*. In their intimate strangeness, and strange intimacy, they bring into play the threshold between inside and outside, allowing the repressed underlying *an-arché* to emerge.

12. The connection between memory and politics has a long history. This link is, however, yet to be fully explored in all its twists and turns, in its decisive yet often underestimated and neglected turning points. Repression of memory clears the city of ghosts; forgetting is foundational.

In this context, it may be useful to read a chapter – perhaps the last or concluding one? – of Athenian democracy, attempting to remove it from monumental history and commemorative narratives. As the textbooks say, post-Periclean Athens entered the crisis of the fourth century BCE. Everything came to a head in the eventful year 403 BCE. The Peloponnesian War in 405 ended with the defeat of Athenian imperialism. To the sound of Spartan flautists, the Great Walls of the *pólis* were destroyed. Internal strife resumed in 404 through the oligarchic violence of the Thirty, i.e. the 'tyrants', as they were called, to exclude them from the city. That bloody oligarchic regime would go down in history as a sort of dictatorship *avant la lettre*. In addition to abolishing the laws of Ephialtes and depriving the people of their power, the Thirty were guilty of extortion and murder. They had persecuted both democrats and their personal enemies with unprecedented cruelty. But the regime collapsed less than a year after the battle in which the exiles prevailed.

The scene in 403 BCE was one of victory: the democratic resistance fighters returned from exile and paraded through the streets of the city, ascending the Acropolis. It would have been a festive sight, had it not been for the fact that each return was much more painful and arduous than expected. The democrats found themselves side by side with yesterday's adversaries. So, what was to be done? How should they act? How could they punish the horrendous crimes committed, and repair the offences done, without rekindling hatred? Any move to right wrongs would be seen as a mere reaction, pure revenge, and would risk reigniting animosity. Athens was a city in recovery, emerging from a long period of conflict that had torn it apart from within. Two transitional governments, the democrats' firm stance, and the intervention of the Spartan king – in 403 and then in 401 – led to an agreement. Reconciliation was proclaimed by means of a decree and an oath. The first decreed: *mè mnesikakeîn*, 'do not remember misfortunes'. The second committed every Athenian citizen not to attack anyone by reproaching them for the past: 'I swear that I will not recall misfortunes':

> I will harbour no grievance [*ou mnesikakés*, literally 'I will not recall misfortunes'] against any citizen, save only the Thirty, the Ten, and the Eleven: and even of them against none who shall consent to render account of his office.[135]

So: have no thoughts about avenging the evils suffered, and do not hold on to the memory of offences done. The verb *mnesikakeîn* combines *mnesi-*, a form derived from the Greek root *mnéme*, memory, and *kaká*, misfortune. It means not only remembering the evil suffered, reactivating resentment in the soul, but also wielding this memory against someone as a weapon of retaliation, an instrument of retribution. It is no coincidence that *mnesikakeîn* is the verb that Plato used to characterize the victorious party, often inclined to reprisals, while in Aristotle – precisely in reference to Athens at that time – it represented the act of bringing a trial for wrongs suffered in the civil war. This meant an act for which the democrats were ultimately responsible.[136]

Once the tyrants were expelled, accused of all the crimes from which Athens needed to be freed, the city decided to forget. A sort of statute of limitations was proclaimed. This was both a form of surveillance of memory, and a preventive erasure. No exceptions were to be made.

One democrat returning from exile who had no intention of forgetting grudges was sentenced to death without trial. He was made into a scapegoat, to provide a warning. Thus, the moderate democrats rebuked and, as a precautionary measure, repressed any advocates of remembrance before they could gain momentum. 'No one ever mentioned the misfortunes again.'[137] While the oligarchs were satisfied with such a policy of forgetting, this was not true of those who had fought for the democracy.

Such was the case of the orator Lysias, a metic aspiring to citizenship, whose words gave vent to resentment and disappointment at the injustice that had gone unpunished. He simply asked for *díke*, a fair trial, on the death of his brother, who had been murdered by one of the Thirty. But the oath of amnesty forbade even any allusion to resentment. Was it not, however, 'shameful' to repudiate all punishment? The city seemed ungrateful to 'those who had risen up for democracy', *stasîantes hupèr tês demokratías*.[138] Lysias's protest was not isolated.

Mè mnesikakeîn is the paradigm of amnesty. It was not the first amnesty in Western history, but the first to become paradigmatic. The decision to forget crimes, but also to institutionally obliterate discord, fixed itself in chronological time. Although the Erinyes, responsible for evoking misfortune, continued to disturb the memory from within, the city sanctioned a democratic reconciliation. The conflict was erased: it was pretended that two opposing sides did not face each other, an altar was erected to *Léthe*, and Oblivion was established in the Acropolis, promoted to the foundation of city life. Loraux writes on this subject: 'As if the memory of the city were founded on the *forgetting of the political as such*.'[139] Once again, it is repressing memories that allows the *pólis* to display a solid political architecture.

The veil of oblivion-by-decree shrouded the murder of Ephialtes, the countless misdeeds, and the wrongs inflicted on the *dêmos* by the oligarchs. It was time for Athenians to rediscover what united them, leaving aside what divided them. And it was precisely the democrats, i.e. the offended party, those who would have had everything to gain by remembering the past, who supported this. A progressive – in the sense of gradual, but we might wonder if it was progressive also in the other sense – oblivion preferred to look ahead. But this could not fail to prompt a backlash and a slip back into the past. The oath sounded like: remember to forget. The need to re-establish continuity through amnesty was a way of thinking about the future in terms of the past, of finding legitimacy in the origin, pretending that, beyond the oligarchic parenthesis, democracy had always existed.[140] Democrats, therefore, were also hardly immune to the archic temptation.

In *Menexenus*, Plato praises the reconciliation of 403 BCE. The relevant passage plays on the ambiguity of the verb *sunémeixan*, referring to the citizens: 'they threw themselves into the fray', arms in hand, brother against brother, 'they mingled', almost rediscovering their old bonds, 'bound themselves together'. The inevitable outcome of war within the family is a family celebration. Even the most violent *stásis* can have a happy ending, provided that *sunghéneia*, kinship by origin, is rediscovered. It is this, for Plato, that guarantees, not in words but in deeds, a solid and fraternal friendship, *homóphulon*, of the same lineage (243e–244a). Thus, in the same text in which Plato distorts democratic isonomy by reducing it to autochthony, Plato seeks in the *arché* of blood and race the kinship-based and familistic bulwark against *stásis*, that is, against the democratic *pólis*.

Aristotle's words are similar in tone when, warning against the risk of stirring up the past, he praises Athenian citizens for being able to adapt to misfortune in the most noble way, such as did not happen in other cities when the democratic faction was victorious. Isocrates had already declared: 'We practice politics well and in the common interest, just as if no misfortune had befallen us.'[141] Through the erasure of conflict, the politics of forgetting prevailed.

Athens would be praised as a model city because of its capacity for reconciliation. In turn, the Athenian *dêmos* would be praised for avoiding further divisions and disputes, marking itself off from other cities as it opted for harmony and stability. The political triumph, as well as the military one, was everywhere confirmed with the refrain: the *dêmos* is *krâton*, the people is triumphant. But by assonance, victory, *níke*, seems to evoke conflict, *neîkos*. And even *krátos*, always accompanied by negative echoes, proves to be a cumbersome word, which refers to the superiority of one side over the other, exposes internal divisions, and reveals the reality of *stásis*. Is amnesty perhaps connected to this? Neutralizing victory means re-establishing continuity, presenting the city as one and indivisible. In order to close the wound, to suture the cut, justice is renounced and trials are not held. The *dêmos* could not give clearer proof of such a step backwards. It was better to relinquish power in order to obtain forgiveness for a victory won by superiority. And even to boast about it. This was, for the moderate Aristotle, the way to 'save democracy', *demokratía sozeîn*.[142] As if exercising power had weakened it. But is it possible to renounce *krátos* and save democracy at the same time? Is this not ultimately a contradiction in terms? We must ask, next, what remains of *demokratía* without *krátos*.

7

ARCHÉ AND *KRÁTOS*: THE TERMS OF POWER

1. Liberalism has shrunk the meaning of the word 'democracy', making it a trite and obvious label, hardened and fixed in place. Democracy has become harder to read, and this has turned the word into an opaque, catch-all term, the formula for a routinized form of representation, the descriptor of a moral institution. If there is an apparent consensus around it, this is echoed by the widespread suspicion that democracy is a power in name only.

From a radical-democratic perspective, it is thus necessary to begin again from the name of power, questioning the etymology of the word *demokratía*. This means examining the semantic latitude of its components, and the problematic interconnection that binds them together. Too often, we imagine that we already know the content of democracy, and thus quickly move on to the next question. But even those who do examine this compound noun more closely generally end up focusing only on the first part, *dêmos*. Thus, *demokratía* is understood to mean the power of the people – and the emphasis and focus is turned to the *subject*.

This has always raised many questions. Indeed, historians, etymologists, and linguists have readily pointed out the dual meaning involved: on the one hand, there is the people as a whole; on the other, the people as a majority, a politicized faction, a party. So, does it mean all or part of the people? This question often serves as the starting point for the observation that the *dêmos* is riven by an internal fault line, which is said to pave the way for its political wrong turns. Such interest in the subject of power often degenerates into a pretext for calling the people itself into the dock – blaming the people for past and future populisms or totalitarianisms. Democracy does not come out well from this reading, either.

Thus, what almost always appears is a *dêmos* without *krátos* – as if it were possible to conceive of democracy while disregarding this second element, which many interpreters prefer to gloss over. In fact, the *dêmos* that has lost any *krátos*, in the multiple senses of the term, is the most meaningful and effective image of present-day democracy.

Such widespread reticence in addressing the question of *krátos* – perhaps akin to that of ancient times – seems all the more striking when we consider that this term indicates democracy's own distinctive form of power. So, we really ought to revisit democracy through the semantic kaleidoscope of *krátos*, exploring its variations over time and its unexpected resources. These cannot be reduced to the negative meaning that has recently cast such defeatist shadows.[1] Shifting attention from the first to the second element does not mean neglecting the *dêmos*, but rather seeing it through the unstable and restless relationship of reciprocity that binds it to *krátos*. Perhaps then it will no longer appear truly as a subject – being neither triumphantly sovereign nor pessimistically subordinate and enslaved.

2. The troubled question of sovereignty is a dividing line in the debate among the various currents of radical thought. On the one hand there are those who – in the manner of Ernesto Laclau, Chantal Mouffe, or Étienne Balibar – hold to the cornerstone of the Rousseauian approach, the sovereign people. On the other hand are those – from Giorgio Agamben to Jacques Rancière – who critique such an approach, on the basis of the violence inherent in the state. Although these different thinkers start from a similar diagnosis of the political landscape, where the decline of classical sovereignty has long been acknowledged, they pursue very different or even diametrically opposed trajectories. If the former seek, through state or supra-state means, to restore and reaffirm the sovereignty of the people, the latter note the dark side of a power made up of walls and exclusions.[2] There would thus seem to be sharp and divisive choice – for, or against, the sovereignty of the people.

A democracy that supports the autonomy of the sovereign people and is based on this principle is again becoming foundationalist – or perhaps never stopped being so. In the beginning, the people establishes itself, it is self-founding, and is thus sovereign and holds power (as if the people ultimately held a sceptre). Against this perspective are those who move in a post-foundationalist vein. They radically question the claim to sovereign power, considering the devastating effects – from the concentration camps of the last century to the more recent necropolitics against migrants – which have been produced even by the most democratic forms. Hence they take their distance from constituent power and instead push for a destitution of power, in the sense that Agamben, for instance, understands this. Following in the wake of Walter Benjamin's text on the 'Critique of Violence', Agamben refers to the power of the multitude to be, and remain, ungovernable.[3]

The destituent power of democracy ends up shaking the people to its core, pushing it to re-evaluate its own supposed sovereignty. In the meantime, it may claim a self-foundation, pretending to have a homogeneous identity, as it commits an act of violence in which it literally discriminates – separating and excluding those who are not part of it. So, the question arises: what is a people? Rancière answers by saying that the 'people' does not exist.[4] For there exist many different criteria and methods of aggregation, starting with the ethnic criteria of land and blood. If elsewhere – in liberal or in republican democracy, but also in the sovereignist currents of radical thought – the people is considered an essential cornerstone, a solid foundation on which state politics is aggregated and constituted, in anarcho-destituent currents it is necessary to deconstruct entities such as 'people' and 'nation' that are substantivized and substantialized. Perhaps no one has done more than Jacques Derrida to pull the rug from underneath nationalistic and identitarian constructs, exposing what they are made of.[5] The denunciation is not directed only at borders, nor even at the reduction of the *dêmos* to the *éthnos*. Rather, it digs down to the violent gesture of sovereign self-assertion.

Here, we must expose the fundamental paradox inherent in every constituent power. Indeed, such a power always remains suspended, for the act of constitution not only establishes an order, but also determines the composition of the people itself. From this, it follows that the people is simultaneously the condition and the result, the subject and object of the constituent process. One may pretend not to see the paradox, flaunting the gesture of foundation and self-foundation. If it is, however, recognized, then there are various ways of addressing the problem. Carl Schmitt did not so much unpick the Gordian knot as cut straight through it. He made an epoch-making decisionist move by casting the nation in its pure homogeneity – a pre-political and pre-legal substance – as the protagonist of constituent violence, in its sovereign will to endow itself with a political form.[6] To clarify, it may be said that what Schmitt presents is not so much an anti-democratic paradigm as an archic pole, the revival and claiming of a foundational *arché*.

Thinkers of modernity from Spinoza to Marx had headed in a completely different direction. Looking beyond the legal and state framework, they saw democracy not as one form of government among others, but as a process in which the constituent power of the people manifests and articulates itself, without ever reaching exhaustion or conclusion. As the order of constitutions is disrupted, the multitude enters the scene. Far removed from the substantial identity of the people, it is riven by permanent discord.[7]

3. The idea that the dominion of the *pólis* could be divided into different forms is already attested in one of Pindar's *Odes*.[8] However, this insight must have been much older, if only because of the possibility of tyranny as a pre-democratic alternative to existing regimes. But the first attestation comes in Herodotus' famous *lógos tripolitikós*. Taken up and adapted by Plato and then by Aristotle, it is most classically formulated in Polybius. The most widespread version, both in monumental history and in political theory, presents the sequence *monarchy–oligarchy–democracy* as a progressive extension of the sphere of power. It moves from one pair of hands, to the few, and then the many. But this extension, however laudable, also brings a degeneration of power, given that to put more people in command is also to ensure greater disagreement. It is no coincidence that Polybius sees therein a degenerative and then evolutionary cycle.[9] But the most important thing is that this sequence, outlined as a chronological succession, also appears in a homogeneous key, differentiated only by the various *bearers* of power. Even those who emphasize the qualitative value of the *dêmos*, which goes beyond the limits of the quantitative series, do not ultimately depart from this reading.

On closer inspection, however, *demokratía* is an unexpected and completely misaligned compound. In a vocabulary that had known no other suffix than *-archía* – starting with *monarchía* – there was a profound change in the way power was understood, and this was bound to influence the subject. This is the sense in which it marks a break. The change is not only because of the assembly of the people, which now becomes the protagonist, but also because the name it takes does not refer to the sovereignty of an archic power. The new term emerges in a sort of an-archy, contrasting with its predecessors. Everyone exercises power; that is, no one – which is why it is called *demo-kratía*. Only a rigid realignment, taking place over the course of centuries, could obscure the rupture that had taken place.

This was noted by certain linguists and philologists – albeit not that many of them – who investigated the etymology of *demokratía*.[10] The most significant article, first published in 1947, was by the linguist Albert Debrunner. In the vocabulary of the *pólis*, the new compound noun must have sounded like an anomaly:

after all, terms used to designate power had for a long time relied on the suffix *-archía*, which served to identify who was in command. Following this series, it may have been reasonable to expect a *demarchía* to come next. So, why did this not happen? Debrunner's answer is twofold: first of all, the compound *dèmarchos* had already been coined to indicate the office of the head of the *demes* of Attica; secondly – and this is the most important reason – given its suffix, the term *demarchía* would have pointed to a situation unimaginable in a democracy. For it would have implied the existence of rulers and ruled.[11]

This thesis has been shared by many, including Meier, who devoted several essays to the topic with a more purely historical approach. He sought to emphasize a division, which turns out to be crucial, between *-archía* and *-kratía*. This serves to outline a triangle of suffixes of power where, between *-archía* and *-kratía*, *-nomía* appears to indicate an important transitional phase.[12] The word *isonomía*, 'the fairest' according to Otanes, was for a time the banner of the struggle for equality, with the effect that the *nómos* would guarantee political equality between those whom nature, *phúsis*, had made different.[13] The demand for *isonomía* thus had a profound political significance. Far from being a call for a merely legal equivalence, it expressed the – in some ways utopian – aspiration that projected the equitable distribution of power onto the *nómos*.[14] Initially, all that was asked for was a greater balance, i.e. involving the assembly in decisions, and openness to the community. When the ideals of isonomy – the antidote to arbitrariness and abuse of power – were contradicted, the word *isokratía* appeared in the constellation of the prefix *isos-*, indicating equality. This should already have been a warning sign. The *dêmos* had aimed at improving its condition in the *pólis*, not at a real overhaul. But as the prospect of equitable distribution began to fade, another way of understanding power made headway. It was more conflictual and openly antagonistic – in a word, democratic.

4. To better frame the terms of power in the *pólis*, we should start from the vacuum of sovereignty that characterized the Greek world in its early days, distinguishing it from other civilizations. The polytheistic horizon is perhaps the most striking proof of this. In Hesiod's *Theogony*, the transmission of power is not only unregulated, but marked by bloody clashes and relentless disputes. Uranus prevents Gaia's children from seeing the light, and she, seeking to avenge them, incites Cronus to castrate his father (*Theogony*, 154–82). In turn, Cronus, who devours his own children, is defeated by the stratagems and violence of Zeus, saved by his mother's

cunning (459–96). Power appears more important than order: Zeus reigns because he was able to subdue his adversaries and, through his victory, gain sovereignty. Aeschylus thus writes in *Prometheus Bound*: 'New gods now rule [*kratoûsi*] on Mount Olympus, and, like a tyrant, Zeus is governing with new-fangled laws, overpowering those gods who were so strong before' (149–51).[15] Chains, yokes, bonds, bits, and whips are the tools of Zeus's sovereignty, maintaining order and justice at his own discretion.[16]

In the face of such divine sovereignty, the submission of mortals can hardly be taken for granted. The concern is, rather, how to thwart and stifle that power, in order to get to grips with one's own fate. Here lies the source of politics. The divine realm does not display unquestioned authority, or any regulated transmission of it. It corresponds to a human realm that is pervaded by sources of conflict, which are reflected in all manner of fields. Discord, dissension, and strife are the markers of a power that proves to be devoid of legitimacy. It is against this backdrop that the *pólis* emerges. Here, the question 'who rules?' soon becomes unavoidable. Which is to say: in whose name, and with what authority? With which *arché*?

The Greek lexicon of sovereignty is varied and includes many terms which, although they often overlap, all have their own specific semantic core and nuances: from *arché* to *krátos*, *kûros*, *exousía*, *dúnamis*, *ischús*, and *bía*. The first two stand out from the others because they became the terms for power in the *pólis*. Relative to these, *kûros*, which indicates decision-making authority, did not establish itself. *Exousía* indicates power, licence, the faculty to do something. The other terms are more connected to physicality and physical strength: *dúnamis* designates power, *ischús* vigour and the capacity for resistance, and *bía* violence.

What needs emphasizing, here, is the close link between power and violence, *krátos* and *bía*.[17] In mythology, *krátos* is an excessive power that asserts itself and becomes overwhelming. It therefore resorts to violence. Thus Zeus, in the indelible image offered by Hesiod, is always accompanied by two characters of Titan origin named Kratos and Bia, Power and Brutal Violence. But the alliance between the two also appears elsewhere, starting with the opening of Aeschylus' *Prometheus Bound*. Such a connection would be unimaginable for *arché*, which imposes itself through its authority. On closer inspection, the underlying contrast that resonates in political vocabulary is the one between *arché* and *krátos*.

5. The uncertainty of its derivation makes it impossible to establish the original meaning of *arché*. The best way to discern its meaning

seems to be that suggested by etymological dictionaries, which refer to the few passages in Homer where the verb *árcho* occurs. The scene depicted is that of a battle where one man, advancing, leads the others. In the *Iliad*, it is said that Ares preceded, *êrche*, the phalanxes.[18] It can thus be summarized in images such as: marching at the head, advancing, being the first. And yet, the first is not destined to remain separate and distant, left isolated in the past. Rather, it is the first step followed by others, the first link in a chain, the first point of a trajectory; from the outset, it presents itself as a determining factor, a foundational beginning.[19] Unsurprisingly, there is a short step from such *beginning* to *commanding*. The military structure encourages this. Who comes first in time, or perhaps space-time, guides, or rather commands, those who follow. This primacy also takes on a political extension,[20] though this is less self-evident.

Arché reflects the two uses of *árchein*: the older one of beginning, initiating, and the later one of commanding. But it actually reinforces their meaning by almost fusing them into a stubborn partnership, an iron coalition: it is the command of the one who begins. The right to command is affirmed in the very act of beginning, and – vice versa – the power to begin is corroborated in the exercise of command. This rigid partnership, sealed in the word *arché*, would last for centuries, as it founded and defined archi-politics. The anarchaeological effort, in its attempt to unsettle and undo the *arché*, is first and foremost a work of distinguishing between principle and command, loosening the link and dissolving the coalition. Yet, from the perspective of the Greek language, the semantic double-sidedness would long be clear. This is demonstrated by the two derived adjectives: *archaîos* for the value of beginning and *archikós* for command, the archaic and the archic.

Arché, unlike *krátos* and other terms of power, is rarely personified. It stands out, anonymous and absolute, in its vertical and indisputable sovereignty.[21] There is no foundational force that grounds it, nor a visible violence that sustains it. Rather, *arché* is itself a source of power, even where it may appear illegitimate. This is why it fits into the vocabulary of sovereignty. It is no coincidence that, as Edmond Lévy has observed, *árchein* is a synonym for *basileúein* and even *turanneúein*. However, three different areas are distinguished: for whereas kingship refers to legitimate power, and tyranny to illegitimate power, *arché* indicates a power that is both effective and recognized. In general, in the Greek imaginary, *arché* belongs to the non-Greek world and comes from there.[22]

So, what should be done with *arché* in the *pólis*? After all, this term – which gives command to those who boast a title from the outset, and threatens to continue in this order – promises to exert such sovereignty over others. It is unsurprising, then, that in political language the opposite of *arché* is *eleuthería*, freedom.[23] It is equally clear that *arché* produces *douleía*, servitude. From this point of view, it is understandable that many interpreters, perhaps also driven by the usual temptation to modernize things, are inclined to conceive *arché* as a political and institutional power. This is emphasized to such an extent that it even shapes the understanding of space: time and again it is claimed that *arché* is the institutionalized pivot, the regulated cornerstone of the *pólis*, whereas the aggressive and insidious *krátos* rages on the outside, between the cities. But starting from such an understanding, it would be hard to imagine how democracy can be admitted in the city. Unless, that is, we resort to the usual taming of democracy or reach for help from Aristotle's *arché politiké* – that is, the device which forbids the power of the people by recentring the city on its archic bulwark.

The terms of power in the *pólis* ought to be conceived the other way around. As Arendt insightfully grasped, the *arché* is an apolitical domain and, as such, falls outside the *pólis*, or rather, constitutes its limit. It is in fact freedom from the *arché*, anarchic *eleuthería*, that opens up the relationships that characterize the political sphere, no longer debased by subordination.

On the other hand, a prudent reticence towards *arché* emerges not only due to abuses and tyrannical tendencies, but also because of the way in which public offices are administered. When the *arché* must, despite everything, make its entrance into the *pólis*, it abandons the rigid verticality of archic power, to be assumed simply as an office. Moreover, it is pluralized in the *archaí*. Within the geometry of the city, each office visually indicates a position. As such, the *arché*, as an office, cannot belong to anyone, because it is always and only a temporarily exercised power. The *árchon* is, in the final analysis, only a substantivized participle.[24] But the democratic treatment of *arché*, divided and distributed among the *archaí*, does not end there. The *árchon* is at the same time *archómenos*: he commands, insofar as he is always already commanded.

The motto 'neither to rule nor to be ruled', *oúte árchein oúte árchesthai*, is the banner and emblem of democracy. These words recur constantly, as if they condensed the key moment of that anarchic destitution of power which has for too long been neglected or passed over in silence.

Yet, this does not escape its detractors – Plato in the lead. He mocks it, without being able to conceal his irritation at this subversion that has so ruinously undermined the *arché*. Anarchy has burst into the city without even an open conflict, but only through a repeated exchange, a constant role reversal that revokes the *arché*. It is now a city of *árchontas archómenoi*, commanders commanded and the commanded in command. Is this just a play on words, a joke, a farce? Far from it. This is how *anarchía* has emerged, and having taken root it 'must penetrate into private homes', *eís te tàs idías oikías*.[25] The warning could not be more serious.

On the opposite side, Herodotus raised the banner of anarchy, staging – in a political vacuum – a discussion of possible forms of government. In it, he has Otanes say the most radical words: *oúte gar árchein oúte árchesthai*, 'neither … to rule nor to be ruled' (III, 83, 8). Even when he renounces power, this withdrawal should not be misunderstood as a retreat into the private *oîkos*. It is, rather, an anarchic exception to the non-politics of the *arché*, to archi-politics.

To take on an *arché* in the *pólis* means to replace someone else, in a role that remains temporary. For an office is nothing more than a temporary exercise of power, or rather, an unavoidable service. It is not enough to divide the *arché* into the plural *archaí*; there must also be succession, a rotation. If the exercise of office cannot be avoided, what neutralizes command is rotation. This circulation of offices, which defines the geometry of the democratic city, interrupts and precludes the trajectory of archic linearity. But while rotation is surely necessary, it does not suffice to forestall the risk of power becoming concentrated in the hands of those who always come forward. There is still the danger that it will become the prerogative of those who imagine they have some superior right of command. This is where sortition comes in, from above. In its vertical fall, it immobilizes every centre of power, undermines every fulcrum from the bottom up, and ensures that everything is emptied out. This sweeps aside any desire for appropriation and foils all such designs.

So, here the rotation of offices is combined with sortition. This is the seventh qualification for authority that contradicts the previous ones, while also revoking its own claim. It is the title of command for those who are not entitled to it. This combination helps to shed light on the commanded commanders and the commanded in command – the subjects who characterize power in the democratic *pólis*. We should recall Aristotle's critical description: 'to govern and be governed in turns', *tò en mérei árchesthai kaí árchein* (*Pol.*, 1327b 3–4). The preference for neither – to prefer being 'under no *arché*' – translates into both. Through the reversibility of roles, no one governs, because all govern. These are the two inseparable faces of the citizen who governs because he is always already governed. On the one hand, there is no first, and no primacy; on the other, *árchesthai* is not 'simply passive'.[26] Merely obedient passivity takes place only outside the *pólis*, in the sphere of the *oîkos*, where the patriarch issues orders and others execute them. The *árchesthai* does not apply to these latter. To be governed is, in fact, to have a part in governing, sharing it thanks to the coincidence of roles.

This is why Aristotle uses the verb *metéchein* when he refers to the characteristics of the citizen. This does not consist in privileges or rights, as they are understood today, but rather in the fact of alternating in office.[27] It is not a question of participating in the sense of taking part, or taking *a part*, but of sharing. One cannot occupy – *katéchein* – an office, nor possess it, nor even hold it; one can only and always share it, divided with others. The expression *metéchein árches*, to share an office, occurs numerous times.[28] The synonym, which is not infrequently used, is in fact *koinoneîn*. An *arché* is admissible in the *pólis* only insofar as it is shared.

6. So what is the meaning of *krátos*, a term which is both so biting and so semantically elusive? The various interpretations that have built up over time generally all stem from Homer.[29] This is not surprising given that, as Simone Weil wrote, 'The true hero, the true subject, the center of the *Iliad*, is force.'[30] But is it only physical force, the kind that subjugates and perhaps kills, in the face of which the body beats a retreat? This seems rather doubtful.

One answer comes from Émile Benveniste, who in his *Dictionary of Indo-European Concepts and Society* devoted a detailed analysis to the complex semantics of *krátos*, in the context of themes relating to royalty.[31] The anthology of passages, taken in particular from the *Iliad*, shows that *krátos* is the ability to win in a trial of strength. In this sense, it 'indicates the superiority of a man, whether he manifests his strength over those of his own camp or the enemy'.[32] Granted by the gods, *krátos* is never solely individual: 'Zeus may confer krátos on one of the two armies engaged. In this case the beneficiary of this superiority is a people, not an individual.'[33] However, this involves not only scenarios of hand-to-hand combat, but also that of the political assembly. It is by speaking, by addressing one's fellow citizens, that one can not just win over others, but win them over through force of persuasion – as most importantly attested by the *Odyssey* (I, 70; XI, 353; XXI, 353). This investigation thus brings to light two meanings of *krátos*. On the one hand, it means superiority or pre-eminence in a test of strength or skill, from which one thus gains an advantage and triumphs. On the other, it means gaining or exercising power. But in the lexical context surrounding *krátos* – a context that is far from homogeneous – Benveniste observes a surprising aspect when the noun is replaced by the adjective *kraterós*. The meanings vary and, indeed, turn out to be opposites: praise and blame, applause and reproach. Thus, for example,

Hecuba addresses Achilles, who has just killed her son Hector, calling him *anèr kraterós*, a 'hard-hearted' man (*Iliad*, XIV, 212).[34] Those who have prevailed can be glorified and praised, but they can also appear cruel and deplorable. From here, it is a short step to the adjective *kratús*, 'hard', and the verb *kratúnein*, 'to harden'. Homer uses it to describe the manoeuvre of the phalanxes as they move in 'a dark mass to battle … horrid with shield and spear' (*Iliad*, IV, 282).

But Benveniste's investigation leaves more than one question unanswered, perhaps because *krátos* is not examined in comparison with *arché*, as would have been desirable. A valuable suggestion comes from the German Hellenist Johann H. H. Schmidt, who in his work *Synonymik der griechischen Sprache*, published in 1879, provides a specific linguistic comparison. While he renders *arché* with the German *Herrschaft*, sovereignty, for *krátos* he proposes *Obmacht*, a very rare term composed of *Macht*, power, and the prefix *ob-*, which indicates superiority. Schmidt thus invites us to look beyond force as such and examine the more peculiarly political value of a power that disrupts the state of calm, breaks the balance, and tips the scales in its own favour.[35] Perhaps better than any other, this German term *Obmacht* translates *krátos* into the political sphere, where it is power that imposes itself and wins, yet still hangs in the balance due to the lack of sovereignty and the constant search for further legitimacy.

Despite the semantic convergence between *árchein* and *krateîn* – or rather, that interpretation which casts them as similar, as if they both boiled down to the exercise of power – they should be considered quite distinct. This becomes clear at many points.[36] The decisive difference lies in this: *árchein* refers to those who command from the beginning, or even to those who command in the meantime, inasmuch as they have been there from the beginning. *Krateîn* is something else: it means to dominate, to conquer, to take possession, and implies those who have gained the upper hand, who have prevailed. In the case of *árchein*, a position of power is always already occupied; it therefore enjoys authority and has the mark of sovereignty. In the case of *krateîn*, one advances towards a power that is not founded, established, that has no official ratification, a power that is attained only through disruptive force. Arising from a contest, it remains a contested power, revealing itself to be a pre-dominance; it is relative and relational. Since it does not exist from the beginning, it comes later and has a history. It tells this history in order to justify itself. It is temporal and temporary, precarious, and possible to revoke. From *krátos*, there always transpires the conflictual gesture from which it arises – hence why it may appear aggressive, almost violent. It represents a victory that is as exciting as it is temporary and uncertain; its power is inevitably wavering and unstable, constantly being put to the test.

It is thus unsurprising that, depending on the perspective, *krátos* may have a derogatory and even denigrating meaning, or else a positive and laudatory one. Ober's proposal, to read *krátos* as a 'collective capacity to do things in the public realm',[37] fits into this interpretative framework. If this apt intuition, which in some ways echoes Arendt, might be further developed, it also bears the risk of blunting the hard edges of the contest and defusing the charge of conflict. It is no coincidence that Ober questions the sense of supremacy. But *krátos*, as many examples show, means to prevail, to have the upper hand. In the case of *demokratía*, it is a predominance that cannot hide the disruptive force from which it sprang. At the heart of victory there is always conflict. It may therefore be understood why – contrary to all expectations and against all common sense – the people is not sovereign.

7. *Demokratía* is habitually translated as 'power of the people', alluding to the political form that establishes its sovereignty. But the *dêmos* is not fixed in an *arché*, and nor does its action fall within the order of *árchein*. The suffix *-kratía*, which should be taken literally, refers to power that bursts forth, to the point of overwhelming even itself. It does not indicate, as in the case of *-archía*, a power established in a principle and based on a foundation. It is already clear, here, that in democracy the 'power of the people' is nothing more than its potential force, which transcends itself by becoming unbound from itself. While the archic logic of sovereign foundation keeps the people at bay, the democratic *krateîn* blocks the way to *archía*, undermining and invalidating it. Here emerges its own open, unfinished nature. It is neither end nor beginning, neither above nor below. Hence the convergence with anarchy. To explore the word *demo-kratía*, to bring to light the hyphen linking the two elements, is a necessary move in radically rethinking their inter-relation, their insurmountable underlying tension. Here, while the *dêmos* assumes the *krátos*, the *krátos* in turn incessantly alters and remoulds the *dêmos*. This is how the repressed anarchic element of democracy is able to re-emerge. Yet, having surfaced only sporadically, this repressed element has not left a lasting mark on the vision of democracy.[38] It is as if on the side of anarchy there had been only the travails of destitution, and on the side of democracy only the concern for the people and its power.

But to understand this, it is necessary to proceed in reverse. In fact, we almost always start from the *dêmos*, the people that has (or does not have) power. This means moving from the subject to the object, as if swallowing an instrumental conception of power that neutralizes it, extinguishes its resources, and defuses its potential. Above all, this dampens the element of conflict. Yet this risks obscuring why the people finds it difficult to admit its victory, to assume its supremacy, to shoulder the power that it has acquired. Behind the Athenian democrats' reticence towards the word 'democracy' there lay – as we have seen – a political unease destined to recur throughout history.

If *krátos* appears to be such a cumbersome word, this is because it signals division within the city, where one part has prevailed over the other. *Krátos* reveals a previous *stásis*. It reveals that the democratic city is, as such, in a state of *stásis*.[39] It reveals the conflict inherent in democracy. To start from *krátos* and then move backwards towards *dêmos* is to start precisely from the division that has always moulded the city. This is what Loraux made clear, albeit by emphasizing internal conflict while leaving the problem of *krátos* and its implications for democracy in the background. The division of the city is never reified and thus cannot be reduced to a separation. While *krátos* must be considered against the backdrop of the *stásis* from which it originates and to which it refers, *stásis* must in turn be seen in the light of *krátos*. In this dynamic, division must always be understood as a conflictual relationship. Among the opposing forces, none ever finally prevails; none has the last word. And we should remember that *krátos* is not domination, but rather a relative and temporary pre-domination.

One side gains the upper hand, as among sailors who find themselves enjoying some advantage when the currents and winds are working in their favour. The wave carrying the majority rises and prevails, breaking the previous balance without in any way creating a new stability. From here stem the accusations against democracy, as to its inconsistency, evanescence, and elusiveness. *Krátos* is an event that occurs, is produced, and reverberates on the *dêmos*; this latter does not therefore control it or have it at its disposal. Hence it would be wrong to think of a subject – the people – as *having* power in the same way that one *has* an object. The instrumental view of *krátos* not only fails to grasp its disruptive power, but also overlooks its repercussions on the *dêmos*, which it in turn destabilizes. It must be supposed that with each wave, the people will reconstitute itself. Democratic power – the capacity to exercise influence through choice, the prevalence of one side – does not maintain the cohesion and compactness of the *dêmos*. It necessarily remains divided.

8. Even today, the difficulty inherent in the concept of 'the people' is that its use can unite and bring together as much as it can separate

and exclude. If the current political vocabulary is almost entirely derived from Latin – just think of terms like multitude, people, or nation – then suggestions, ideas, and concerns may also be drawn from Greek, which is less absent than it may seem.

In a masterful article on the historical semantics of *dêmos*, Pierre Lévêque traced its origin to the root **da-*, meaning division or distribution.[40] Since the language of Homer's day, the word has had a dual meaning, referring both to a part of a territory and to those who inhabit it.[41] But the turning point came when the democratic revolution took *dêmos* out of everyday language and elevated it to a criterion for both the division and the unification of the *pólis*. Thanks to the measures taken by Cleisthenes, other groups based on the principles of *genos* and aristocracy were thus ousted. In this unprecedented redistribution, the *deme* inaugurated the political bond between citizens, who as *demoti* were no longer called by their father's name but by that of the *deme*.

A new protagonist in Greek political life, the *dêmos* prevails over rival terms, starting with *lâos*, which designates a group of individuals, often warriors, bound by a chief and subject to his command.[42] Benveniste specifies: '*lâos* is the name of the people insofar as they are capable of bearing arms.'[43] The *Iliad* brings to light the antagonistic trait of the *dêmos*: a community without leaders, which is formed in opposition to kings, the *basileîs*. This contrast would re-emerge in a more acute form as an opposition between the people and the aristocrats. Therefore, we also encounter the expressions *oi polloí*, the many, or even *plêthos*, the majority which may be seen as a multitude. On the other hand, *óchlos* has a derogatory meaning, designating the indistinct crowd, the turbulent rabble, the dehumanized dregs, dominated only by instincts. But there is no use in saying that a political battle destined to last for so many centuries is already fought out in the names chosen. The scandal over the majority that votes – and, through voting, makes its own decisions, asserts itself and prevails – has its echoes even in contemporary debate. Is this not itself the violent trait of democracy? The majority that prevails over the minority, ending up crushing it? The *plêthos* that has the power to decide? The disapproval on this score has been passed down through the monumental history, which revives and hardens this critique. From the critics of that distant past to today's liberals, there is a chorus of protests against the power of the majority. Alcibiades' accusation stands out. In a dialogue with Pericles, he does not mince his words as he accuses that majority power of being violent and coercive. He refers to a *krátos*. The multitude takes advantage of being stronger than the rich and prescribes the law.[44] Is democracy not, then, anti-democratic, since it could turn out to be the power of the many over the few? This is an unacceptable oppression, especially as the 'many' in question are, in fact, the poor, the ignorant, lacking in intelligence and full of *húbris*, brazen and impossible to tame.

But the harshest criticism – needless to say – comes from the Anonymous Athenian, the Old Oligarch. In his pamphlet, he repeats the accusation that democracy is the rule of the incompetent mob. He adds – and this is the novel element – that the politics of the people responds to its own interests, not those of the community. In short, the incompetent are at least consistent; the *dêmos* knows what it is doing. This leads to the idea that democracy is a regime that favours the poor. And the contrast between the people and the nobles could not be more acute. Employing a skilful stylistic device that runs through the pages of the pamphlet, the Anonymous Athenian moves from the *dêmos* to the masses, the *plêthos*, and then to the *óchlos*, the crowd, to arrive at the poor, the scoundrels, the good-for-nothings, the reckless. This would be the worst part of the city, opposed by the nobles, the rich, and the honest. And such a situation is due to power over the sea and the power of the sea. Behind democracy lies thalassocracy.[45] The thesis is this: since it is 'the people who man the ships', and Athens derives its power from the sea, Athens is necessarily a democracy (1, 2).[46] Once again, sailors – rowers, helmsmen, riggers, etc. – the people of anarchy, are called into question.

The image of a divided city remains. Above all, there remains discord, in the way of understanding the *dêmos* and the power that it exercises through voting. But it is the victory itself that is so disturbing. For the partisans of democracy, it goes without saying that the choice of the majority – of those who can amass the most votes – is, in each case, the decision taken in the name of the city assembly. For its detractors, however, this is nothing more than a way of imposing the will of the majority on the minority. The dispute over the *dêmos* is linked to the even more bitter dispute over *demokratía*, a polemical term brandished as an insult and used as a stigma. On the other hand, *dêmos* in the political context means not only the people as the citizens of a *pólis*, spatially understood as a gathered assembly, but also democracy itself. As we have seen, the expression *kataleuîn dêmon* means both to dissolve the people, to destroy it, and to ruin or overthrow democracy.

Among today's interpreters there is now, justifiably, a widespread suspicion of the reading that has long dominated the tradition. This latter served to promote and fix in place a discrediting conception of democracy. A cornerstone of this reading is Aristotle's reduction of the *dêmos* to a part of the citizens, the majority consisting of the poor, the lower class, the masses opposed to the elite.[47] Aristotle is certainly right to suggest that with democracy the poor exercise power – but only in the sense that they are the vast majority of the *pólis*. However, it cannot be deduced from this that the *dêmos* is to be understood as a class, in the economic sense.[48] From the viewpoint of democracy and its history, the *dêmos* is a political criterion, indeed *the* criterion that brings politics into being. Therefore, we can say with Rancière that the *dêmos* is the poor, not as an economically disadvantaged group, but rather as those who do not 'count', having no title or qualification to be counted.[49] The *dêmos* are those who do not belong to the order of the *arché*.

The division of the *demes* – the redistribution introduced by Cleisthenes – was a revolutionary gesture already long before the modern beheading of the king. The guillotine breaks the unity of the 'king's two bodies': indeed, in cleanly separating them, and deposing the unifying power of sovereignty, it causes an unprecedented dismemberment. Henceforth, individuals can no longer recognize themselves in the body of the kingdom to which they had previously belonged.[50] But this disidentification did not require the sacrifice of the sovereign body. It is the people, not the king, that has two bodies. In this lies the very possibility of politics.

The *dêmos* is constituted *against* the beginning and *against* command, breaking the *arché*. The new distribution of the *demes* in Athens broke the principle of birth, and so too its heir, the principle of wealth. The contingent place of birth is transformed into a place where the contingency of dwelling destitutes paternal power. The foundational principle of place, the dominion of autochthony, is scattered. The *dêmos* is not *éthnos*: it is not based on ties of blood and soil. The people always exists in the unfounded place of politics. As such, it has no pre-existing identity, but is constantly recomposing itself, dividing and redefining itself. The *dêmos* is a division of the beginning, but also a division of command. It is the political partition of those without a part, of those who have no title to command, who do not belong to the order of any *arché*. The power of the people resides in this subversion.

9. Democracy is traditionally imagined to originate from a supposed founding centre, an *arché* from which the *pólis* radiates. This architectural image is merely an optical projection – and through the course of time also a mythical one – of the ways in which political theory, following in the wake of monumental history, has understood democracy. Such interpretations have taken democracy for one form of regime among others, another more or less successful system of government. Assumed as a timeless archetype, situated

within a tripartite hierarchy, democracy is thought to be distinguished by its particular distribution of power and, resulting from this, a greater difficulty in governing. Such a view imagines democracy as a quantitative multiplication of command which risks diluting and muddying it, exploding the boundary between outside and inside. When democracy is judged by the yardstick of stability and evaluated in view of some transcendental end – the common good in which all discord is meant to dissolve – it is forcibly reduced to an archic model. Yet, in the background, its element of disorder remains inescapable. The indeterminacy inherent in democracy, its dissolution of all fixed bearings, raises fears that it will descend into confusion and chaos. Since ancient times, this accusation has been repeated in different forms and terms, reviving a litany of suspicion, mistrust, and discredit. Democracy is a hazardous adventure full of unexpected happenings. The spectre of anarchy, highlighted by Plato and Aristotle, peers out also in the contemporary landscape, in the complaints about democracy's inefficiency and delays, where rules and regulations are suggested to improve governance, and where authoritarian solutions are openly discussed.

But in our efforts to get to the root of the question, we have seen something else. In the *radicalism* of democracy – in what from an archic standpoint appears to be nothing more than threatening disorder and disturbing chaos – resides the *an-arché* that leaves a fundamental mark on democracy. Precisely because democracy is unfounded from its very inception, it can only survive thanks to the political bond that is inaugurated through this *an-arché*. When we conceive disorder, magma, emptiness, groundlessness in these terms, this allows us first of all to conceive an an-archic politics, dismantling the metaphysical fulcrum on which classical anarchism rests. It also allows us to interpret the current context according to coordinates that have not yet been experimented with. It may well be that the threat hanging over us is not the spectre of anarchy, but rather the nightmare of the *arché*.

Here, we are proposing that politics may be considered in the tension between an archic and an opposite anarchic pole, between which there emerges a broad continuum. There can, in fact, be a more and a less. Democracy can maintain itself, with all its difficulties, in its structural anarchy. Or, it can be pushed towards an *arché* which – while supposed to uphold it – in fact closes democracy down, walls it in and fences it off. What has often been called the archic device pushes in this direction: it delegitimizes and depletes the force of *krátos*, reducing it to the power of *arché* – the command of the beginning and the beginning of command. As now hardly needs pointing out, this also serves to oust politics itself.

In discussions of totalitarianism, with its connection to total power and the totalizing dimension, we risk failing to bring to light the question of the foundation. It would perhaps, then, be more appropriate to consider the tension between the two poles just mentioned, and to examine this archic device. Totalitarianism has become a limit-label, a prohibition sign, a perennial warning; it is now the name of a bogeyman of the past, of a crazed digression in European history. Not by accident, it has given way to terms such as authoritarianism, despotism, and autocracy, all ultimately used in a generic anti-democratic sense. But the threat has not disappeared and the risk remains inherent in democracy. This, however, is hardly apparent if we think of this threat in terms of a random deviation or a coup pulled off by some usurper. Perhaps no one has emphasized this point better than Claude Lefort: 'Totalitarianism can only be explained, in my view, by understanding its relationship with democracy.'[51] In other words, totalitarianism appears in history at the same time as democracy and constitutes its internal danger. It is thus an attempt to occupy the place of power that must instead remain empty. Lefort identifies the distinctive feature of democracy in a now famous phrase: 'the place of power becomes an empty place'.[52] However effective, the image of emptiness, accompanied by that of indeterminacy, still leaves room for the idea of an almost inevitable drift, or of an external force that overwhelms it.

It is quite another thing to look at democracy in the tension between the archic and anarchic poles. This is a path that Abensour partly headed along in examining the strange attraction of totalitarian regimes to architecture, 'as if totalitarianism had found therein the ideal terrain for its own proper element, the *arché*'.[53] Instead of allowing cohabitation in a differentiated space, architecture establishes a compact space that has nothing either public or political about it. However, the archic device, as understood here, goes beyond a static *arché* and becomes a key to understanding the contemporary scenario.

10. We may observe two trends in politics today: an archaic trend, which revives the identity of the beginning; and an archic trend, which reaffirms the identity of command. While the one may present itself as the negation of the other, most often they converge. These two powers of the *arché*, which are apparently alternative but ultimately complementary, are the two faces of the present moment that reveal the crisis of democracy and the absence of politics. There can be politics where democracy interrupts and separates the *arché*. We have seen that democracy involves a double interruption. In addition to breaking the circle of a beginning that commands and a

command that begins, it also interrupts the *arché* in both its senses. It abrogates the birth that orders and disposes: that is, natural authority, the line of filiation, the transmission of one's property and properties, the bonds of blood and soil, the right of inheritance, the code of autochthony – in short, the archaic form of community. But it also interrupts *arché* understood as the power of beginning that is legitimized today in state command.

Today's depoliticization should be seen not only as a matter of the familial *oîkos* and the economy prevailing within the *pólis*. For it also expresses a reduction of *krátos* to the *arché*. This leads to the political impotence of the people, which no longer has the ability to intervene. To find it would mean the people undoing the established roles and even dividing itself, thanks to its potential for conflict.

Notes

1 Democracy in Radical Thought

1 For an overview, see D. Comtesse, O. Flügel-Martinsen, F. Martinsen, and M. Nonhoff (eds.), *Radikale Demokratietheorie. Ein Handbuch*, Frankfurt: Suhrkamp, 2019.
2 Karl Marx, 'Contribution to the Critique of Hegel's Philosophy of Law', in *Marx-Engels Collected Works* (henceforth *MECW*), Vol. 3, London: Lawrence & Wishart, 1975, p. 182.
3 Karl Marx, 'Zur Kritik der Hegelschen Rechtsphilosophie. Einleitung', in *Werke – Artikel – Entwürfe. März 1843 bis August 1844*, in *Marx-Engels-Gesamtausgabe (MEGA)*, Vol. I/2, Berlin-Brandeburgische Akademie der Wissenschaften, Berlin: De Gruyter, 2009, p. 172.
4 This did happen in certain strands of orthodox Marxism, which misrepresented Marx's critical project, reducing it to an essentialist anthropology and philosophy of history.
5 Karl Marx and Friedrich Engels, 'The Manifesto of the Communist Party', in *MECW*, Vol. 6, 1976, p. 488.
6 Karl Marx, 'The Eighteenth Brumaire of Louis Bonaparte', in *MECW*, Vol. 11, 1979, p. 103.
7 Dante Alighieri, *Convivio*, Book IV, Chapter 4, Lansing translation.
8 Editions in other languages aptly chose the subtitle as a title, but the Italian one maintained the original order. Ernesto Laclau and Chantal Mouffe, *Hegemony and Socialist Strategy: Towards a Radical Democratic Politics*, London: Verso, 1985.
9 Ibid., pp. 152ff.
10 Jacques Derrida, *Rogues: Two Essays on Reason*, translated by Pascale-Anne Brault and Michael Naas, Stanford, CA: Stanford University Press, 2005, pp. 78ff.
11 The expression 'negative democracy' was coined by Pierre Rosanvallon, *La Contre-Démocratie. La politique à l'âge de la défiance*, Paris: Seuil, 2006, p. 20.

12 Claude Lefort, 'Relecture' (1988), in Edgar Morin, Claude Lefort, and Cornelius Castoriadis, *Mai 68. La Brèche, suivi de Vingt ans après*, Paris: Fayard, 2008, p. 275.
13 Miguel Abensour, *Democracy Against the State: Marx and the Machiavellian Movement*, translated by Max Blechman, Cambridge: Polity, 2011, pp. xxiii ff.
14 Ibid., pp. xl–xli.
15 Jacques Rancière, *Dis-agreement: Politics and Philosophy*, translated by Julie Rose, Minneapolis: University of Minnesota Press, 1999.
16 Jacques Rancière, 'Ten Theses on Politics', *Theory & Event* 5:3, 2001.
17 Jacques Rancière, *Hatred of Democracy*, translated by Steve Corcoran, London: Verso, 2014, p. 58.
18 Jean-Luc Nancy, *The Truth of Democracy*, translated by Pascale-Anne Brault and Michael Naas, New York: Fordham University Press, 2010, p. 31.
19 Miguel Abensour, '"Savage Democracy" and "Principle of Anarchy"', *Philosophy & Social Criticism* 28:6, 2002, pp. 703–26, reproduced as an appendix in *Democracy Against the State*.
20 Ibid.
21 Reiner Schürmann, *Heidegger on Being and Acting: From Principles to Anarchy*, Indianapolis: Indiana University Press, 1990. See also his 'Political Thinking in Heidegger', in *Social Research* 45:1, 1978, pp. 191–221.
22 Schürmann, *Heidegger on Being and Acting*, p. 6.
23 Abensour returned to the theme of anarchy and anarchism in another essay: Miguel Abensour, 'L'anarchie entre métapolitique et politique', *Les Cahiers philosophiques de Strasbourg* 14, 2002, pp. 109–31. However, democracy does not appear in this text.
24 Abensour, '"Savage Democracy" and "Principle of Anarchy"', in *Democracy Against the State*, p. 121.
25 Oliver Marchart, *Die politische Differenz. Zum Denken des Politischen bei Nancy, Lefort, Badiou, Laclau und Agamben*, Frankfurt: Suhrkamp, 2010, pp. 8, 11ff., 59ff.
26 German has the single term *Fundamentalismus*, and thus it is not possible to disambiguate these meanings.
27 TN: *rimosso*, repressed in the psychoanalytic sense.
28 Marchart, *Die politische Differenz*, p. 16.
29 Ibid., p. 67.
30 Martin Heidegger, *Vom Wesen des Grundes*, Frankfurt: Vittorio Klostermann, 1949; *Contributions to Philosophy (Of the Event)*, Bloomington: Indiana University Press, 2012, pp. 231ff.
31 Herbert Marcuse, *One-Dimensional Man*, London: Routledge, 2002; Paul Piccone et al., 'Marcuse's Heideggerian Marxism', *Telos* 6, 1970, pp. 36–46; Richard Wolin, 'Herbert Marcuse: From Existential Marxism to Left Heideggerianism', in *Heidegger's Children: Hannah Arendt, Karl Löwith, Hans Jonas, and Herbert Marcuse*, Princeton, NJ: Princeton University Press, 2001, pp. 135–72. Wolin, however, uses the expression in a pejorative sense.
32 See Daniel Janicaud, *Heidegger en France*, 2 vols, Paris: Albin Michel, 2001, Vol. I, pp. 291–300.

33 Marchart, *Die politische Differenz*, pp. 14ff.
34 Ibid., p. 362.
35 Nancy relates the history of the Centre with an autobiographical touch in his dialogue with Peter Engelmann. See Jean-Luc Nancy, *Demokratie und Gemeinschaft. Im Gespräch mit Peter Engelmann*, Vienna: Passagen, 2015, pp. 54ff.
36 See Philippe Lacoue-Labarthe and Jean-Luc Nancy (eds.), *Le Retrait du politique*, Paris: Galilée, 1983, pp. 183–99.
37 See Philippe Lacoue-Labarthe and Jean-Luc Nancy, *Retreating the Political*, edited by Simon Parks, London: Routledge, 1997, pp. 112ff.
38 In the difference between politics and the political Marchart saw a renewed proposal of Heidegger's ontological difference between entity and Being. See Marchart, *Die politische Differenz*, pp. 32ff.
39 Claude Lefort, 'The Question of Democracy', in *Democracy and Political Theory*, translated by David Macey, Minneapolis: University of Minnesota Press, 1988, p. 10.
40 Ibid., p. 11.
41 In Pierre Rosanvallon, *Democracy Past and Future*, edited by Samuel Moyn, New York: Columbia University Press, 2006, p. 36.
42 See Jacques Derrida, *The Politics of Friendship*, translated by George Collins, London: Verso, 2005.
43 Lacoue-Labarthe and Nancy, *Retreating the Political*, p. 125.
44 Rancière, *Dis-agreement*, p. 65.

2 Anarchaeology: A Philosophical Excavation

1 The aphorism is attributed to Bernard of Chartres, quoted by John of Salisbury in the *Metalogicon* (III, 4).
2 Friedrich Nietzsche, 'On the Utility and Liability of History for Life', in *Unfashionable Observations*, translated by Richard T. Gray, Stanford, CA: Stanford University Press, 1995, p. 99.
3 Ibid., p. 100.
4 Moses I. Finley, *Democracy Ancient and Modern*, London: Hogarth, 1985, pp. 13–14.
5 Paul Veyne, 'Did the Greeks Invent Democracy?', *Diogenes* 31:124, 1983, pp. 1–32.
6 The expression 'Greek miracle' appears in a text by Renan from 1876. See Ernest Renan, 'Prière sur l'Acropole', in *Œuvres complètes*, edited by Henriette Psichari, Paris: Calmann-Lévy, 1947–61, Vol. II, pp. 50–1.
7 See John Bloxham, *Ancient Greece and American Conservatism: Classical Influences on the Modern Right*, London: I. B. Tauris, 2018, in particular pp. 224.
8 Johann Joachim Winckelmann, *History of the Art of Antiquity*, Boston: J. R. Osgood, 1880. On Hegel, see Jacques Taminiaux, *La Nostalgie de la Grèce à l'aube de l'Idéalisme allemand. Kant et les Grecs dans l'itinéraire de Schiller, de Hölderlin et de Hegel*, The Hague: Nijhoff, 1967; Dominique Janicaud, *Hegel et le destin de la Grèce*, Paris: Vrin, 1975, and especially pp. 27–48 on 'La constitution de l'idéal de la belle totalité'.

9 See how this theme was taken up in Leo Strauss, *Natural Right and History*, Chicago: University of Chicago Press, 1953.
10 Cornelius Castoriadis, *Ce qui fait la Grèce 1. D'Homère à Héraclite, Séminaires 1982–1983 (La création humaine II)*, edited by Enrique Escobar, Myrto Gondicas, and Pascal Vernay, preface by Pierre Vidal-Naquet, Paris: Seuil, 2004, p. 62.
11 See Pierre Vidal-Naquet, 'L'Iliade sans travesti', in Homer, *Iliade*, Paris: Gallimard, 1975, pp. 5–32.
12 See Diodorus Siculus V, 9. See, on this point, Robert J. Buck, 'Communalism in the Lipari Islands (Diod. 5. 9. 4)', in *Classical Philology* 54:1, 1959, pp. 33–9.
13 See Tyrtaeus, fr. 6 Diehl; Terpander fr. 6 Diehl. See William George Forrest, *History of Sparta*, New York: W. W. Norton, 1968.
14 See Plutarch, *Life of Lycurgus*, VI, 2, and David Asheri, 'The Prehistory of the Word "Democracy" (δημοκρατία*)', *Mediterraneo antico. Economie, società, culture* 5:1, 2002, pp. 1–7; some believe there are traces of the document in Tyrtaeus. On the myths and mysteries of Sparta, see Edmond Lévy, *Sparte. Histoire politique et sociale jusqu'à la conquête romaine*, Paris: Seuil, 2015.
15 See Eric W. Robinson, *The First Democracies: Early Popular Governments Outside Athens*, Stuttgart: Steiner, 1997, pp. 90–101; Paolo Costantini, 'Legge di Chio', *Axon* 1:1, 2017, pp. 53–62.
16 See Ainsley T. Embree, 'Oriental Despotism: A Note on the History of an Idea', *Societas. A Review of Social History* 1:30, 1971, pp. 255–69. On the persistence of the cliché, see Edward Said, *Orientalism*, New York: Pantheon Books, 1978.
17 W. G. Forrest, *The Emergence of Greek Democracy*, London: Weidenfeld and Nicolson, 1966.
18 Claude Mossé, *Histoire d'une démocratie: Athènes. Des origines à la conquête macédonienne*, Paris: Seuil, 1971.
19 See Thucydides, II, 65, 9. On this, see Luciano Canfora, *La democrazia. Storia di un'ideologia*, Bari: Laterza, 2004, p. 13.
20 Hans Vorländer, *Demokratie. Geschichte, Formen, Theorien*, Munich: Beck, 2020, p. 13.
21 Tellingly, it is absent from the etymologies of Isidore of Seville. It is also missing in *Mediae latinitatis lexicon minus*, edited by Jan Frederik Niermeyer et al., Leiden: Brill, 1976.
22 See Kostas Vlassopoulos, *Unthinking the Greek Polis: Ancient Greek History beyond Eurocentrism*, Cambridge: Cambridge University Press, 2007.
23 Marcel Detienne, 'Comparabilities Viewed from the Vantage Point of Politics', in *The Greeks and Us*, Cambridge: Polity, 2005, pp. 113ff.
24 Marc Abélès, *Le Lieu du politique*, Paris: Société d'ethnologie, 1983.
25 See Chapters 5 and 6.
26 Marcel Detienne (ed.), *Qui veut prendre la parole?*, preface by Pierre Rosanvallon, Paris: Seuil 2003. This volume brings together contributions from scholars in various fields, including history, anthropology, and political science. They comparatively study the modes of political assembly, with a view to rethinking *communitas*.
27 Pierre Vidal-Naquet, *Politics Ancient and Modern*, Cambridge: Polity,

1995; Pierre Vidal-Naquet, *The Atlantis Story: A Short History of Plato's Myth*, Liverpool: Liverpool University Press, 2007.

28 On the question of *Allópolis*, I refer the reader to my own *The Political Vocation of Philosophy*, Cambridge: Polity, 2021.

29 Cornelius Castoriadis, *Ce qui fait la Grèce 2. La Cité et les lois, Séminaires 1983–1984 (La création humaine III)*, edited by Enrique Escobar, Myrto Gondicas, and Pascal Vernay, Paris: Seuil, 2008, p. 25.

30 Castoriadis also emphasizes these binaries. See ibid., p. 41.

31 The myth of Sparta carved a path for itself through the centuries, and one can hardly overlook its Nazi offshoots. See Johann Chapoutot, *Greeks, Romans, Germans: How the Nazis Usurped Europe's Classical Past*, translated by Richard R. Nybakken, Berkeley: University of California Press, 2016.

32 Nicole Loraux and Pierre Vidal-Naquet, 'The Formation of Bourgeois Athens', in Vidal-Naquet, *Politics Ancient and Modern*.

33 Ibid., p. 83.

34 Benjamin Constant, 'The Liberty of Ancients Compared with that of Moderns', in *Political Writings*, translated by Biancamaria Fontana, Cambridge: Cambridge University Press, 1988, p. 317.

35 Ibid., p. 311.

36 Ibid., p. 316.

37 See François Hartog, *Le XIXe siècle et l'histoire. Le cas de Fustel de Coulanges*, Paris: PUF, 1988. See Numa Denis Fustel de Coulanges, *The Ancient City: A Study on the Religion, Laws, and Institutions of Greece and Rome*, translated by Willard Small, Baltimore: Johns Hopkins University Press, 1980. George Grote is also vulnerable to the accusation of modernization, despite the credit he is due for focusing attention on politics. For a brief overview, which only covers the first half of the twentieth century, see Carmine Ampolo, 'Per una storia delle storie greche', in *I Greci. Storia, cultura, arte, società*, edited by Salvatore Settis, Turin: Einaudi, 1996, Vol. I, pp. 1015–88.

38 For example, Victor Ehrenberg, who defines Coulanges' work as 'in substance and in method fanciful, but a great concept'. Ehrenberg, *The Greek State*, New York: W. W. Norton, 1964, p. 245. In this long note, Ehrenberg reconstructs the main phases in historical studies of the ancient city.

39 See Castoriadis, *Ce qui fait la Grèce 1*, pp. 35ff.; and his 'La démocratie athénienne: fausses et vraies questions', in *La Montée de l'insignificance. Les carrefours du labyrinthe 4*, Paris: Seuil, 1996, pp. 220–33.

40 Michel Foucault, *The Archaeology of Knowledge and the Discourse on Language*, translated by A. M. Sheridan Smith, New York: Pantheon, 1972, p. 137.

41 Martin Heidegger, *Being and Time*, translated by John Macquarrie and Edward Robinson, Oxford: Blackwell, 2001, p. 43.

42 Foucault, *The Archaeology of Knowledge*, p. 129.

43 Michel Foucault, 'Nietzsche, Genealogy, History', in *Language, Counter-Memory, Practice*, Ithaca, NY: Cornell University Press, 1977, p. 144.

44 Giorgio Agamben, 'Philosophical Archaeology', *Law and Critique* 20:3, 2009, pp. 211–31, citation from p. 217.

45 Foucault, 'Nietzsche, Genealogy, History'; Friedrich Nietzsche, *On the Genealogy of Morality*, translated by Carol Diethe, Cambridge: Cambridge University Press, 2006.
46 Franz Overbeck, 'Kirchenlexikon Materialien. Christentum und Kultur', edited by Barbara von Reibnitz, in *Werke und Nachlass*, VI, I, Stuttgart-Weimar: Metzler, 1996, pp. 53–7.
47 Agamben, 'Philosophical Archaeology'.
48 Michel Foucault, 'The Order of Discourse', in Robert Young (ed.), *Untying the Text: A Post-Structuralist Reader*, Boston: Routledge, 1981.
49 Immanuel Kant, 'Lose Blätter zu den Fortschritten der Metaphysik', in *Gesammelte Schriften, Akademie Ausgabe*, III, Berlin: De Gruyter, 1942, p. 343.
50 Agamben, 'Philosophical Archaeology'.
51 Jacques Derrida, *Resistances of Psychoanalysis*, translated by Peggy Kamuf, Pascale-Anne Brault, and Michael Naas, Stanford, CA: University of California, 1998, p. 27.
52 See Jacques Derrida, 'Différance', in *Margins of Philosophy*, translated by Alan Bass, Chicago: University of Chicago Press, 1984.
53 Agamben, 'Philosophical Archaeology'.
54 Michel Foucault, *On the Government of the Living: Lectures at the Collège de France, 1979–1980*, translated by Graham Burchell, Basingstoke: Palgrave Macmillan, 2014, p. 79.
55 Hence Foucault's importance among the various tendencies of today's new anarchism. See Todd May, 'Anarchism from Foucault to Rancière', in Randall Amster et al. (eds.), *Contemporary Anarchist Studies: An Introductory Anthology of Anarchy in the Academy*, London: Routledge, 2009, pp. 11–17; Catherine Malabou, *Au voleur! Anarchisme et philosophie*, Paris: PUF, 2022, pp. 205–64.
56 Foucault, *On the Government of the Living*, p. 79.
57 Thucydides, *The History of the Peloponnesian War*, translated by Richard Crawley.
58 This is emphasized by many interpreters. See Eugen Täubler, *Die Archaeologie des Thukydides*, Leipzig-Berlin: Teubner, 1927, pp. 89ff.
59 See Luciano Canfora, 'L'inizio della storia secondo i Greci', *Quaderni di storia* 33, 1991, p. 9.
60 Giovanni Parmeggiani, 'L'heurein senza saphes: Tucidide e la conoscenza del passato. Tucidide e la conoscenza del passato', *Ancient Society* 33, 2003, pp. 235–83.
61 Cornelius Castoriadis, *Ce qui fait la Grèce 3. Thucydide, la force et le droit. Séminaires 1984–1985 (La création humaine IV)*, edited by Enrique Escobar, Myrto Gondicas, and Pascal Vernay, Paris: Seuil, 2011, p. 122.
62 Hannah Arendt, 'The Crisis in Education', in *Between Past and Future: Six Exercises in Political Thought*, New York: Viking Press, 1960.
63 See Cornelius Castoriadis, 'La source hongroise', in *Quelle démocratie?*, Vol. 1: *Écrits politiques 1945–1997*, Vol. III, Paris: Sandre, 2013, pp. 593ff.
64 Hannah Arendt, 'Introduction: Walter Benjamin, 1892–1940', in

Walter Benjamin, *Illuminations*, New York: Schocken Books, 2007, p. 42.

65 As aptly underlined by Adriana Cavarero, in speaking of a 'surging democracy': *Surging Democracy: Notes on Hannah Arendt's Political Thought*, Stanford, CA: Stanford University Press, 2021.

66 Hannah Arendt, 'What Is Freedom?', in *Between Past and Future*, p. 169.

67 See Castoriadis, 'La démocratie athénienne: fausses et vraies questions', p. 221.

68 See Cornelius Castoriadis, 'Pouvoir politique, autonomie', in *Le Monde morcelé. Les carrefours du labyrinthe 3*, Paris: Seuil, 2000, pp. 154–6.

69 Cornelius Castoriadis, 'La "polis" grecque et la création de la démocratie', in *Domaines de l'homme. Les carrefours du labyrinthe 2*, Paris: Seuil, 1986, p. 329.

70 See Castoriadis, *Ce qui fait la Grèce 3*, p. 223; *Ce qui fait la Grèce 1*, p. 40; *Ce qui fait la Grèce 2*, p. 170.

71 Castoriadis, *Ce qui fait la Grèce 3*, p. 180.

72 Walter Benjamin, 'The Translator's Task', translated by Steven Rendall, in *TTR: traduction, terminologie, rédaction* 10:2, 1997, pp. 151–65.

73 Walter Benjamin, *Ursprung des deutschen Trauerspiels*, in *Gesammelte Schriften*, Vol. I/1, edited by R. Tiedemann and H. Schweppenhäuser, Frankfurt: Suhrkamp, 1991, p. 226 (*Origin of the German Trauerspiel*, translated by Howard Eiland, Cambridge, MA: Harvard University Press, 2019).

74 Martin Heidegger, 'The Origin of the Work of Art', in Heidegger, *The Basic Writings*, edited by David Farrell Krell, New York: Harper Collins, 2008.

75 Benjamin, *Origin of the German Trauerspiel*, pp. 24–5.

76 See Catherine Collobert, 'Penser avec les Grecs ou la tâche d'une philosophie à venir', in Collobert (ed.), *L'Avenir de la philosophie est-il grec?*, Montreal: Fides, 2002, pp. 115–31.

77 Martin Heidegger, *Sojourns: The Journey to Greece*, translated by John Panteleimon Manoussakis, New York: State University of New York Press, 2005.

78 Hans-Georg Gadamer, 'Die griechische Philosophie und das moderne Denken', in *Gesammelte Werke,* Vol. 6: *Griechische Philosophie II*, Tübingen: Mohr Siebeck, 1985.

79 Nietzsche, 'On the Utility and Liability of History for Life', p. 130.

80 See Nicole Loraux, 'Éloge de l'anachronisme en histoire', in *La Tragédie d'Athènes. La politique entre l'ombre et l'utopie*, Paris: Seuil, 2005, pp. 173–90. See also Roberto Esposito, 'Anacronismi', in *Termini della politica*, Vol. II, Milan: Mimesis, 2018, pp. 161–74.

3 The Spectre of Anarchy

1 Jacques Derrida, *Archive Fever: A Freudian Impression*, Chicago: University of Chicago Press, 1996.

2 Enzo Melandri, *La linea e il circolo. Studio logico-filosofico sull'analogia*,

with introductory essay by Giorgio Agamben, Macerata: Quodlibet, 2004.

3 Ibid.

4 See Chapter 7.

5 Nicole Loraux, *The Divided City: On Memory and Forgetting in Ancient Athens*, translated by Corinne Pache and Jeff Fort, New York: Zone Books, 2006.

6 Jacqueline de Romilly, *Problèmes de la démocratie grecque*, Paris: Hermann, 2006, pp. 73ff.

7 Aristotle, *Athenaion Politeia*, XIII, 1 (translation by Harris Rackham); cf. also *Politics*, 1272b 12 (all citations from Benjamin Jowett's translation).

8 An echo of this meaning is preserved in the Roman *Interregnum*, the year when the magistracy is vacant. See P. C. Ludz and C. Meier, 'Anarchie, Anarchismus, Anarchist', in O. Brunner, W. Conze, and R. Koselleck (eds.), *Geschichtliche Grundbegriffe. Historisches Lexikon zur politisch-sozialen Sprache in Deutschland*, Vol. I (A–D), Stuttgart: Klett-Cotta, 1992, pp. 49–109, in particular pp. 50–5.

9 In Edward P. Coleridge's translation, the 'unruliness of sailors'.

10 In Edward P. Coleridge's translation.

11 In James Petch's translation, this appears as an alternative translation.

12 See Herodotus, IX, 23, 2; Thucydides, VI, 72, 3ff.; see also Xenophon, *Anabasis*, III, 2, 19.

13 Max Nettlau, *Geschichte der Anarchie, I. Der Vorfrühling der Anarchie. Ihre historische Entwicklung von den Anfängen bis zum Jahre 1864* (1927), Berlin: Bibliothek Thélème, 1993, p. 17.

14 Translation by Herbert Weir Smyth.

15 Sophocles, *Antigone*, translated by Richard Jebb.

16 De Romilly takes a different view in *Problèmes de la démocratie grecque*, p. 81.

17 Plato, *The Republic*, translated by Paul Shorey.

18 Plato, *Laws*, translation by R. G. Bury.

19 See Rancière, *Hatred of Democracy*.

20 Translated by Edmund Spencer Bouchier.

21 See Hans-Georg Gadamer, *Truth and Method*, New York: Seabury Press, 1975.

22 Schürmann, *Heidegger on Being and Acting*, p. 40.

23 Ibid., p. 85.

24 Manfred Riedel, *Metaphysik und Metapolitik. Studien zu Aristoteles und zur politischen Sprache der neuzeitlichen Philosophie*, Frankfurt: Suhrkamp, 1982, pp. 65–73.

25 Ibid., p. 43. In the various political theories the approaches may change but the reference to the *pros hen* remains.

26 Schürmann, *Heidegger on Being and Acting*, p. 10.

27 A similar strategy is employed by Isocrates, XII, 118. On the *damnatio memoriae* to which democracy is condemned, see Chapter 6.

28 The *méson* is not the crux of things, as claimed by Loraux, who thus ends up underestimating the way in which *arché* is placed at the centre. See Loraux, *The Divided City*. The opposite operation, i.e. the reappropriation of the *méson* in a re-established *arché*, is, however, problematic.

29 See Pierre Aubenque, 'Aristote et la démocratie', in his and Alonso Tordesillas' edited volume, *Aristote politique. Études sur la politique d'Aristote*, Paris: PUF, 1993, pp. 257–64.

30 Aristotle had already clarified the idea of the perfect community at the beginning of *Politics*, 1252b 31–2.

31 See Aristotle, *Politics*, 1291b 31–1292a 38; 1292b 22–1293a 11.

32 See Giuseppe Cambiano, *Come nave in tempesta. Il governo della città in Platone e Aristotele*, Rome: Laterza, 2016, pp. 73ff.; Fulvia De Luise, 'I filosofi antichi e l'esperienza della democrazia. Tra principio di rotazione e principio di qualità', *Teoria politica* 7, 2017, pp. 407–16. On the question of merit and *mésoi*, see also Enrico Berti, 'Aristotele e la democrazia', in Cristina Rossitto, Alessandra Coppola, and Franco Biasutti (eds.), *Aristotele e la storia*, Padua: Cleup, 2013, pp. 31–52.

33 See, for example, Dmitri Courant, 'Sortition and Democratic Principles: A Comparative Analysis', in John Gastil and Erik Olin Wright (eds.), *Legislature by Lot: Transformative Designs for Deliberative Democracy*, London: Verso, 2019, pp. 229–48; Gil Delannoi, Oliver Dowlen, and Peter Stone, *The Lottery as a Democratic Institution*, Dublin: SciencesPo, 2011; Lyn Carson and Brian Martin, *Random Selection in Politics*, Westport, CT: Praeger, 1999; Yves Sintomer, *Petite histoire de l'expérimentation démocratique: Tirage au sort et politique d'Athènes à nos jours*, Paris: La Découverte, 2011; Yves Sintomer, 'Sortition and Politics: From Radical to Deliberative Democracy – and Back?', in Dino Piovan and Giovanni Giorgini (eds.), *Brill's Companion to the Reception of Athenian Democracy: From the Late Middle Ages to the Contemporary Era*, Leiden: Brill, 2021, pp. 490–521.

34 Bernard Manin, *Principes du gouvernement représentatif*, Paris: Calmann-Lévy, 1995, pp. 65.

35 This does not mean that this practice had a religious character, as some interpreters have believed, considering it a bizarre and inexplicable practice. See De Coulanges, *The Ancient City*, and Gustave Glotz, *The Greek City and Its Institutions*, London: Routledge, 1929, pp. 209ff. *Klêros* is a noun whose corresponding verb is *kleróo*, to draw lots. Obtaining a position by drawing lots is indicated by the verb *lancháno*. The *klêros*, the object used for drawing lots, was a piece of wood or often a (white or black) bean. See Plutarch, *Life of Pericles*, XXVII. Many texts refer to offices 'assigned by beans': see, for example, Herodotus, VI, 109; Thucydides, VIII, 66; Aristotle, *Athenaion Politeia*, XXXII, 1. Later, the method was refined with the use of the *klerotérion*, a sophisticated machine in which the names to be drawn were inserted. Archaeological research has confirmed its existence. See Sterling Dow, 'Aristotle, the Kleroteria and the Courts', *Harvard Studies in Classical Philology* 50, 1939, pp. 1–34.

36 On the organization of sortition, see J. W. Headlam, *Election by Lot at Athens* (1891), Cambridge: Cambridge University Press, 1933. See also E. S. Staveley, *Greek and Roman Voting and Elections*, Ithaca, NY: Cornell University Press, 1972; Moses I. Finley, *Politics in the Ancient World*, Cambridge: Cambridge University Press, 1983.

37 Aristotle, *Rhetoric*, translated by W. Rhys Roberts.

38 This is echoed in the positions of those with an elitist approach who, more or less explicitly, call for epistemocracy.
39 See for instance Euripides, *The Suppliants*, 409–20. Thucydides is silent on this count in Pericles' funeral oration.
40 Mogens Herman Hansen, *The Athenian Democracy in the Age of Demosthenes*, Oxford: Blackwell, 1991. This is an abbreviated version of a much more extensive work published in Danish in six volumes: *Det Athenske Demokrati u 4 årch. F. Kr.*, Copenhagen: Museum Tusculanum Press, 1977–81. In it, the author focuses on the Athenian institutions of the fourth century, up to their final collapse in 322 BCE, emphasizing the lack of sources for the previous period.
41 See Rancière, *The Hatred of Democracy*, pp. 58ff.
42 Plato, *Protagoras*, 319d. See also a similar passage in Xenophon, *Memorabilia*, I, 2, 9.
43 See Plato, *Protagoras*, 322c–323a.

4 Tragedy and Politics

1 See Gregory Vlastos, 'Equality and Justice in Early Greek Cosmologies', *Classical Philology* 42:3, 1947, pp. 156–78; Marcel Detienne, 'En Grèce archaïque: géométrie, politique et société', *Annales* 20:3, 1956, pp. 425–41.
2 Jean-Pierre Vernant, 'Geometry and Spherical Astronomy in the First Greek Cosmology', in *Myth and Thought Among the Greeks*, London: Routledge, 1983. See also his *The Origins of Greek Thought*, Ithaca, NY: Cornell University Press, 1984.
3 Vernant, 'Geometry and Spherical Astronomy', p. 184.
4 Ibid., p. 187.
5 A. D. Godley translation, edited.
6 Vernant, 'Geometry and Spherical Astronomy'.
7 Charles H. Kahn, *Anaximander and the Origins of Greek Cosmology*, New York: Columbia University Press, 1960.
8 Ibid., p. 56.
9 Hippolytus, *Refutation of all Heresies*, I, 6 (Diels Kranz B 22).
10 On this verb, see Chapter 7.
11 See Aristotle, *Physics*, 203b 7ff.
12 Cornelius Castoriadis, 'La pensée politique', in *Ce qui fait la Grèce 1*, p. 278. Here we find a polemic against Heidegger which, although it reappears in other texts, unfortunately never appears to be sustained through argument.
13 Cornelius Castoriadis, 'The Greek Polis and the Creation of Democracy', *Graduate Faculty Philosophy Journal* 9:2, 1983, pp. 79–115, this from p. 95.
14 Ibid. See also Stathis Gourgouris, 'Democracy Is a Tragic Regime', *Modern Language Association* 129:4, 2014, pp. 809–18.
15 Castoriadis, 'La pensée politique'.
16 *Húbris* is, in fact, one of the charges most often levelled by its detractors against the *dêmos* and its rule.
17 Martin Heidegger, *Introduction to Metaphysics*, New Haven, CT: Yale

University Press, 2000, pp. 166ff. He would continue to return to the verses of *Antigone*, using Hölderlin's German translation.

18 See Cornelius Castoriadis, 'Anthropogonie chez Eschyle et autocréation de l'homme chez Sophocle', in *Figures du pensable. Les carrefours du labyrinthe* 6, Paris: Seuil, 1999, pp. 30ff.; Jean-Pierre Vernant, 'Tensions and Ambiguities in Greek Tragedy', in Vernant and Pierre Vidal-Naquet, *Myth and Tragedy in Ancient Greece*, New York: Zone Books, 1998, pp. 29ff.

19 George Steiner, *Antigones*, Oxford: Clarendon Press, 1984, p. 184.

20 Massimo Cacciari, 'La parola che uccide', in Sophocles, *Antigone*, edited by Massimo Cacciari, Turin: Einaudi, 2007, p. xi.

21 See Christian Meier, *The Political Art of Greek Tragedy*, Cambridge: Polity, 1993; Vernant and Vidal-Naquet, *Myth and Tragedy in Ancient Greece*; J. Peter Euben, *The Tragedy of Political Theory: The Road Not Taken*, Princeton, NJ: Princeton University Press, 1990; many of the essays included in John J. Winkler and Froma I. Zeitlin (eds.), *Nothing To Do with Dionysos? Athenian Drama in its Social Context*, Princeton, NJ: Princeton University Press, 1990; Peter J. Ahresdorf, *Greek Tragedy and Political Philosophy: Rationalism and Religion in Sophocles' Theban Plays*, Cambridge: Cambridge University Press, 2009; D. M. Carter (ed.), *Why Athens? A Reappraisal of Tragic Politics*, Oxford: Oxford University Press, 2011.

22 In this sense, Aeschylus' *Eumenides* marked an exception; see Chapter 6.

23 Jacob Burckhardt, *History of Greek Culture*, New York: Ungar, 1963, p. 227.

24 Arthur Pickard-Cambridge, *The Dramatic Festivals of Athens*, Oxford: Clarendon Press, 1968, pp. 58ff., 84ff.

25 The theatre was initially a trapezoidal structure, reassembled each time for the festivities and not very suitable for assemblies. Only much later, around 340 BCE, was it built in stone in its familiar circular form.

26 Vernant, 'Tensions and Ambiguities', p. 32.

27 Wilhelm Nestle, *Vom Mythos zum Logos. Die Selbstentfaltung des griechischen Denkens von Homer bis auf die Sophistik und Sokrates*, Stuttgart: Kröner, 1940.

28 Vernant, 'Tensions and Ambiguities', pp. 34ff.

29 Vernant and Vidal-Naquet, *Myth and Tragedy in Ancient Greece*, pp. 92, 145.

30 Friedrich Nietzsche, *The Birth of Tragedy*, London: T. N. Foulis, 1910, p. 69.

31 Ibid., p. 56.

32 Ibid.

33 On this, see Lawrence J. Hatab, *A Nietzschean Defense of Democracy*, La Salle, IL: Open Court, 1995; Urs Marti, '*Der grosse Pöbel- und Sklavenaufstand'. Nietzsches Auseinandersetzung mit Revolution und Demokratie*, Stuttgart: Metzler, 1995, in particular pp. 189–235; see Herman W. Siemens and Vasti Roodt (eds.), *Nietzsche, Power and Politics: Rethinking Nietzsche's Legacy for Political Thought*, Berlin: De Gruyter, 2009.

34 Euben, *The Tragedy of Political Theory*, p. 147; Nicole Loraux, *La Voix endeuillée. Essai sur la tragédie grecque*, Paris: Gallimard, 1999, pp. 88ff.
35 On the presence of foreigners and the composition of the chorus, see Pierre Vidal-Naquet, *Le Miroir brisé*, Paris: Les Belles Lettres, 2002.
36 See Richard Halpern, 'Theater and Democratic Thought: Arendt to Rancière', *Critical Inquiry* 37:3, 2011, pp. 545–72; Jacques Rancière, *Le Philosophe et ses pauvres*, Paris: Flammarion, 2007.
37 Henri Francotte, *La pólis grecque. Recherches sur la formation et l'organisation des cités, des ligues et des confédérations dans la Grèce ancienne*, Paderborn: Schöningh, 1907, pp. 24ff. Francotte examines how the new Greek political structure took shape by eradicating the principle of nobility, which conferred immense power above all on the families of the Eupatridae.
38 James Redfield, 'Homo Domesticus', in Jean-Pierre Vernant (ed.), *The Greeks*, Chicago: University of Chicago Press, 1995, p. 153.
39 On the role of slaves, see Yvon Garlan, *Les Esclaves en Grèce ancienne*, Paris: La Découverte, 1982.
40 See Homer, *Iliad*, XXIII, 832–35; *Odyssey*, IV, 318. The Homeric *oîkos* must have been more extensive than the classical *oîkos* because it also included a number of noble companions who lived with the master of the house. However, the similarity to the property of the classical era, as described by Xenophon in the *Oeconomicus* and by Aristotle in Book I of the *Politics*, remains.
41 W. K. Lacey, *The Family in Classical Greece*, London: Thames and Hudson, 1968, pp. 21ff. On abandonment, see David Asheri, 'L'*oikos eremos* nel diritto successorio attico', *Archivio giuridico* 159, 1960, 7–24.
42 See Otto Brunner, 'Das "ganze Haus" und die alteuropäische "Oekonomik"', in *Neue Wege der Verfassungs- und Sozialgeschichte*, Göttingen: Vandenhoeck u. Ruprecht, 1968, pp. 103–27.
43 See Ehrenberg, *The Greek State*.
44 In the *Homeric Hymn to Hestia* (I), 11–12, the term *epichtónioi* appears to indicate 'on Earth'.
45 *Homeric Hymn to Aphrodite* (I) 30.
46 *Homeric Hymn to Hermes* (I) 14–15, translated by H. G. Evelyn-White.
47 Vernant, 'Hestia-Hermes', in *Myth and Thought Among the Greeks*, p. 130.
48 Louis Gernet, 'Sur le symbolisme politique en Grèce ancienne: le foyer commun', *Cahiers internationaux de sociologie* 101, 1996, pp. 247–65.
49 Artemidorus, *The Interpretation of Dreams – Oneirocritica*, Park Ridge, NJ: Noyes Press, 1975, p. 38.
50 See Pindar, *Nemean Odes*, XI, 1–9.
51 See Vernant, 'Hestia-Hermes'.
52 Sappho, *Fragments*, translated by Hugh Lloyd-Jones.
53 Lefort, 'The Question of Democracy'.
54 Christian Meier, *Die Entstehung des Politischen bei den Griechen*, Frankfurt: Suhrkamp, 1983, p. 12.
55 Bruno Snell, *The Discovery of the Mind: The Greek Origins of European Thought*, Oxford: Blackwell, 1953. The substantivized adjective is used

to designate citizenship (Herodotus, VII, 107; Thucydides, VIII, 93, 3) or in the plural to indicate political affairs (Thucydides, II, 40).

56 See Demosthenes, IX, 48; Aristotle, *Athenaion Politeia*, XIV, 3 and XVI, 2. See Meier, *Die Entstehung des Politischen bei den Griechen*.

57 This is the essay on the 'theological politics' of Aeschylus' *Eumenides*. The dedication reads: '*Carolo Schmitt, tou politikoú investigatori illustri*'. Meier, *Die Entstehung des Politischen bei den Griechen*, pp. 144ff.

58 Carl Schmitt, 'Political Theology', in *Political Theology: Four Chapters on the Concept of Sovereignty*, Chicago: University of Chicago Press, 1985, pp. 36ff.

59 Meier, *Die Entstehung des Politischen bei den Griechen*, p. 17.

60 Ibid.

61 Ibid., pp. 30–1.

62 Ibid., p. 33. This provides Meier with a way of referring to Schmitt's involvement in Nazism.

63 Ibid., p. 37.

64 Ibid., p. 40.

65 Ibid., p. 152.

66 Ibid., p. 38.

67 It is worth noting that Meier also cites Arendt; he was thus familiar with her thinking, although he does not discuss her theories in depth. See ibid., pp. 46, 79, 256, 269, 319, 343, 359, 371, 498, 512.

68 But on the problematic nature of Pericles' epitaph, see Chapter 6.

69 Paul Veyne, 'Did the Greeks Know Democracy?', *Economy and Society* 34:2, 2005, pp. 322–45, here from p. 344.

70 Meier, *Die Entstehung des Politischen bei den Griechen*, p. 53.

71 Carl Schmitt, *Land and Sea: A World-Historical Meditation*, New York: Telos Press, 2015.

72 Massimo Cacciari, *L'arcipelago*, Milan: Adelphi, 1997, p. 23.

73 According to the famous metaphor. Cf. Plato, *The Republic*, 487a 1–489a 2; Aristotle, *Politics*, 1276b 20.

74 Claude Lefort, 'Hannah Arendt and the Question of the Political', in *Democracy and Political Theory*, Minneapolis: University of Minnesota Press, 1988, p. 50.

75 Dolf Sternberger, 'Die versunkene Stadt. Über Hannah Arendts Idee der Politik', *Merkur* 30:341, 1976, p. 935.

76 Hannah Arendt and Dolf Sternberger, *Ich bin Dir halt ein bißchen zu revolutionär. Briefwechsel 1946 bis 1975*, edited by Udo Bermbach, Berlin: Rowohlt, 2019.

77 Sternberger, 'Die versunkene Stadt', p. 939. Herodotus, III, 83, 8. On this passage, see Chapter 5.

78 Sternberger, 'Die versunkene Stadt', p. 941.

79 Walter Benjamin, 'Zum Wahrnehmungsproblem', in *Gesammelte Schriften*, Vol. VI, edited by Rolf Tiedemann and Hermann Schweppenhäuser, Frankfurt: Suhrkamp, 1991, p. 66.

80 Jürgen Habermas, 'Hannah Arendts Begriff der Macht', *Merkur* 30:341, 1976, pp. 946–61.

81 Sternberger, 'Die versunkene Stadt', p. 945.

82 Hannah Arendt, *The Human Condition*, Chicago: University of

Chicago Press, p. 24. The German edition uses the term *unpolitisch*. This version, prepared by Arendt, leaves less room for misunderstanding, because *Herrschaft*, power in the sense of domination, and *Regierung*, government, and the two related verbs *herrschen* and *regieren*, are in general kept distinct, where in English *rule* and *to rule* are used.

83 Ibid.

84 Ibid.

85 Ibid., pp. 32–3.

86 Ibid., p. 38.

87 Ibid., p. 55.

88 Hannah Arendt, *On Revolution*, New York: Penguin Books, 1990, p. 30.

89 Ibid., pp. 30–1.

90 Ibid., p. 31.

91 Arendt, *The Human Condition*, p. 24. On Arendt's relation to Marx and her highly controversial criticism, see Simona Forti, *Hannah Arendt tra filosofia e politica*, Milan: Bruno Mondadori, 2006, pp. 83ff.

92 Hannah Arendt, *The Promise of Politics*, edited by Jerome Kohn, New York: Schocken, 2005, p. 94.

93 See Oliver Marchart, *Neu beginnen. Hannah Arendt, die Revolution und die Globalisierung*, Vienna: Turia + Kant, 2005. See also Facundo Vega, 'On Bad Weather, Heidegger, Arendt, and Political Beginnings', in Christoph F. E. Holzhey and Arnd Wedemeyer (eds.), *Weathering: Ecologies of Exposure*, Berlin: ICI Berlin Press, 2020, pp. 227–43.

94 Arendt, *On Revolution*, pp. 30ff.; *The Human Condition*, pp. 177ff.; 'What Is Freedom', in *Between Past and Future*, pp. 165ff. In her *Denktagebuch* both *arché* and *árchein* appear: Ursula Ludz and Ingeborg Nordmann (eds.), Hannah Arendt, *Denktagebuch: 1950–1973*, Munich: Piper, 2002.

95 See also Patchen Markell, 'The Rule of the People: Arendt, Archê, and Democracy', *The American Political Science Review* 100:1, 2006, pp. 1–14; Annabel Herzog, 'Political Itineraries and Anarchic Cosmopolitanism in the Thought of Hannah Arendt', *Inquiry* 47:1, 2004, pp. 20–41.

96 Hannah Arendt, *The Life of the Mind*, Boston: Harcourt, 1981.

97 Hannah Arendt, *Lectures on Kant's Political Philosophy*, Chicago: University of Chicago Press, 1982.

98 See Arendt, *The Life of the Mind*; Aristotle, *Politics*, 1324a 16.

5 Refugee Women, and the Victory of the People

1 Pierre Vidal-Naquet, 'Esclavage et gynécocratie dans la tradition, le mythe, l'utopie', in *Le Chasseur noir. Formes de pensée et formes de société dans le monde grec* (1981), Paris: La Découverte, 2005, p. 269.

2 Philip Brook Manville, *The Origins of Citizenship in Ancient Athens*, Princeton, NJ: Princeton University Press, 2016, pp. 3ff.

3 See Polybius XII, 5, 10–11. See S. G. Pembroke, 'Locre et Tarente: le rôle des femmes dans la fondation de deux colonies grecques', *Annales* 25:5, 1970, pp. 1241–67.

4 It is worth noting that here, in addition to the traditional role reversal typical of comedy, the disguises that took place during the festivals of Athena Skira also play a role.

5 See E. Cantarella, *L'ambiguo malanno. Condizione e immagine della donna nell'antichità greca e romana*, Milan: Feltrinelli, 2013, pp. 34ff.

6 This is rightly pointed out by Vidal-Naquet, 'Esclavage et gynécocratie dans la tradition', p. 287.

7 See Nicole Loraux, 'La cité, l'historien, les femmes', in *La Grèce hors d'elle et autres textes. Écrits 1973–2003*, edited by M. Cohen-Halimi, Paris: Klincksieck, 2023, pp. 301ff. On women's role in the civil war in Corcyra, see Chapter 6.

8 Until a few decades ago, the tragedy of the Suppliants was considered the oldest and was dated to around 490 BCE; but in 1952, a lucky discovery of a papyrus (P.Oxy 2256 fr. 3) allowed another hypothesis to be advanced, which is now widely accepted.

9 A. F. Garvie, *Aeschylus' 'Supplices': Play and Trilogy*, Cambridge: Cambridge University Press, 1969.

10 Julia Kristeva, *Strangers to Ourselves*, New York: Columbia University Press, 1991, p. 43.

11 See Maria Pia Beriotto, *Le Danaidi. Storia di un mito nella letteratura greca*, Alessandria: Edizioni dell'Orso, 2016.

12 Aeschylus, *The Suppliant Women*, translated by Herbert Weir Smyth (translation altered).

13 See Laurent Barry, 'Étranges étrangères. Les sombres fleurs des "Suppliantes" d'Eschyle', in Françoise Héritier and Margarita Xanthakou (eds.), *Corps et affects*, Paris: Odile Jacob, 2004, pp. 93–104. See also Claudia Passariello, 'La supplica paradossale delle Danaidi di Eschilo', in ὅρμος – *Ricerche di Storia Antica* 3, 2011, pp. 305–17.

14 The supplicant, *hikétes*, connected with the verb *híko*, etymologically means 'he who comes'. He differs from the stranger, the *xénos*, because while the latter stops at the threshold waiting to be received, the supplicant approaches, crosses the threshold and begs to be welcomed, with the ritual attitude of supplication. See Liana Lomiento, 'Girovaghi, migranti, forestieri: i volti della "xenia" nella Grecia antica. Le fonti letterarie', *Quaderni urbinati di cultura classica* 117:3, 2017, pp. 173–91; Ulrike Riemer and Peter Riemer, *Xenophobie-Philoxenie. Vom Umgang mit Fremden in der Antike*, Stuttgart: Steiner, 2005.

15 It is difficult to believe that Aeschylus could have coined these compounds and periphrases if he had not known what democracy meant. This is explained by Victor Ehrenberg, 'Origins of Democracy', *Historia. Zeitschrift für alte Geschichte* 1:4, 1950, p. 524. See also Monica Centanni, 'Démou kratoùsa cheír: Aesch. Suppl. 604', in *Mythologeîn. Mito e forme di discorso nel mondo antico. Studi in onore di Giovanni Cerri*, edited by A. Gostoli, R. Velardi, and M. Colantonio, Pisa: Fabrizio Serra, 2015, pp. 221–6.

16 The Danaïdes present marriage between cousins as incest, even though it was widely accepted in the Greek world of the fifth century BCE. See Edmond Lévy, 'Inceste, mariage et sexualité dans les "Suppliantes" d'Eschyle', in *La Femme dans le monde méditerranéen*,

Lyon: Maison de l'Orient et de la Méditerranée Jean Pouilloux, 1985, pp. 29–45.

17 Marcel Detienne, 'Les danaïdes entre elles ou la violence fondatrice du mariage', *Arethusa* 21:2, 1988, pp. 159–75.

18 On this, see Donatella Di Cesare, *Resident Foreigners: A Philosophy of Migration*, Cambridge: Polity, 2020.

19 See Aeschylus, *The Persians*, 213–14; 241–3.

20 'The Athenian demos … (a) confirms the right of the cleruchs settled in Salamis to reside there permanently.' Marcus N. Tod, *A Selection of Greek Historical Inscriptions*, Vol. I, Oxford: Clarendon Press, 1946, no. 11; Russell Meiggs and David Lewis, *A Selection of Greek Historical Inscriptions to the End of the Fifth Century B.C.*, Oxford: Clarendon Press, 1969, no. 14.

21 Ibid. This complete formula indicates two votes, one by the council and one by the popular assembly.

22 As assumed by Ehrenberg, 'Origins of Democracy', pp. 538ff.; but see especially Eugenio Lanzillotta, 'Sulla formazione del concetto di democrazia', in *Alle radici della democrazia. Dalla polis al dibattito costituzionale contemporaneo*, Rome: Carocci, 1998, pp. 20–3.

23 Tod, *A Selection of Greek Historical Inscriptions*, 954. See Monica Centanni, *La nascita della politica. La Costituzione di Atene*, Venice: Editrice Cafoscarina, 2011, pp. 182ff., 185ff.

24 See, for example, Lanzillotta, 'Sulla formazione del concetto di democrazia', p. 18; Domenico Musti, *Demokratía. Origini di un'idea*, Bari: Laterza, 1995, pp. 12ff. But this view is widespread almost everywhere, in secondary literature and in textbooks.

25 See Jules Isaac, *Les Oligarques: Essai d'histoire partiale*, Paris: Calmann-Lévy, 1994.

26 Loraux, 'Éloge de l'anachronisme en histoire', p. 182. These pages contain a polemic with Luciano Canfora, which sometimes takes on overly harsh tones. All the more so because, although perhaps granted excessive importance, the text of the Anonymous Athenian, which Canfora attributes to the oligarch Critias, is nevertheless a significant source in which the term *demokratía* appears.

27 See Nicole Loraux, *L'Invention d'Athènes. Histoire de l'oraison funèbre dans la cité classique*, Paris: EHESS, 1981, pp. 334ff.

28 Herodotus, IV, 137, 9; VI, 43, 12–15. Translation by George Rawlinson.

29 Herodotus, VI, 43, 3; VI, 131, 1. The passage on Cleisthenes became a source for Aristotle.

30 See Klaus Brinmann, 'Die Verfassungsdebatte bei Herodot 3, 80–82 und Dareios' Aufstieg zur Königsherrschaft', *Hermes* 104:3, 1976, pp. 266–79.

31 See Edmond Lévy, '"Archè" chez Hérodote', in *Φιλολογία, Mélanges offerts à Michel Casevitz*, Lyon: Maison de l'Orient et de la Méditerranée Jean Pouilloux, 2006, pp. 89–98.

32 *Plêthos* always indicates multiplicity. See Pierre Chantraine, *Dictionnaire étymologique de la langue grecque. Histoire des mots*, Paris: Klincksieck, 1968–80, Vol. II, pp. 902ff., 927ff.

33 Jean-Luc Breuil, 'De κράτος à δημοκρατίη. Une famille de mots chez Hérodote', *Ktèma* 20, 1995, pp. 71–84.

34 The term *stasiótes*, derived from *stásis*, means 'partisan', 'supporting a party', 'belonging to a political faction'.
35 Here, freedom could border on an aristocratic freedom – see, for example, Herodotus, IV, 35 – if it were not qualified by the sharing required in isonomy.
36 The foreigners must have been mostly allies.
37 See Musti, *Demokratía. Origini di un'idea*, pp. 3ff.
38 See Konrad Gaiser, *Das Staatsmodell des Thukydides. Zur Rede des Perikles für die Gefallenen*, Heidelberg: Kerle, 1975.
39 See Gregory Vlastos, 'Isonomia politiké', in Jürgen Mau and Ernst Günther Schmidt (eds.), *Isonomia. Studien zur Gleichheitsvorstellung im griechischen Denken*, Berlin: Akademie-Verlag, 1964, pp. 1–35, at p. 29.
40 See Jakob A. O. Larsen, 'Cleisthenes and the Development of the Theory of Democracy at Athens', in Milton R. Konvitz and Arthur E. Murphy (eds.), *Essays in Political Theory: Presented to George H. Sabine*, Ithaca, NY: Cornell University Press, 1948, pp. 1–16, at p. 13; Claude Mossé, *Les Institutions politiques grecques à l'époque classique*, Paris: Armand Colin, 1967, p. 155; Georg Peter Landmann, 'Das Lob Athens in der Grabrede des Perikles (Thukydides II 34–41)', *Museum Helveticum* 31:2, 1974, p. 80.
41 See Luciano Canfora, 'Studi sull'Athenaion Politeia pseudosenofontea', *Memorie dell'Accademia delle Scienze di Torino* 4, 1980, pp. 1–109, at p. 38.
42 The authenticity of the dialogue, long disputed, is no longer an issue and is generally accepted. There was no lack of evidence even before: Aristotle, *Rhetoric*, I 1367b; III 1415b.
43 Translated by Walter Rangeley Maitland Lamb.
44 On autochthony, a myth which is today more powerful than ever, see Di Cesare, *Resident Foreigners*, section 3.6.
45 Nicole Loraux, *Born of the Earth: Myth and Politics in Athens*, Ithaca, NY: Cornell University Press, 2000.
46 The *phratría* was the smallest and most important basic community. See Stephen D. Lambert, *The Phratries of Attica*, Ann Arbor: University of Michigan Press, 1993.
47 Christian Meier, *Entstehung des Begriffs 'Demokratie'. Vier Prolegomena zu einer historischen Theorie*, Frankfurt: Suhrkamp, 2015 (2nd edition), p. 68. Even in comedies the term appears rarely, although in Aristophanes' *The Knights*, the Demos is the protagonist. In his *The Frogs*, staged in 405 BCE, a striking joke is put in Euripides' mouth, where the tragedian boasts of having had 'the woman' speak, and the 'slave, the master, maiden, the old woman, too. … I was doing my work the democratic way' (952, translated by Ian Johnston).
48 This is attested, among other things, by the texts of Isocrates. See Isocrates, IV, 39; XII, 118.
49 See Alexander Fuks, *The Ancestral Constitution: Four Studies in Athenian Party Politics at the End of the Fifth Century B.C.* (1953), edited by R. J. Goldstein, London: Routledge, 2009.
50 On the variations and changes in this word, see Meier, *Entstehung des Begriffs 'Demokratie'*, pp. 61ff.
51 See Thucydides, III, 62, 4.

6 *Stásis*: Twists and Turns in the History of the *Pólis*

1 Sheldon S. Wolin, 'Transgression, Equality, and Voice', in *Fugitive Democracy and Other Essays*, edited by Nicholas Xenos, Princeton, NJ: Princeton University Press, 2016, pp. 53–76. See also his *Politics and Vision: Continuity and Innovation in Western Political Thought*, Princeton, NJ: Princeton University Press, 2004, pp. 601ff.
2 Wolin, 'Transgression, Equality, and Voice', p. 57.
3 Sheldon S. Wolin, 'Norm and Form: The Constitutionalizing of Democracy', in *Fugitive Democracy and Other Essays*, p. 83.
4 Wolin, 'Fugitive Democracy', in *Fugitive Democracy and Other Essays*, p. 107.
5 Ibid.
6 Wolin, *Fugitive Democracy and Other Essays*, pp. 459ff.; Josiah Ober, '"I Besieged That Man": Democracy's Revolutionary Start', in Kurt Raaflaub, Josiah Ober, and Robert Wallace, *Origins of Democracy in Ancient Greece*, Berkeley: University of California Press, 2007. Confirmation of the affinities between Wolin and Ober can be found in the volume containing contributions by both authors: Josiah Ober and Charles Hedrick (eds.), *Dēmokratia: A Conversation on Democracies, Ancient and Modern*, Princeton, NJ: Princeton University Press, 1996.
7 See Josiah Ober, *Mass and Elite in Democratic Athens: Rhetoric, Ideology, and the Power of the People*, Princeton, NJ: Princeton University Press, 1989; *The Athenian Revolution: Essays on Ancient Greek Democracy and Political Theory*, Princeton, NJ: Princeton University Press, 1996.
8 See Josiah Ober, 'The Original Meaning of "Democracy": Capacity to Do Things, Not Majority Rule', *Constellations* 15:1, 2008, pp. 3–9. For a discussion of this topic, see Chapter 7.
9 Josiah Ober, *Demopolis: Democracy before Liberalism in Theory and Practice*, Cambridge: Cambridge University Press, 2017.
10 New perspectives on this topic are opened up by Roberto Esposito, *Instituting Thought: Three Paradigms of Political Ontology*, Cambridge: Polity, 2021.
11 Mogens Herman Hansen, 'On the Importance of Institutions in an Analysis of Athenian Democracy', in *The Athenian Ecclesia II: A Collection of Articles, 1983–1989*, Copenhagen: Museum Tusculanum, 1989, pp. 263–9.
12 *Athenaion Politeia*, Rackham translation.
13 Vernant, *Origins of Greek Thought*, p. 85.
14 See Robert W. Wallace, 'Charismatic Leaders', in Kurt A. Raaflaub and Hans van Wees (eds.), *A Companion to Archaic Greece: A Blackwell Companion to the Ancient World*, Oxford: Blackwell, 2009, pp. 411–26. See also Diego Lanza, *Il tiranno e il suo pubblico*, Turin: Einaudi, 1977.
15 See Aristotle, fragment 548 (Rose) (= Schol. in Pind., Olymp., 10, 17 i).
16 Plutarch, *Moralia*, 304. Aristotle had spoken of *ataxía kaí anarchía*, 'disorder and anarchy'. See Aristotle, *Politics*, 1302b 30, 1304b 334–40; see also 13a 16–19.

17 Solon, 31 G.-P.[2] (37 W.[2]), 8–9; Aristotle, *Athenaion Politeia*, XII, 65, Rackham translation.
18 Solon, 29 G.-P.[2] (32 W.[2]), 1–2; Plutarch, *Life of Solon*, XIV, 5, translation by Bernadotte Perrin.
19 See Loraux, 'Solon au milieu de la lice', in *La Tragédie d'Athènes*, pp. 145–60.
20 Hesiod, *Works and Days*, 27–34, 342–52.
21 It is no coincidence that in the first half of the sixth century BCE, the *agorá* changed from a private space to a public one. See Kurt Raaflaub, 'Die Anfänge des politischen Denkens bei den Griechen', *Historische Zeitschrift*, 248, 1989, pp. 1–32. Michael Stahl, 'Solon F 3D. Die Geburtsstunde des demokratischen Gedankens', *Gymnasium* 99, 1992, pp. 385–408; Christian Meier, *The Greek Discovery of Politics*, Cambridge, MA: Harvard University Press, 1990; see also his *Entstehung des Begriffs 'Demokratie'*, pp. 70ff.
22 Solon, 3 G.-P.[2] (4 W.[2]), 26–31; translation by B. H. Fowler.
23 See Peter Spahn, 'Oikos und Polis. Beobachtungen zum Prozess des Polisbildung bei Hesiod, Solon und Aischylos', *Historische Zeitschrift*, 231, 1980, pp. 545–50.
24 Solon, 30 G.-P[2] (36 W.[2]), 27; *Ath. Pol.*, XII, 53–4, Rackham translation.
25 Solon 30 G.-P.[2] (36 W.[2]), 5–7; *Ath. Pol.*, XII, 32–4, Rackham translation.
26 See Louis Gernet, *Anthropologie de la Grèce antique*, Paris: Maspero, 1968, p. 369.
27 On *eunomía* and *isonomía*, see Victor Ehrenberg, 'Eunomia', in *Aspects of the Ancient World*, Oxford: Blackwell, 1946, pp. 70–94, and his 'Origins of Democracy', pp. 530ff.; Gregory Vlastos, 'Isonomia', *The American Journal of Philosophy*, 74:4, 1953, pp. 350ff.
28 The first citation is from Plutarch, *Life of Solon*, XVIII, 4 (see 5–6); the second from Aristotle, *Athenaion Politeia*, XII, 1–2 (in Aristotle's text, *ghéras*, privileges, appears instead of *krátos*). See Solon, 35 G.-P.[2] (30 W.[2]).
29 See Ober, *The Athenian Revolution*, pp. 46–9.
30 See Rosalind Thomas, *Oral Tradition and Written Record in Classical Athens*, Cambridge: Cambridge University Press, 1989, pp. 245ff.
31 The terms used by Herodotus are, for example, *moiran*, 'part', or even *tòn démon prosetairízetai*, 'brought the common people of Athens entirely over to his own side'. See Herodotus, V, 66–9, Rawlinson translation, edited.
32 Meier describes the resistance of the people as 'singular'. See Christian Meier, 'Clisthène et le problème politique de la polis grecque', *Revue Internationale des Droits de l'Antiquité* 20, 1973, pp. 135ff.
33 See Nicole Loraux, 'Clisthène, diviseur-lieur d'Athènes', *L'Inactuel* 8, 1997, pp. 5–27, reprinted in her *La Grèce hors d'elle et autres textes*, pp. 801–22.
34 In Ian Johnston's translation.
35 Pierre Lévêque and Pierre Vidal-Naquet, *Cleisthenes the Athenian: An Essay on the Representation of Space and Time in Greek Political Thought from the End of the Sixth Century to the Death of Plato*, New York: Humanity Books, 1996; see also Martin Ostwald, *Nomos and the*

Beginning of the Athenian Democracy, Oxford: Clarendon Press, 1969, in particular pp. 154ff.

36 In G. C. McCauley's translation.

37 Rawlinson translation.

38 While '[t]hese reforms made the constitution much more democratic than that of Solon' (*Ath. Pol.*, XXII, 1), it is reported that 'the constitution of Cleisthenes was not democratic but similar to that of Solon' (XXIX, 3).

39 See Jean-Pierre Vernant, 'Space and Political Organization in Ancient Greece', in *Myth and Thought Among the Greeks*, pp. 212ff.

40 Lévêque and Vidal-Naquet, *Cleisthenes the Athenian*, p. 7.

41 Francotte, *La pólis grecque*, p. 29.

42 Gustave Glotz, *Histoire grecque, I. Des origines aux guerres médiques*, Paris: PUF, 1925, pp. 464ff.; see also his *La Solidarité de la famille dans le droit criminel en Grèce*, Paris: Fontemoing, 1904.

43 See Aristotle, *Athenaion Politeia*, XXI, 4; *Politics*, 1275b 37.

44 Lévêque and Vidal-Naquet, *Cleisthenes the Athenian*. Although weakened, the *ghéne* nevertheless resisted. On the *phulé* as the ancient nucleus of the *pólis*, see Gregory Nagy, 'Mythical Foundation of Greek Society and the Concept of the City-State', in *Greek Mythology and Poetics*, Ithaca, NY: Cornell University Press, 1990, pp. 276–93. See also Françoise Ruzé, 'Les tribus et la décision politique dans les cités grecques archaïques et classiques', *Ktèma* 8, 1983, pp. 300ff.

45 Rather than a Pythagorean influence, it must be imagined that Cleisthenes resorted to the numbering system that writing had already spread in the public sphere, opposed to the duodecimal system. See Vernant, 'Space and Political Organization', p. 217.

46 See Louis Gernet, 'Sur le symbolisme politique en Grèce ancienne: le Foyer Commun', *Cahiers internationaux de sociologie* 11, 1951, pp. 21–43.

47 See Manville, *The Origins of Citizenship in Ancient Athens*.

48 See Francotte, *La pólis grecque*, pp. 30ff.

49 This is also the thesis of Lévêque and Vidal-Naquet, *Cleisthenes the Athenian*, p. 9. See also Finley, *Politics in the Ancient World*.

50 Aristotle, *Politics*, 1275a 7–9, Rackham translation.

51 Michel Clerc, *Les Métèques athéniens*, Paris: Thorin, 1893, pp. 328, 336ff.

52 On the differentiation of these groups and on the metics, see Deborah Kamen, *Status in Classical Athens*, Princeton, NJ: Princeton University Press, 2013, pp. 43ff.

53 See Giannalberto Luzi, 'I nuovi cittadini di Clistene (Aristotele, Polit., 3, 2, 3 [1275b])', *Annali della Scuola Normale Superiore di Pisa* 10:1, 1980, pp. 71–8.

54 This is, for example, Meier's thesis in his *Die Entstehung des Politischen bei den Griechen*.

55 *Chôra* refers not only to the idea of containing, but also to separation. On *chôra* as mother and nurturer, see Nicole Loraux, *Les Enfants d'Athéna. Idées athéniennes sur la citoyenneté et la division des sexes*, Paris: Maspero, 1981, pp. 65ff.

56 See Fritz Gschnitzer, 'Abitanti senza diritto di cittadinanza: non liberi e stranieri', in Settis (ed.), *I Greci. Storia, cultura, arte, società*,

Vol. II, 2, 1997, pp. 403–21. See also Jakob Seibert, *Die politischen Flüchtlinge und Verbannten in der griechischen Geschichte*, Darmstadt: Wissenschaftliche Buchgesellschaft, 1979; David Whitehead, *The Ideology of the Athenian Metic*, Cambridge: Cambridge Philological Society, 1977; M. J. Osborne, *Naturalization in Athens*, 4 vols, Brussels: Paleis der Academiën, 1981–83.

57 TN: Or as the original Italian has it, 'Brothers of Attica', a pun on the name of contemporary Italy's nationalist ruling party, Fratelli d'Italia.

58 Plutarch, *Life of Cimon*, XV, 2.

59 For Solon, the Areopagus was, together with the assembly, the supreme body of control; thus the city, 'with its two councils, riding as it were at double anchor, would be less tossed by the surges, and would keep its populace in greater quiet'. See Plutarch, *Life of Solon*, XIX, 2, translated by Bernadotte Perrin.

60 See R. W. Wallace, 'Ephialtes and the Areopagos', *Greek, Roman and Byzantine Studies* 25:3, 1974, pp. 266–9. It is also difficult to know for sure how many members there were.

61 Aristotle, *Athenaion Politeia*, XXV, 2. On this, see Nicole and Patrice Loraux, 'L'Athenaion politeia avec et sans Athéniens' (1991), in Loraux, *La Grèce hors d'elle et autres textes*, pp. 645–63. See also T. E. Rihll, 'Democracy Denied: Why Ephialtes Attacked the Areopagus', *The Journal of Hellenic Studies* 115, 1995, pp. 87–98.

62 The meaning of the expression *prostátes toû démou* is unclear; it could refer both to the leader and protector of the people and to those who, through proposals and discussions, ensured the functioning of the popular assembly. See W. Robert Connolly, *The New Politicians of Fifth-Century Athens*, Princeton, NJ: Princeton University Press, 1971, pp. 110ff.; P. J. Rhodes, *A Commentary on the Aristotelian 'Athenaion Politeia'*, Oxford: Clarendon Press, 1981, pp. 347ff.

63 On Ephialtes' name, see R. Arena, 'Di un possibile rapporto Ophélandros: Ophéles e dei nomi dell'incubo in greco', *Annali della Facoltà di Lettere e Filosofia dell'Università di Macerata* 7, 1974, pp. 291–310.

64 Luigi Piccirilli, *Efialte*, Genoa: il melangolo, 1988, p. 73.

65 See Plutarch, *Life of Pericles*, VII, 8; the reference here is to a passage from Plato, *Republic*, 562c–d.

66 Plutarch, *Life of Cimon*, XV, 2, translated by Bernadotte Perrin.

67 As suggested by Loraux, *The Divided City*, p. 71.

68 See Diodorus Siculus, XI, 77, 2–6; *tês núktos anairetheis*. The expression is similar to that used by Aristotle, *Athenaion Politeia*, XXV, 4 and by Plutarch, *Life of Pericles*, X, 8. It is a euphemistic formula that Thucydides uses for seditious homicides. See Loraux, 'Thucydide et la sédition dans les mots', *La Tragédie d'Athènes*, pp. 81–107. For a detailed historical reconstruction and discussion of the sources, see the chapter on the assassination in Piccirilli, *Efialte*, pp. 71ff.

69 See Plutarch, *Life of Pericles*, XV, 1; Thucydides, II, 65, 9; and Plutarch, *Life of Pericles*, IX, 1. Pericles became *prostátes* after Ephialtes' death. See Gaetano de Sanctis, *Pericle*, Milan: Principato, 1944, p. 65; see also *Atthís. Storia della repubblica ateniese dalle origini all'età di Pericle* (1912), Florence: La Nuova Italia, 1975.

70 Yet, the oligarchs surely did remember them. As soon as the Thirty came to power in 404 BCE, they abolished Ephialtes' laws.
71 See Karl Reinhardt, *Aischylos als Regisseur und Theologe*, Bern: Francke, 1949, pp. 149ff.
72 Translated by Herbert Weir Smyth.
73 Aeschylus calls the Furies 'daughters of the night': *Eumenides*, 321, 416, 745, 845, 1034. See Clémence Ramnoux, *La Nuit et les enfants de la Nuit dans la tradition grecque*, Paris: Flammarion, 1959. See also Froma I. Zeitlin, 'The Dynamics of Misogyny: Myth and Myth-Making in the Oresteia', *Aretusa* 11:1–2, 1978, pp. 149–84.
74 On the relationship between the Furies and the city, see Vincenzo di Benedetto, *L'ideologia del potere e la tragedia greca*, Turin: Einaudi, 1978, pp. 230ff.
75 Translated by Herbert Weir Smyth.
76 See Jean-Pierre Vernant, 'Aeschylus, the Past and the Present', in Vernant and Vidal-Naquet, *Myth and Tragedy in Ancient Greece*, pp. 249ff.
77 Meier, *Die Entstehung des Politischen bei den Griechen*.
78 Ibid., pp. 164ff.
79 Ibid., p. 219.
80 Ibid., p. 189.
81 Ibid., p. 299.
82 Ibid., p. 223.
83 See Aristotle, *Politics*, 1255b 20, 1277b 9, 1254b 2, 1259b 1.
84 Meier, *Die Entstehung des Politischen bei den Griechen*, p. 235.
85 This is clearly highlighted by Gabriele Pedullà in his introduction to the Italian edition. See Pedullà, 'Introduzione', in Nicole Loraux, *La città divisa*, Vicenza: Neri Pozzi, 2006, p. 48.
86 Loraux, 'La cité grecque pense l'un et le deux', in *La Tragédie d'Athènes*, pp. 129–30.
87 Loraux, *L'Invention d'Athènes*, p. 11.
88 Louis Althusser, 'Idéologie et appareils idéologiques d'État (Notes pour une recherche)', *La Pensée* 151, 1970, republished in *Positions, 1964–1975*, Paris: Les Éditions sociales, 1976, p. 104.
89 Claude Lefort, 'On the Genesis of Ideology in Modern Societies', *Canadian Journal of Political and Social Theory/Revue canadienne de théorie politique et sociale* 7:1–2, 1983.
90 Loraux, *L'Invention d'Athènes*, p. 511.
91 See Cornelius Castoriadis, *The Imaginary Institution of Society*, Cambridge: Polity, 2005. We can understand why in a seminar held at the EHESS in 1985 (his comments were published after his death), Castoriadis refers critically to the way Loraux uses 'imaginary'. See Castoriadis, *Ce qui fait la Grèce 3*, pp. 226–7. In turn, Loraux emphasizes – in the 1993 preface to *L'Invention d'Athènes* – the vagueness of that notion in her own interpretation, to the point that it can be dispensed with. Loraux, *L'Invention d'Athènes*, p. 19.
92 See Castoriadis, *Ce qui fait la Grèce 3*, pp. 22ff.; *Ce qui fait la Grèce 2*, pp. 125ff.
93 The research work carried out over more than twenty years is evidenced not only by her various volumes on specific topics, but also in the collection of essays edited by Michèle Cohen-Halimi (Loraux,

La Grèce hors d'elle et autres textes), cited above, which contains texts from 1973 to 2003.

94 Pierre Clastres, *Society Against the State: Essays in Political Anthropology*, New York: Zone Books, 1989, pp. 186ff.

95 See Nicole Loraux, 'Notes sur l'un, le deux et le multiple', in Miguel Abensour (ed.), *L'Esprit des lois sauvages. Pierre Clastres ou une nouvelle anthropologie politique*, Paris: Seuil, 1987, p. 163. The conference dedicated to Clastres had already taken place in May 1982; Loraux's paper was published several years later.

96 See Nicole Loraux, 'La cité grecque pense l'un et le deux', in *La Tragédie d'Athènes*, pp. 129–30; Pierre Clastres, *Archeology of Violence*, Los Angeles: Semiotext(e), 2010.

97 Loraux, *The Divided City*, pp. 50–1.

98 Ibid., p. 20.

99 For a critique of the metaphysics of conflict, see Donatella Di Cesare, *The Time of Revolt*, Cambridge: Polity, 2021.

100 Jean-Pierre Vernant, 'Introduction', in *Problèmes de la guerre en Grèce ancienne*, The Hague: Mouton, 1968.

101 Loraux, *The Divided City*, p. 53.

102 Ibid., p. 93.

103 Gustave Glotz, *La Cité grecque. Le développement des institutions*, Paris: Albin Michel, 1968, pp. 113ff.

104 Theognis, 39–40; Plato, *Laws*, 744d.

105 Loraux, *The Divided City*, p. 97.

106 Henri Van Effenterre, *La Cité grecque. Des origines à la défaite de Marathon*, Paris: Hachette, 1985, p. 25.

107 'Politics of Brothers', in Loraux, *The Divided City*, pp. 197ff.

108 See Thucydides, III, 70–84.

109 Nicole Loraux, 'Corcyre, 427–Paris, 1871', in *La Tragédie d'Athènes*, pp. 48ff. Overall, however, the comparison is unconvincing and many aspects remain unclear. For a detailed analysis of Thucydides' passages, see U. Fantasia, 'Corcira 427–425: anatomia di una "stasis"', in C. Bearzot and F. Landucci (eds.), *Partiti e fazioni nell'esperienza politica greca*, Milan: Vita e Pensiero, 2008, pp. 167–201.

110 Alcaeus, 208 a, I Voigt.

111 Chantraine, *Dictionnaire étymologique de la langue grecque*, Vol. IV, p. 1044.

112 See Émile Benveniste, 'Deux modèles linguistiques de la cité', in *Problèmes de linguistique générale*, Paris: Gallimard, 1980, Vol. II, p. 277. See also Paula Botteri, '"Stasis": le mot grec, la chose romaine', *Mètis. Anthropologie des mondes grecs anciens* 4:1, 1989, pp. 87–100.

113 Santo Mazzarino, *Il pensiero storico classico*, Bari: Laterza, 1973, Vol. II, 2, p. 183. On its cosmic sense, see Arendt, *On Revolution*, pp. 42ff.

114 See Mazzarino, *Il pensiero storico classico*, pp. 183ff. See also his *Fra Oriente e Occidente. Ricerche di storia greca arcaica* (1947), Turin: Bollati Boringhieri, 2007, pp. 229ff. On the ambiguities in Mazzarino, see Nicole Loraux, 'Santo Mazzarino, la stásis et la "revolution"', in *La Tragédie d'Athènes*, pp. 161–71; her criticism, however, seems rather excessive.

115 Finley, *Politics in the Ancient World*, pp. 105ff.

116 From *stasiázo* and *stasiótes*. For a philological analysis, see Paola

Radici Colace and Emilia Sergi, 'Stasis nel lessico politico greco', *Annali della Scuola Normale Superiore di Pisa* 4:5, 2000, pp. 223–36.
117 *Stásis émphulos* already appears in Solon 3 G.-O.[2] (4 W.[2]); Herodotus, VIII, 3, 1.
118 Hans-Joachim Gehrke, *Stasis. Untersuchungen zu den inneren Kriegen in den griechischen Staaten des 5. und 4. Jahrhunderts v. Chr.*, Munich: Beck, 1985, pp. 350ff.
119 See Thomas Hobbes, *Leviathan*, Cambridge: Cambridge University Press, 1996; Max Weber, *Economy and Society: An Outline of Interpretive Sociology*, Berkeley: University of California Press, 1978.
120 On this, see Moshe Berent's study, '"Stasis", or the Greek Invention of Politics', *History of Political Thought* 19:3, 1998, pp. 331–62.
121 A partial exception was represented by Sparta and the Athenian navy. The use of militias for internal purposes, on the other hand, was characteristic of tyrannical interventions. See Andrew Lintott, *Violence, Civil Strife, and Revolution in the Classical City: 750–330 BC*, Baltimore: Johns Hopkins University Press, 1982, pp. 26ff.
122 See Loraux, *The Divided City*, p. 42.
123 Aristotle, *Athenaion Politeia*, VIII, 5. Translation edited: in Rackham's translation *pólis* and its cognates are rendered as 'state'. See Plutarch, *Life of Solon*, XX. The authenticity of this law has long been the subject of controversy, not so much on account of its content as because of its attribution to Solon, the moderate of the centre.
124 See Hans-Joachim Gehrke, 'Zwischen Freundschaft und Programm. Politische Parteiung im Athen des 5. Jahrhunderts v. Chr.', *Historische Zeitschrift* 239, 1984, pp. 529–64.
125 Ampolo had already floated the idea of a founding evil. See Carmine Ampolo and Giovanni Ciappelli, 'Commentary', in Anthony Mohlo, Kurt Raaflaub, and Julia Emlen (eds.), *City States in Classical Antiquity and Medieval Italy: Athens and Rome, Florence and Venice*, Stuttgart: Franz Steiner, 1991, pp. 115–16.
126 Gehrke, *Stasis*, pp. 368ff.
127 See G. E. M. de Sainte-Croix, *The Class Struggle in the Ancient Greek World: From the Archaic Age to the Arab Conquests*, London: Duckworth, 1981, pp. 268ff.; Finley, *Politics in the Ancient World.*
128 Loraux, 'Corcyre 427–Paris, 1871', p. 35.
129 Ibid., pp. 35–8.
130 Aristotle, *Politics*, V, 1301 a, 37–9.
131 It is worth noting, however, that Loraux – unlike Agamben – strangely does not take into consideration Arendt's thinking on this decisive issue.
132 Giorgio Agamben, *Stasis: Civil War as a Political Paradigm*, Edinburgh: Edinburgh University Press, 2015, p. 13.
133 Ibid., p. 16.
134 This was not a slave revolt. There were, indeed, not many such revolts, because slaves were not a class and were part of the private sphere. See Berent, '"Stasis"', pp. 338ff.; Vidal-Naquet, 'Esclavage et gynécocratie dans la tradition, le mythe, l'utopie', pp. 269ff.
135 The formula of the oath is taken from Andocides, I, 90, translated by Kenneth John Maidment. Aristotle, *Athenaion Politeia*, XXXIX,

6, quotes it indirectly. Xenophon, *Hellenica*, XI, 4, 20–2. For a complete bibliography of the oath, see Thomas Clark Loening, *The Reconciliation Agreement of 403/402 BC in Athens: Its Content and Application*, Stuttgart: Steiner, 1987.

136 See Plato, *Epistles*, VII, 336e–337a; Aristotle, *Athenaion Politeia*, XL, 2.

137 Aristotle, *Athenaion Politeia*, XL, 2. See also Isocrates, XVIII, 2–3.

138 See Lysias, XII, 79–84; *Epitaph*, 61.

139 Loraux, *The Divided City*, p. 42.

140 In his first speech to the assembly of all Athenians, Thrasybulus calls for the application of 'the ancient laws', *toîs nómois toîs archaîois*. See Xenophon, *Hellenica*, II, 4, 42.

141 Aristotle, *Athenaion Politeia*, XL, 2–3; Isocrates, XVIII, 46, trans. LaRue Van Hook.

142 Aristotle, *Athenaion Politeia*, XL, 2.

7 *Arché* and *Krátos*: The Terms of Power

1 Just think of the wide use of the Anonymous Athenian's text as a source, and the suggested reading of it.

2 For an overview, see Daniel Loick, *Kritik der Souveränität*, Frankfurt: Suhrkamp, 2012.

3 See Giorgio Agamben, *The Use of Bodies*, Stanford, CA: Stanford University Press, 2016; Walter Benjamin, 'Critique of Violence', in *Selected Writings, Volume 1, 1913–1926*, Cambridge, MA: The Belknap Press of Harvard University Press, 1996. Benjamin speaks of 'Entsetzung des Rechtes', 'deposition of the law'.

4 Jacques Rancière, 'The Populism That Is Not to Be Found', in *What Is a People?*, New York: Columbia University Press, 2016.

5 Jacques Derrida, 'The Politics of Friendship', *American Imago* 50:3, 1993, pp. 353–91.

6 Carl Schmitt, 'The Political Component of the Modern Constitution', in *Constitutional Theory*, Durham, NC: Duke University Press, 2008, §§ 17–18.

7 See Donatella Di Cesare, 'La democrazia anarchica di Spinoza', in Pina Totaro and Giovanni Licata (eds.), *Letture di Spinoza per il nuovo millennio*, Rome: Sapienza University Press, 2023, pp. 63–74.

8 Pindar, *Pythian Odes*, II, 86ff.

9 See Polybius, IV, 4–10. On the *lógos tripolitikós* and this hierarchy, see what has already been said in Chapter 4. See Herodotus, III, 80–2; Aristotle, *Politics*, 1279a–b.

10 However, countless comments point towards the already habitual version.

11 See Albert Debrunner, 'Δημοκρατία', in *Festschrift für Edouard Tièche, Schriften der literarischen Gesellschaft Bern*, 6, Bern: Lang, 1947, pp. 11–24, reprinted in Konrad H. Kinzl (ed.), *Demokratia. Der Weg zur Demokratie bei den Griechen*, preface by Kurt A. Raaflaub, Darmstadt: Wissenschaftliche Buchgesellschaft, 1995, pp. 55–86, in particular pp. 65ff. The *démarchos* was a magistrate in ancient Chios. The function then spread and even in late Athens the *démarchoi* were those who administered the *demes* of Attica.

12 Meier, *Entstehung des Begriffs 'Demokratie'*, pp. 47ff.
13 On the contrast between *nómos* and *phúsis* in the Greek world, the work by Felix Heinimann, *Nomos und Physis. Herkunft und Bedeutung einer Antithese im griechischen Denken des 5. Jahrhunderts*, Basel: Reinhard, 1965, remains key.
14 See Hans Schaefer, *Staatsform und Politik. Untersuchungen zur griechischen Geschichte des 6. und 5. Jahrhunderts*, Leipzig: Dieterich'sche Buchhandlung, 1932, p. 106.
15 Translated by Ian Johnston.
16 Marcel Detienne and Jean-Pierre Vernant, *Cunning Intelligence in Greek Culture and Society*, Chicago: University of Chicago Press, 1991, pp. 82ff.
17 In German, these would be *Macht* and *Gewalt*. See Christian Meier, 'Macht, Gewalt', in Otto Brunner, Werner Conze, and Reinhart Koselleck (eds.), *Geschichtliche Grundbegriffe. Historisches Lexikon zur politisch-sozialen Sprache in Deutschland*, Stuttgart: Klett-Cotta, 1982, Vol. III, pp. 820–30.
18 See Homer, *Iliad*, V, 592; XVI, 65; *Odyssey*, III, 68; VIII, 105–8; XIV, 230.
19 See C. Joachim Classen, 'APXH – Its Earliest Use', *Scripta Classica Israelitica* 15, 1996, pp. 20–4. Philosophers use *arché* to indicate principles, the first elements, the causes. On this subject, see Malcolm Schofield, 'APXH', *Hyperboreus* 3, 1997, pp. 218–35. Its first use is owed to Anaximander – see Chapter 3. Lucia Marrucci, in *Kratos e arche. Funzioni drammatiche del potere*, Amsterdam: Hakkert, 2010, interprets it in an almost opposite way to the one proposed here, and finds herself in a rather isolated position.
20 This is a source for metaphors of power through which the king is imagined appearing first in a procession or battle and referred to as princeps or *Fürst*.
21 This aspect already appears in Pindar, *Odes*, 2, 64.
22 See Lévy, '"Archè" chez Hérodote', pp. 89ff.; and 'Basileus et turannos chez Hérodote', *Ktèma* 18, 1993, pp. 12ff.
23 See Fredrik Sixtensson, *Dēmokratia: The Prehistory of a Word in Relation to the Greek Typology of Constitutions*, Uppsala: Uppsala University Press, 2021, p. 57.
24 It is not *árchos*, which is found in Homeric language.
25 See Plato, *Republic*, 562d–563e.
26 Castoriadis expresses this insight in a footnote, *Ce qui fait la Grèce 2*, p. 201; see also Stathis Gourgouris, 'Arché', in J. M. Bernstein et al. (eds.), *Political Concepts: A Critical Lexicon*, New York: Fordham University Press, 2018, pp. 5–24.
27 See Martin Ostwald, 'Shares and Rights: "Citizenship" Greek Style and American Style', in Ober and Hedrick (eds.), *Demokratia*, pp. 49–61; R. K. Sinclair, *Democracy and Participation in Athens*, Cambridge: Cambridge University Press, 1988.
28 Aristotle, *Politics*, 1268a 24, 1272a 16, 1293a 3–4, 1294a 12–14, 1297b 4–6, 1302b 26–7, 1306b 10–11, 1332a 32–5.
29 See Jean-Luc Breuil, 'Kratos et sa famille chez Homère: étude sémantique', in *Études homériques. Séminaire de recherche sous la direction*

de M. Casevitz, Lyon: Maison de l'Orient et de la Méditerranée Jean Pouilloux, 1989, pp. 17–53.

30 Simone Weil, *The Iliad, or the Poem of Force*, Wallingford, PA: Pendle Hill, 1991.

31 Émile Benveniste, *Dictionary of Indo-European Concepts and Society*, Chicago: HAU Books, 2016.

32 Ibid., p. 365.

33 Ibid.

34 Translated by Samuel Butler.

35 Johann H. H. Schmidt, *Synonymik der griechischen Sprache*, 3 vols, Leipzig: Teubner, 1879, Vol. III, pp. 668ff. Schmidt specifies 'Die Macht, welche den Ausschlag gibt'.

36 See, for example, Sophocles, *Oedipus at Colonus*, 66 (translation by Ian Johnston): 'Who governs [*árchei*] them? Do they have a king, or is there a popular assembly?'

37 Ober, 'The Original Meaning of "Democracy"', pp. 3–9.

38 Vardoulakis rightly points this out with regard to Agamben. See Dimitris Vardoulakis, 'Stasis: Notes Toward Agonistic Democracy', *Theory and Event* 20:3, 2017, p. 716.

39 See Dimitris Vardoulakis, *Stasis before the State: Nine Theses on Agonistic Democracy*, New York: Fordham University Press, 2018, pp. 11ff.

40 See Pierre Lévêque, 'Répartition et démocratie. À propos de la racine *da-', *Esprit* 12, 1993, pp. 34–9.

41 See Homer, *Iliad*, V, 710; III, 50.

42 See Marie-Joséphine Werling, *Le dèmos avant la démocratie. Mots, concepts, réalités historiques*, Paris: Presses universitaires de Paris ouest, 2010.

43 Benveniste, *Dictionary of Indo-European Concepts and Society*, p. 378.

44 Xenophon, *Memorabilia*, I, 2, 42–5.

45 On the relationship between democracy and thalassocracy, see Jochen Bleicken, *Die athenische Demokratie*, Paderborn: Schöningh, 1994 (2nd edition), pp. 42ff., 453ff.

46 Pseudo-Xenophon (Old Oligarch), *Constitution of the Athenians*, translated by E. C. Marchant.

47 Aristotle, *Politics*, 1278b, 1290a 30–b 20. But see also Plato, *Republic*, 565e.

48 This is made clear in the essay by Daniela Cammack, 'The Demos in Democracy', *The Classical Quarterly* 69:1, 2019, pp. 45ff.

49 Rancière, *Dis-agreement*, pp. 38ff.

50 Ernst Kantorowicz, *The King's Two Bodies: A Study in Mediaeval Political Theology*, Princeton, NJ: Princeton University Press, 1957, Chapter 5; Claude Lefort, *L'Invention démocratique* (1981), Paris: Fayard, 1994 (revised and expanded edition), pp. 171ff.; Lefort, 'The Question of Democracy'.

51 Claude Lefort, 'L'image du corps et le totalitarisme', in *L'Invention démocratique. Les limites de la domination totalitaire*, Paris: Fayard, 1981, p. 170.

52 Lefort, 'The Question of Democracy', p. 152.

53 Miguel Abensour, *Della compattezza. Architetture e totalitarismi*, Milan: Jaca Book, 2012, p. 71.

Index